Ordnance Survey
York
and the Moors
Landranger Guidebook

JARROLD

How to use this Guide

Pre-planning:
First look at the KEY MAP section – this shows the area covered, the towns and villages and the starting point for 12 Walks and 10 Tours. If you are unfamiliar with the area, look up some of the towns and villages in the PLACES OF INTEREST section. The WALKS or TOURS will provide further local information. The introductions will give you a feeling for the history, landscape and wildlife of the area.

On the Spot:
From your chosen base, explore the area by road or on foot. Stars after a place name indicate that it is featured in the PLACES OF INTEREST section (this is necessary as it is not possible to include every village and town because of space limitations). Some 28 places of interest are accompanied by maps to enable you to plan a short stroll. The scale of these is 2½ INCHES to 1 MILE (see CONVENTIONAL SIGNS for rights of way etc).

Landranger Maps:
These are the natural companion to the Guide. Places of interest are identified first with the number of the Landranger Map on which it appears (sometimes more than one). This is followed by two letters indicating the National Grid Square and by a 4-figure reference number. To locate any place or feature referred to on the relevant Landranger map, first read the two figures along the north or south edges of the map, then the two figures along the east or west edges. Trace the lines adjacent to each of the two sets of figures across the map face, and the point where they intersect will be the south-west corner of the grid square in which the place or feature lies.

Acknowledgements

We would like to thank those individuals and organisations who helped in the preparation of this book: The Department of Tourism and Amenities, Scarborough; the Yorkshire and Humberside Tourist Board and The Moors Centre, Danby Lodge. John Rushton, author of the excellent book 'The Ryedale Story', was kind enough to read the Gazetteer, while Ian Sampson checked it for accuracy. Charles Kightly wrote the York Walk; Pat Morris the Natural History section, Allan Berends wrote the entry on Whitby and Colin Winchester the Walks and Tours. Stan Morse provided the artwork; The Sutcliffe Gallery, Whitby the photograph of the harbour; and the Jorvik Centre the Viking illustration.

Ordnance Survey   ISBN 0-319-00145-8
Jarrold Publishing ISBN 0-7117-0567-4

First published 1988 by Ordnance Survey and Jarrold Publishing
Reprinted 1991

Ordnance Survey   Jarrold Publishing
Romsey Road   Barrack Street
Maybush   Norwich NR3 1TR
Southampton SO9 4DH

Printed in Great Britain by Jarrold Printing, Norwich. 2/91

Contents

KEY MAP INDEX

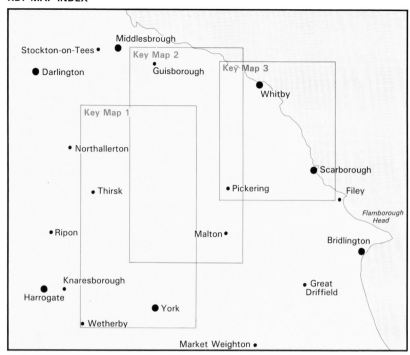

Key Map 2

Key Map 3

Key Map 1

- Stockton-on-Tees
- ● Middlesbrough
- ● Darlington
- ● Guisborough
- ● Whitby
- ● Northallerton
- ● Thirsk
- ● Scarborough
- Filey
- ● Pickering
- *Flamborough Head*
- ● Ripon
- Malton ●
- ● Bridlington
- Knaresborough
- ● Harrogate
- ● Great Driffield
- ● York
- ● Wetherby
- Market Weighton ●

🥾 6	Motor and Cycle Tour Start
👟 9	Walk Start
👟	Mini-Walk Start

LANDRANGER MAPS OF YORK AND THE MOORS

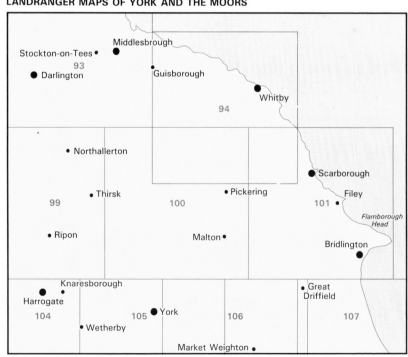

- Stockton-on-Tees ●
- ● Middlesbrough
- 93
- ● Darlington
- ● Guisborough
- ● Whitby
- 94
- ● Northallerton
- ● Scarborough
- ● Thirsk
- ● Pickering
- Filey
- 99
- 100
- 101
- *Flamborough Head*
- ● Ripon
- Malton ●
- ● Bridlington
- Knaresborough
- ● Great Driffield
- ● Harrogate
- 104
- 105
- ● York
- 106
- 107
- ● Wetherby
- Market Weighton ●

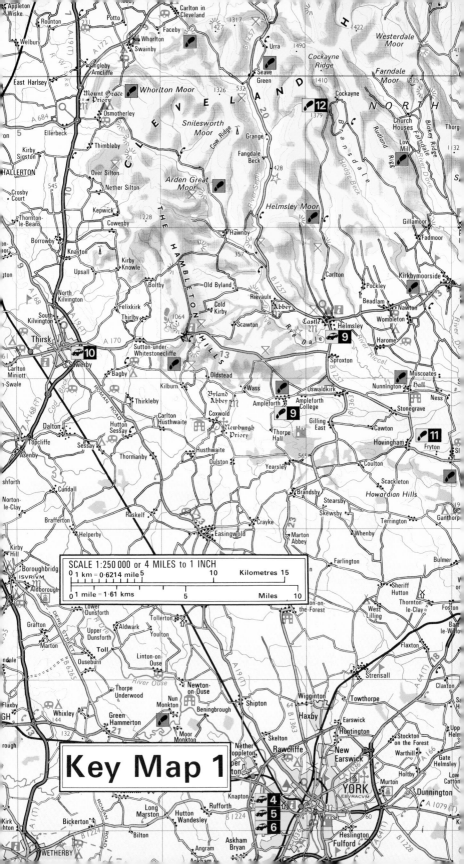

Key Map 1

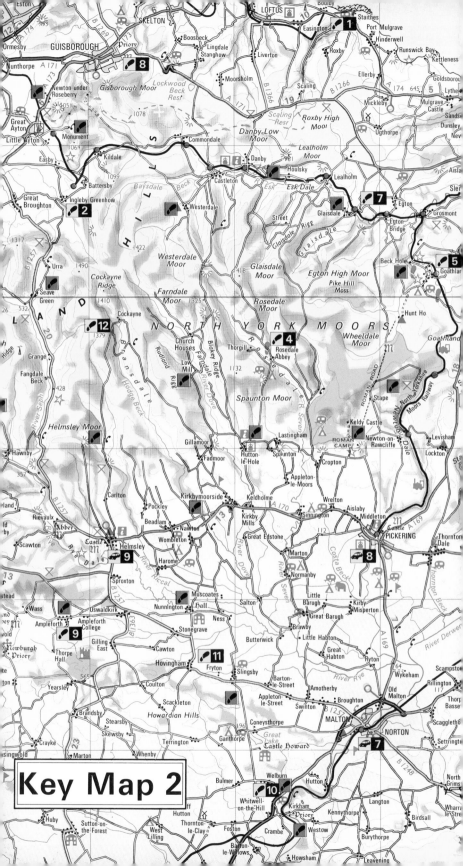

Key Map 2

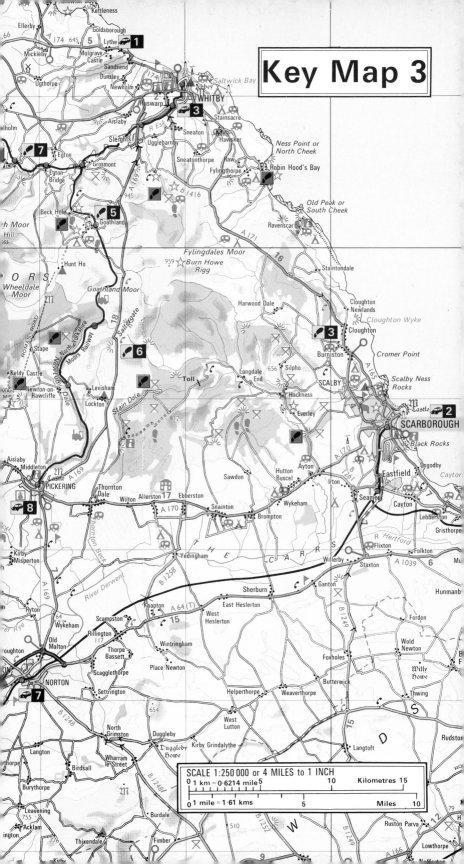

Introduction

York

No visitor to the city of York can escape its history. The suburbs are not remarkable, but the buildings which press close to the medieval city wall begin to borrow something from the atmosphere inside, as if it radiates from the honey-coloured stone of the wall itself or seeps through the ancient gates.

Within the walls the sense of history is intense. It is not only that a large number of early buildings have survived. Nor is it the scrupulous attention of the civic authority who have ensured that even the facades of fast food chains and betting shops do not obtrude and who have placed informative plaques throughout the city which, like footnotes in a text, are constant reminders of York's past. All these factors help of course but there is also an unmistakable atmosphere, a distillation of all the lives of all the generations of the city's past. As fanciful as this sounds, it is true.

All ancient cities are 'recordings' of the past, as if stone can, over time, take on the qualities of magnetic tape. Usually the impressions are indistinct and fragmentary: York, paved with stone and encircled with stone, records the past with the clarity of a compact disc. Perhaps it is this fact which has prompted commercially-minded entrepreneurs to organise 'ghost tours' of the city.

Historically, spiritually, York is the second city of England after London. There were times in its history when it vied with the southern capital; King George VI said 'the history of York, is the history of England'. The reason that York has seen 2,000 years of continuous human habitation is because it is a natural communication centre: it is situated in low-lying country where the Vale of York forms a natural north-south corridor. The first settlement was Roman. The fort, which they called Eboracum, was built by Roman engineers at the point where the smaller river Foss joins the mighty Ouse – then still tidal and giving them a vital link to the sea.

There is no archaeological evidence of any earlier settlement on the site, although the area is rich in Iron Age forts and the banks of the river had provided rich pickings since the earliest period of Man's prehistory after the Ice Age. But the true history of York dates from the arrival of The Roman *'Legio IX Hispana'*,

whose 6,000 soldiers had come to subdue the confederation of Celtic tribes known as the Brigantes in AD 71.

During the four centuries of Roman occupation, York became an important outpost of the empire. At its height, the legionary fortress covered more than fifty acres: it was protected by high walls and towers designed to take ballistae, the giant catapults used by the legions. Eboracum was equipped with all the facilities of a major command centre: in addition to the Principia, or headquarters, and the barracks, there were officers' houses, baths and an elaborate system of sewers. Wharves and warehouses lined the banks of the Ouse, and a prosperous civil community grew up on the far bank. Roman York was visited by several emperors, including Hadrian, Constantine and Caracala. Severus and Constantius died there. Perhaps these important visitors were entertained in the great dining room on a terrace overlooking the river which has recently been excavated.

The excellent Yorkshire Museum contains many fascinating artefacts from the Roman period, but the city itself still remembers its Roman past. Walk down Chapter House Street beside the Treasurer's House to the north of the Minster – it is the Via Decumana. The modern Stonegate follows the Via Praetoria; Petergate is the Via Principalis. The Minster itself is built over the Principia. Although it was two centuries after the Romans left before a Christian church was built on the site of the Principia, there was an early Christian community in Roman York which sent a bishop to the Church Council at Arles in AD 314. To this day the Archbishop of York signs himself 'Ebor'. A more poignant reminder of the early Christian community than items of ecclesiastical history is the inscription found with the body of a young woman buried outside the city walls at this time: 'soror ave vivas in deo' which means 'hail, sister, may you live in God'.

As the Anglo-Saxon people gradually came to dominate the Romano-British in the centuries after the Romans left, so Roman Eboracum became Saxon Eoforwic. Although the Anglo-Saxons maintained many of the larger Roman buildings, it is clear from archaeological evidence that much of the road system was neglected. Earth ramparts covered the Roman walls, although one tower of limestone slabs built during this period is still visible behind the Yorkshire Museum. The grid pattern of Roman streets was broken by the curve of modern Mick-

York Minster

legate when the old Roman bridge became unusable and a route needed to be made to the new Saxon structure built on the site of the modern Ouse Bridge.

Perhaps the most significant event of the Anglo-Saxon period in York's history was the Christian baptism – on Easter Day, AD 627 – of the Anglian king Edwin. A small wooden church had been built for the occasion. Its precise position is not known, but over the centuries it was to grow into York Minster.

On 1 November AD 866, while the Angles were engaged in one of their interminable civil wars, the Vikings captured York. The Danish Vikings were to make a lasting impression on the city which they called Jorvik. Although Viking York was a city built largely of wood, modern archaeological methods – helped by the waterlogged soil which preserves wood and leather – have revealed more than 15,000 items from this period. The brilliant excavation in Coppergate and the Jorvik Viking Centre have enabled the modern visitor to look back into history to a time when York was capital of a Danish empire: The streets of modern York have

their own links with the Viking age. Look for the streetnames ending in '-gate': it is nothing to do with gates, 'gata' is Old Norse for street. It is clear that many of the street patterns of the present day city date from the tenth century.

The Norman invasion was to have a devastating effect on the city precisely because of its strong sense of Scandinavian identity. The inhabitants of York were extremely hostile to the Normans. William the Conqueror ordered the building of the first castle in 1068. This stronghold was manned with 500 knights, but it was successfully attacked in the following year. It was repaired and another built on the other side of the Ouse. Both were attacked and destroyed by an Anglo-Danish force. William himself took charge, spending the Christmas of 1069 in York while rebuilding recommenced. One fortification became York Castle, the other stood on what is now Baile Hill. Modern Foss Islands Road marks the position of the new water defences he had built. From this position of strength William began his campaign of devastation which has become known as 'the

Early Man

Late Neolithic 2500 BC

The Beaker people arrived in Britain from the continent at about this time: their culture is named after the characteristic drinking cup or beaker they placed with burials. Very gradually they intermixed with the existing Neolithic (Stone Age) population and introduced bronze metalworking for tools and weapons – although flint and stone still continued to be used as a major resource until the later period of the Bronze Age.

Large numbers of round barrows (Tumulus or Cairn on OS maps) were built, rather than the long barrows of the Neolithic period, and ceremonial stone circles and alignments were constructed. Only a few of these more elaborate monuments survive in the Moors area.

Early Bronze Age 1700 BC.

This period saw a marked increase in social organisation. Territories were marked out by round

Harrowing of the North'. The policy was as effective as it was ruthless. Stability restored and Norman domination complete, the new archbishop Thomas of Bayeux began to build a new church on the site of the Saxon one which had been burnt during William's campaign of terror.

The new Norman church was built on the site of the Roman Principia and re-worked stone from the Roman buildings was used in its construction. It lasted about 150 years and its splendid crypt can still be seen below the choir. Work on the Minster as we see it today was begun in the thirteenth century and was to take 250 years to complete. The stone walls which circle the city – incorporating earlier Roman and Saxon elements – reached their final form over the same period.

If the history of York is the history of England, then the history of the Minster is the history of York. Many cities have no heart, but York does: every day of the year the doors open at seven o'clock, and every day there are services to the God whose place this is. The Mother Church of the Northern Province of the Church of England is dedicated to St Peter, 'the rock': it is the largest Gothic cathedral north of the Alps, and it rises like a great spiritual power station above the city.

'Minster' is a Saxon word meaning a centre for evangelism. York Minster is a living, functioning church just as it has always been: a place of prayer and worship, and a sanctuary. But the building, which can be seen or glimpsed from almost every part of the city, is also a repository for the hopes and aspirations of the kings and nobles, the merchants and ordinary people who have spent their lives in York over nineteen centuries.

The Minster as History

The Minster is entered from the west door which leads into the nave: this part of the cathedral was begun in 1291 and completed in the 1350s. If you walk to the centre of the nave and turn to face the door you have entered you will see above it the great west window which dates from 1338. Above the left corner is the south-west tower which has a peal of twelve bells. York's medieval brass foundry was in the area known as Bedern – a

barrows. There was permanent settlement in the valleys and seasonal mixed farming on the moorland hills.

Bronze Age 1300 BC.

Major social changes are known to have occurred in the region at about this time due to land deterioration and the pressure of an increasing population. Massive linear earthworks defining territorial boundaries and defensive hillforts were starting to be built suggesting the emergence of tribal organisation. The production of flint and stone artefacts ceased at about this time as bronze became the major item of prestige. Examples of decorative bronze pins and armlets, military swords and spearheads and craftsmen's tools such as axes, chisels and gouges have been found in the Moors area, especially concentrated on the more fertile Tabular Hills; a gold torc also found here indicates a wealthy and prosperous society.

Iron Age 600 BC.

From this period until the Roman Conquest, waves of immigrants from Europe settled in Britain. They brought with them the use of iron for weapons and implements, and intensified mixed farming.

About 400 BC.

A sophisticated culture with characteristic art style, influenced by Greek traditions, spread from the continent to Britain, bringing with it a distinctive language known as Celtic. A tribal society reflecting this culture settled in eastern Yorkshire and on the fringes of the Tabular Hills. These were the Parisi, who built unique square barrows for burial, some of which contained dismantled chariots or carts and rich grave goods. To the north and west of the Parisi was another, vast, territory belonging to the Brigantian tribe. The age of the Celtic tribal chieftan had arrived.
(All dates are approximate)

passage off St Andrewgate. Archae-ologists have discovered furnaces and the remains of clay moulds for the bells. Above the right corner is the north-west tower which houses Great Peter, a six-teen ton bell which has the deepest tone of any bell in Europe.

The railway which brought Great Peter to York in 1845 was the creation of George Hudson, three times Lord Mayor and known as 'The Railway King'. Hudson it was who said to George Stevenson 'Make all t'railways cum t'York'. A true Victorian entrepreneur, his turbulent career ended in disgrace over financial manipulation and he died in penury. But it was Hudson's vision which made York a key part of England's rail network, a fact which stimulated industry in the town, particularly the great chocolate compa-nies Terry and Rowntree on whom so much of York's prosperity has depended. George Hudson's true monument is York's continuing railway industry whose heart is the magnificent Victorian Station completed in 1877 – but spare a thought for the old rogue when Great Peter tolls at noon each day.

In York Minster's nave if you look up – and above all else gothic architecture is designed to make you do that – you will see that it is decorated with shields high up on the stonework on either side. These depict the arms of the benefactors of the Minster and the barons who fought in the long wars against Scotland. In 1314 Ed-ward II and his nobles prayed for victory at the cathedral on their way to the Battle of Bannockburn. Their prayers were in vain, but their shields can be seen in the clerestory windows.

Walking down the nave to the crossing and transepts gives the visitor the best view of the Minster's stained glass. The great west window, now being restored, is known from its heart-shaped stone tracery as 'the heart of Yorkshire', and depicts some of the principal events in the life of Christ. These events were included in York's famous Mystery Plays which told the Bible story from the Crea-tion to the Last Judgment. Originally they were performed by the city's craft guilds – also known as 'masteries' or 'mysteries' – and it is recorded that they were per-formed for Richard III, England's last truly Northern king and not as bad as the Tudors painted him.

One of the cathedral's greatest glories is its glass. The north transept contains one of the most beautiful stained glass windows in the world, 'The Five Sisters'. Each of the thirteenth-century lancet win-

Middlesbrough from Eston Nab

dows is over fifty feet tall and glazed with grey-green 'grisaille' glass. The beauty of the design made an impression on Sir Basil Spence (architect of Coventry Ca-thedral) that was to stay with him throu-ghout his career. The windows inspired Charles Dickens to write a story about its origin in Nicholas Nickelby. Another chapter in York's history is recalled by the devotion of two women of the city who organised the re-leading of The Five Sisters window in 1925 with medieval lead found at Rievaulx Abbey. All works of art need repair, and their work was dedicated to making the window a me-morial to all the women of the Empire who died in the Great War.

The humiliating and harsh terms of the Treaty of Versailles, economic collapse and the rise of Fascism in Europe brought a second World War only fourteen years after the restoration of The Five Sisters window. The astronomical clock to the right of the window in the north transept is a memorial to the 18,000 men of the RAF and other air forces stationed in the North who lost their lives in World War Two.

In the south transept is the famous Rose Window which is said to comme-morate the marriage of Henry VII and Elizabeth of York and the end of the Wars of the Roses. Ironically the window celebrates an event which marked a turn in York's fortunes. For, under the Tudors, the all-important wool industry went into sharp decline, and there were outbreaks of epidemic witnessed by plague pits which have been found in the city.

At the east end of the Minster is the

Ruswarp near Whitby

east window, physically the most impressive work of the medieval glaziers whose workshops were situated in the area of present-day St Helen's Square. The window is the size of a tennis court and takes as its theme the Latin quotation at the apex: Ego Sum, Alpha et Omega – 'I am the Beginning and the End'.

It is not possible to list all the treasures of York Minster within the confines of this introduction. Nor is it important. What is important is for the visitor to understand that this is the heart of York: the Minster is both the spiritual centre of the city and the repository of an infinite number of clues to its long history. Several times fire has threatened to destroy the building: when a deranged man called Jonathan Martin set fire to hymn and prayer books after evensong in 1829 (he died in Bedlam); when a careless workman left a candle alight in the south-west tower; and in 1984 when it was struck by lightning. Still York Minster survived.

During the Civil War, York was besieged by 40,000 Parliamentarian troops. Relieved by Charles I's nephew, Prince Rupert, it was finally taken after his crushing defeat at Marston Moor. Many of York's buildings were damaged, but Sir Thomas Fairfax, the leading Parliamentarian Yorkshireman, prevented the usual destruction of church decoration by fanatical iconoclasts. Again York Minster survived.

The powerful forces of the Industrial Revolution – so important to the history of the North and the foundation of Britain's prosperity in the nineteenth century – had needs which York could not supply. The city became a social and cultural centre whose domestic and civil architec-

ture from the Georgian and Early Victorian period can still be enjoyed today, but a backwater in the minds of the great industrial barons whose world was manufacturing industry and the new cities which grew around it.

In our post-industrial age the importance of cities like York, which now has a thriving university opened in 1963, is better understood. Of course York, like all cities, needs industries to survive. Tourism is vitally important today, and of this new industry York Minster is – again – the heart.

The Vale of York

To the west of York is the fertile agricultural land of the Vale of York, a flat landscape which continues north towards Thirsk drained by the Ouse, Nidd, Wharfe and their many tributaries. It was across this terrain that Prince Rupert's cavalry rode in 1644, skilfully evading three Parliamentarian armies to relieve the siege of York. Brave as a lion, he then attacked the main Roundhead force. The battle fought during a summer thunderstorm between the villages of Long Marston and Tockwith was a terrible defeat for Rupert and his cause: the Battle of Marston Moor.

In prehistoric times the Vale of York was boggy and heavily wooded, but the soils left after the last glaciation were rich and easily worked. Once cleared and properly drained the area gave a good living to Bronze and Iron Age farmers, and successive generations of Celts, Saxons, Danes and their descendants up to the present day.

The Howardian Hills and The Vale of Pickering

To the north of the undulating Howardian Hills is the Vale of Pickering. This is the drainage basin where the Riccal, Dove, Seven and Rye rivers, and Costa and Thornton Becks, take the water from the high moors down into the Derwent. The names of the rivers show some Norse elements but most have Celtic origins. When the Celts were driven higher and higher into the moors by waves of Saxon invaders they left not only their homes and farms, but also their gods. Water had great significance for the Celts. Rivers and estuaries were inhabited by supernatural beings, some benign, some malevolent: something worth remembering as you cross and re-cross the many stone bridges.

The watery landscape of the Vale of Pickering is a creation of the ice which left deposits of gravel and sand overlaying the Jurassic bedrock. As a result some streams are fast-running, some slow; all follow unpredictable and often surprising courses. The great ice sheet has left glacial erratics over the whole region, some boulders are larvikite and rhomb-porphyry carried all the way from southern Norway.

Geologically the Howardian Hills are a continuation of the Hambledon Hills, but their character is different. As the roads rise and turn, there are sudden beautiful views of the lower ground. At the eastern end of the hills towards Malton is the great Baroque house which Sir John Vanbrugh built for the third Earl of Carlisle, Charles Howard, between 1700 and 1737. Vast, beautiful and magnificent, Castle Howard is as improbable as a dinosaur on the landscape, and as unforgettable.

Whitby Abbey

The Coast

Although you will look in vain for the idealised 'Fair' of the song, Scarborough is one of the most pleasant seaside resorts on the East Coast. A spa town, built for leisure and relaxation, it has all the features the English seaside should have: cliffs, a castle, a harbour and lighthouse, parks, a funfair and a sandy beach with donkeys. Above the town, on the South

Anglo Saxons

In the early fifth century – after the Roman province of Britain had been abandoned – the principal threat to the British came from the northern Celtic kingdoms of the Picts and Scots. Tradition holds that one British king, Vortigern, decided to invite Saxon mercenaries – who had earlier been used by the Romans – to help defend his kingdom against Pictish incursions.

The Saxons were one of a variety of Germanic peoples, including also the Angles and Jutes, who had occupied the continental seaboard from

Friesland to Denmark. The unfortunate Vortigern was to regret his invitation: some 500 years after Julius Caesar, the Saxons, Angles and Jutes also came, saw and eventually conquered. The Anglo-Saxon kingdoms in the area of York were known as Deira, which was later absorbed by the vast and powerful Northumbrian kingdom. Repeated migration from the fifth to the ninth century saw the creation of numerous Anglo-Saxon kingdoms spread over a vast area. The 'Angles' had come to rule much of what we now think of as 'England'.

Cliff and around North Bay, the well-kept stuccoed Victorian hotels and private houses confront the sea like wedding cakes iced in white and pastel colours. The heavily eroded cliff below the castle is a nesting place for a colony of gulls, whose noisy domestic arrangements almost drown the endless crashing of the North Sea on the Black Rocks below.

From Ravenscar there are magnificent views back to Scarborough and along the coast. According to the Old Norse Kormak's Saga, 'Scarborough' is Scarthi's burgh – that is 'the fortress town founded by Scarthi', a nickname meaning harelipped. But the meaning for Ravenscar must be more straightforward. 'Scar' can also mean a rocky ravine and if not ravens, other members of the crow family are still much in evidence clinging with difficulty to the telephone wires along the cliffs and perched on the drystone walls.

The remorseless erosion of the North Sea has created a wonderful landscape of collapsed cliffs which are host to a rich variety of plants, animals and birds. From the high points, depending on the season and the weather, you can watch a vast expanse of North Sea in every one of its moods from blue Mediterranean stillness to a fury of white-topped waves racing to dash themselves against the cliffs in their age-old battle with the land. For walkers, the Cleveland Way is the best means of enjoying this stretch of coast, and many of the best views are only accessible on foot.

The coast near Robin Hood's Bay

Beyond Ravenscar, between South Cheek and North Cheek, is Robin Hood's Bay. Here, the encroaching sea has created an equilibrium where land and sea together form a beautiful varied landscape. The peaceful little fishing village could almost make you forget what a hard living the sea offered when that was the only trade.

Whitby, like all ports, is full of interest. Working boats, large and small, as well as pleasure craft, crowd the harbour and the estuary of the River Esk which bisects the town. Leland, writing in the sixteenth century, called Whitby 'a great fischar toune', and a rich variety, caught the same morning, can still be eaten in waterfront restaurants. The old town nestles on the east bank of the Esk, above it are the wonderful Georgian parish church and the thirteenth-century ruins of Whitby Abbey, originally founded by St Hilda in AD 657. Built in sandstone from the Howardian Hills, the Abbey looks down on today's fishing and cargo ships as once it looked down on Viking ships and Norman ships and the whaling fleets of the eighteenth century. The Abbey will also have seen the sailing of the Whitby

ships Endeavour, Resolution, Adventure and Discovery which took Captain James Cook, a Staithes man, on his voyages of discovery.

The coast north of Whitby is one of the most beautiful in England. Runswick Bay below Kettleness offers magnificent views and visitors should not miss the village of Staithes – Staithes where cottages cling precariously to the steep sides of a wooded valley cut by a stream, and where the flat stones of the little harbour make the air pungent with seaweed at low tide.

At the northern-most extremity is Boulby Head. Grim-faced and dangerous, this is where the Moors meet the North Sea – at 690 ft the highest point on the east coast of England.

The Moors

The Moors – taking the whole west to east span from the Cleveland Hills to the coast – is a landscape moulded out of opposites and opposing forces, a place of stark contrasts both natural and man-made.

The forces which moulded the landscape over unimaginable periods of geological time are those which can still be seen at work today on the coast, which

Whitby in 1880 by F.M. Sutcliffe

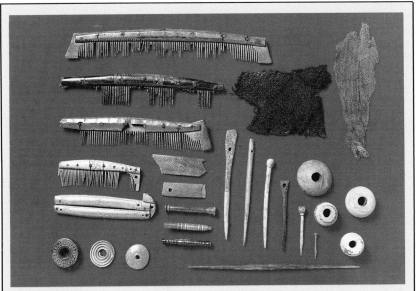

The Vikings

Tenth century bone and antler combs, pins, spindle whorls and textiles from Viking York

Spring came as a mixed blessing to the Anglo-Saxons of the eighth and early ninth centuries. The warm weather and favourable winds brought shiploads of marauding pagan pirates from Scandinavia across the North Sea. These were the Vikings – a name that in translation probably means 'frequenters of the sea-creeks and inlets'.

Yorkshire was attacked by Viking ships from Denmark. For a time the rich summer plunder of Christian monasteries and productive Saxon farms and villages was enough, but gradually boats wintered in England and sporadic raiding became an organised invasion and then settlement.

The vast settlement area governed by the Danelaw stretched from the Thames in the south, Watling Street in the west and the Tees to the north. Between 1016 and 1042 AD most of England was ruled by Danish kings: firstly by Canute (Cnut) and then successively by his sons. York (Jorvik) was the capital of the Danish (and for a while Irish-Norse) kingdom and the Jorvik Viking Centre in Coppergate is a brilliant reconstruction of this international trading settlement.

loses up to three feet a year to the sea in some places. Because, although glaciers greatly changed the lower country which surrounds the moors, and ice carved out the dales, the high moors are the creation of the sea.

The bedrock of the moors was created in the shallow seas of the Jurassic period more than 150 million years ago. For millions of years the layers built up until, about 80 million years ago, forces in the earth's crust raised up the ocean floor to create what geologists call 'the Cleveland Dome'. This structure was eroded by the sea and re-submerged, before rising once again to form the beginning of a landscape we would recognise. Further erosions, mainly from water, shaped today's moors. Stand anywhere on this coast where the moors meet the ocean and you can watch the sea remorselessly reclaiming her own.

The time spans of geology are vast: if the history of the world is represented by one year, the most primitive form of life (blue green algae, again from the sea) only emerges during the last hour on New Year's Eve. In the light of this it seems incredible that Man has had any impact on the landscape: but he has and

The Romans

The invasion of Britain under the Emperor Claudius in AD 43 marks the end of prehistory and the beginning of written history. Rome wanted Britain for the usual colonial reasons. The island was rich in raw materials, particularly lead and other metals. There was also a cereal surplus and high quality wool which was highly prized. In addition, the ostentatious Celtic aristocracy were a good market for Roman manufactured goods.

The Romans secured the new province with their usual efficiency and ruthlessness (after one rebellion more than 70,000 people were put to the sword). Thousands of miles of well-engineered roads were built and a network of towns and military bases. Although Britain was always a relatively minor province, by the third century a Romano-British middle class were enjoying the advantages of civilisation and of being part of the world's largest empire.

York was one of the great towns of late Roman Britain: it was raised to the status of colonia and made capital of Britannia Inferior, the northern half of the province. As part of the web of empire, York saw at different times military units from the Balkans and Greece, North Africa, the Danube and the Tigris. In the stone sewers beneath modern York a fragment of material woven from Chinese silk has been found, and Yorkshire jet has been unearthed in the Rhineland. So significant was York that Constantine was declared emperor there in AD 306.

As the Roman empire began to crumble towards the end of the fourth century, the Romano-British ruling class became increasingly restive. The tax burden was heavy as the empire fought to hold back the barbarians, and Rome was less concerned with a distant province than with saving itself. The early fifth century saw the withdrawal of Roman troops and officials from Britain as the province was severed from the Roman Empire.

he continues to.

Early Man first cleared the forests which covered all but the high moors with stone axes and with fire: carefully controlled winter burning of the heather is used today to provide ideal conditions for the red grouse. It is poignant to watch the Charlie Chaplin progress of a young red grouse in the late spring and early summer, knowing that when autumn comes it will face a deadly barrage from the West End gunmakers' finest creations.

From the desolation of the highest moors, which can only be reached on foot, the extent to which Man has already encroached is apparent. The tamer beauty of the lush green patchwork quilt of fields, seamed with drystone walls and hawthorn, is in vivid contrast to the purple-brown moorland above. A greater threat than agriculture is afforestation which even the steepest and highest land can support. Serried ranks of fir and spruce already mock the natural beauty of some of the high ridges, giving them the primped appearance of newly-combed hair.

It is time now for Man's intrusion to stop, but the changes of the past are what give the North Yorkshire Moors their endlessly changing perspectives, the contrasts which are the secret of their beauty. One of the most powerful agents of change in the past were the many religious orders, whose ruined abbeys are among the area's most beautiful monuments. The first, today the most haunting, was Whitby. Here the Saxon princess, St Hilda, founded a monastic order for nuns and monks in AD 657. It was the Synod of Whitby in AD 664 which brought together the southern and northern churches of England in one communion.

The Vikings destroyed the first abbey in AD 866, but in AD 1078 a Norman, Reinfrid, who had been a key figure in the genocidal 'Harrowing of the North' – perhaps out of guilt – founded a new monastery of Benedictines on the sacred site. It was both politically and 'spiritually' expedient for the Normans to grant land to religious orders. Soon there were many abbeys around the Moors, notably at Byland and Rievaulx. There is an old saying that cats and clerics quickly find the most comfortable place in a room, and the modern visitor could be forgiven for looking at the beautiful countryside around Byland and Rievaulx and supposing that it was a comfortable life. The soft, rolling country, lush with pasture and shaded by great oaks is as beautiful as

Staithes

any in England.

The Cistercians who founded the abbeys were in fact ascetics who found the Benedictine order too lax: they 'revelled in their poverty'. But the poverty was not to last. The monastic estates soon became the most powerful economic force in Yorkshire. Rievaulx had an estimated 14,000 sheep on the moors and traded with Florence and all the major European cities. Nor was sheep farming the only industry they controlled: the Cistercians also exploited the iron from the moors and mined for coal. The monastic estates were vast and their tenants constantly improved farming techniques under their intelligent guidance.

It is no exaggeration to say that these religious orders layed the foundations of modern industry and agriculture in Yorkshire. The great wealth they amassed in the process did not go unnoticed. Henry VIII's Dissolution of the Monasteries was not simply of political significance in his engineered split with Rome, it was an economic move. In a few short years he shifted the wealth of England from the Church to the civil population. The wool industry the monks had created remained an important feature of Yorkshire's economy after the Dissolution, but great hardship resulted from the loss of the organisational ability of the various orders and the parcelling-up of the estates to the 'get rich quick' elements of the day.

Sheep still abound. Sheep farming is a hard way of life for men and the animals that help them. The men look forward to their sons taking over the harder work, and the sheepdogs to a year or two of watching the young dog run where they once did before their muzzles became grey and their joints a little stiff. Sheep are part of the Moors: they shape them, they determine the way many people live and are themselves part of the landscape.

The Natural History of York and the North York Moors

The heather moors

Few natural regions of England are so clearly defined as the uplands of North Yorkshire. They rise steeply in the west and south from the relatively flat farmland of the Cleveland Plain and the Vale of York. Sutton Bank is the most spectacular part of the southern escarpment, with wonderful views from the well-placed Visitors Centre. To the north and east, the area ends abruptly at the coast, with the cliff at Boulby forming the highest point on the east coast of England. Within this upland area, some 553 square miles was designated as the North York Moors National Park in 1952. The Park encompasses two types of landscape whose differences are clearly visible: the predominantly green areas are pastureland and trees, the rest is mostly purple and brown heather moorland. The heather is seen at its best in late summer and covers the largest area of heather moor in England – one of the main reasons for the National Park designation.

The two kinds of scenery reflect different wildlife communities and, to a considerable extent, are the result of differences in the underlying geology. The limestone areas to the south, around Hutton-le-Hole, being different from the sandstone to the north. With the passage of time, the limestone weathers down to produce nutrient-rich alkaline soils on well-drained rock. The sandstones erode slowly to form poor acidic soils, deficient in nutrients. Moreover, the sandstones tend to be less permeable to water, impeding drainage and encouraging the formation of bogs. These are characterised by soggy cushions of Sphagnum moss, a plant which holds water like a sponge and withdraws what little nutrients are present, making it hard for other plants to grow in competition.

Sphagnum bogs become extensive where there is abundant rain and poor drainage. However, these bogs are less prominent than in parts of the Pennines which are higher. The Pennines catch most of the moisture coming from the west and leave the North York Moors in a 'rain shadow'. Another distinctive plant of acid boggy areas is the so-called Cotton grass (actually a sedge with a wispy

Ellers Wood near Hawnby

cotton-wool topknot). Cotton grass is typical of the moors, but absent from the dry calcareous regions to the south.

The cold acid waters in peat bogs do not encourage decomposition, with the result that dead vegetable material – particularly the blankets of Sphagnum – gradually accumulates to form peat. This process raises the level of the bog and in time its surface begins to become dry, especially in summer. Where the bogs are dry enough – on top or at the edges – heather begins to grow and may take over. Large areas of the moors are now clad in heather (mostly Calluna), bilberry and grasses, growing on a thick layer of peat formed long ago. Today this is often well-drained and dry, so that if a fire is not controlled the peat may begin to burn too and be difficult to extinguish.

The peat bogs and acid soils are unsuitable for earthworms, and many worm-eaters are consequently rare or absent. Moles and the common shrew are not found on the moors, but are abundant in the worm-rich soils to the south. Instead pigmy shrews thrive, evidently able to survive on the insects and spiders which are surprisingly abundant in the dry shelter of heather clumps. The invertebrates also support characteristic upland birds such as the meadow pippit. In turn these are the food of merlins, rapidly becoming one of Britain's rarest birds due to the loss of open upland habitat to forestry. The merlin is our smallest bird of prey and is usually seen, if at all, skimming low over the hillside, rapidly disappearing from sight. The male is slate grey above, the female grey-brown. Lapwing, curlew and redshank breed on the moors and common sandpipers live along the

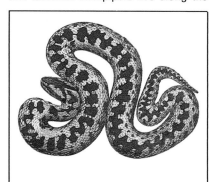

Male adders are boldly marked in contrasting black and white; they rarely reach 20 inches in length

Common buzzards soar on broad wings, making a cat-like mewing call. They feed mainly on rabbits and other small mammals, birds, insects and carrion. They nest in trees and on rocky ledges; both parents incubate the eggs.

plovers, curlew and other waders remain around the coasts, ring ouzels fly south to Africa, returning in April.

The red grouse, perhaps more than any other bird, typifies the heather moors at all times of the year. It lives and breeds only in this habitat and is the only bird which is found in Britain and nowhere else. Heather shoots are its main food, and the nutritional quality of the heather affects the density of grouse populations. The males are darker than females and have gleaming bright red wattles over the eyes during the breeding season. They defend a territory vigorously in the spring, standing prominently on a hummock or outcrop crying indignantly "go-back, go-back, go-back grrrr" at all intruders whether they be hikers or other grouse. The territory needs to be large enough to support the adult birds and their offspring, and will have to be larger where the heather is nutritionally poor.

To improve heather quality and encourage young growth, it is customary to organise controlled burning of strips of the moor. Different parts of the moor are treated in this way each year. Sometimes fertilisers may be added to improve the growth and quality of the new heather and to increase grouse densities. Patches of burnt ground and the lines of stone and peat shooting butts are a reminder that moorland management means that some of the grouse will end up being shot. However, high density grouse populations are particularly prone to disease and shooting lessens the risk of epidemics. Shooting also provides a way for landowners to earn income from the moors as an alternative to having more sheep or conifer plantations, both of which would further reduce the remaining remnants of beautiful heather moors and their associated wildlife.

Burning the moor in small patches leaves plenty of old heather in which the birds can shelter and nest. The females lay an average of seven or eight mottled yellow eggs which they incubate for about three weeks. The female bird's barred and spotted brown plumage camouflages her and her eggs, and she sits tight even when approached by foxes, dogs or people. The male is more conspicuous and keeps well away. The eggs all hatch together and the chicks, in camouflage-coloured down, all leave immediately to hide in the heather. They feed themselves, with a little help from the parents but are vulnerable to predation, starvation and inclement weather. Those that survive the first precarious

stony streams, but on the whole the North York Moors are less well endowed with birds than most other upland areas in Britain. In winter, the majority of the birds migrate, leaving the moors desolate and empty.

The wheatear is a characteristic upland bird. One of the first spring migrants to arrive, its white rump is very distinctive as it flits from rock to rock. Its preference is for areas of short grass, shorn by the wind or the nibbling of sheep. It normally avoids long heather and lays its pale blue eggs in a nest in a grassy tussock or tucked in the lee of a boulder. The golden plover is another bird found in the uplands. It too prefers grassy areas among the heather, though not with too many sheep or people.

The ring ouzel – upland cousin of the blackbird – frequents the stone walls and boulder-strewn hillsides. It is usually first detected by its loud whistle or song, though both are usually difficult to hear above the noise of the wind. The ring ouzel's song is disjointed and untidy-sounding, not at all like the leisurely melody of the blackbird. Like most of the typical moorland birds, it deserts the high ground in winter. Whereas many of the

Hasty Bank near Urra

week of life can soon fly and are independent at about six weeks. They do not normally go very far away, not least because their moorland habitat is restricted. Most die within a mile of where they were hatched and the North York Moors grouse population seems to be largely self-contained, separate from others in the Pennines and elsewhere.

As well as helping the grouse, controlled moor burning clears the ground and offers a chance for pioneering plants like mosses to become dominant for a while, adding interesting species as well as colour and texture to the moorland scene. Provided the fire is controlled, brief and not too hot, new growth soon occurs. This also prevents large areas of very old dry heather developing in which fires – if started accidentally – can be devastating. If heather fires are not controlled properly, the underlying peat may ignite and smoulder for days. The heat generated kills everything: plants, insects, even the heat tolerant heather seeds. This creates a black scar on the landscape, an open invitation for invasion by bracken.

Already some 20 per cent of the National Park is covered by bracken, which continues to spread. The problem is that bracken swamps almost everything else. Few things can grow under the dense cover which it provides in summer or

survive being smothered by the blanket of dead fronds which accumulate each year. These dry fronds are prone to fire, killing all but the bracken's resistant underground root system which can then regenerate the bracken sward with renewed vigour, all competition removed. Moreover, few things eat bracken, so it is not controlled by grazing animals. Nor does it support many insects, or provide fruits or flowers to support other creatures. It is a thoroughly selfish, invasive, ecological bully which is almost impossible to control except by using special herbicides. The alternative of repeated cutting and rolling at vulnerable times of the year is expensive and difficult to apply on steep or rocky hillsides.

Sheep are another important part of the landscape and – like bracken – are to a considerable extent responsible for creating it. Their constant nibbling suppresses the growth of shrubs and young trees, and encourages the development of grass. Some tough and unpalatable grasses escape and form tussocks or spriggy tufts; the softer, more edible species are nibbled back to form a dense turf. This is particularly evident in the pastures of course, but also on the roadsides over the moors where some 50,000 sheep roam freely.

Sheep (and moor burning) maintain the open wild landscape necessary for many other plants and animals. The sharp hooves of the sheep cut deeply into soft peat leaving exposed patches vulnerable to erosion. However, this type of damage is less severe than in the Pennines, partly because there are fewer people adding their trampling to the effects of the sheep. Also the moors receive less rain than the Pennines, so peat is not so likely to be washed away once it is broken up by walkers and animals. If sheep are excluded by fencing off areas, long grass and thickets develop which ultimately become woodland – the original and natural climax vegetation before the advent of Man. It is therefore important that the numbers of sheep are regulated. The optimum density varies on different parts of the moors. Few places can support more than one per acre, usually there ought to be less than half that number. Sheep also need to be kept off some areas altogether to permit young trees to grow.

Wheeldale Lodge

Since the 1920s forest has once more begun to clothe the hills: mostly this is not by natural colonisation. The Forestry Commission owns over 15 per cent of the National Park. Forestry grants have encouraged the planting of extensive conifer plantations on poor-quality land unsuited to other forms of profitable activity. Conifers are usually used because they grow fast on poor soils. Alien species such as spruce are often chosen rather than our native conifer, the Scots pine. They form dense, even-age stands of only one or two species. Their branches, especially spruce, cast dense shade and obliterate most other plants.

Conifer plantations also affect the

Roe deer inhabit the conifer plantations and are rarey seen among the trees. The spotted kids are born in May and June. Roe bucks have small spikey antlers 6 inches long

The conifer plantations harbour roe deer which nibble the young trees and distort their growth. The deer are shy and unlikely to be seen in the dense thickets, though they may emerge at dusk and dawn. When disturbed they usually disappear quietly, but sometimes bound away showing their conspicuous white rump patch. The alarm call of the roe deer is a sharp bark, easily mistaken for that of a dog. The males are territorial and roe deer usually live singly or in small family groups, not the large herds typical of park species such as fallow and red deer.

Although 'wild' in the sense of being open and desolate, the moors are nevertheless not natural. The landscape is a product of centuries of manipulation by Man and his domestic animals. Some activities – such as potash mining or erections like radio masts – are visually intrusive and of no benefit to wildlife. However, many other practices – particularly those associated with farming – are highly beneficial in promoting fine scenery and a rich diversity of wildlife. Unfortunately, economic survival on upland farms is increasingly difficult. This encourages a more intensive use of the land.

Fertilisers, pesticides and other agricultural chemicals are used to increase productivity but at the expense of reducing the variety of wild flowers and insects. Improving the grasslands by better drainage or adding fertiliser allows more sheep to be kept, but probably means fewer birds. Often farms are just too small or the soil and climate too intractable, especially on the high moors. For this reason many people have been forced to leave the land for jobs elsewhere. While this is primarily a socio-economic problem, it does also have profound effects on wildlife. Fewer farmhands means that stone walls and fences are not repaired. Sheep then gain access to areas from which they were excluded, ending the prospects of natural regeneration of woodland and devastating delicate woodland flowers.

The heather moors need people to manage them, or they face encroachment by bracken or coarse grasses. The poor economic returns from upland farming enhance the attractiveness of tree planting grants and the potential employment prospects provided by the development of forestry. Undesirable though these influences and changes may seem, they are a reminder of the continuing processes that have fashioned the landscape and its wildlife down the ages. Our countryside

drainage of the land and, for complex reasons, increase the acidity of ground water and the streams, ponds and rivers nearby. This represents a potential danger to the long-term health of various forms of aquatic life, including insects and the dippers which feed on them. The plantations form dark green, angular blots on the landscape which are low in wildlife interest and consequently somewhat unpopular. However, they do provide shelter for animals such as deer, and promote some species of fungi and birds which might otherwise not be present. Scottish crossbills for instance, may be seen here during most winters. There is even the prospect that the pine marten may return from near-extinction to inhabit these new forests and it has been reported in North Yorkshire several times recently.

The early stages of plantation growth often form valuable habitats after fencing out the sheep and before the dense canopy closes over and casts its dark shadow. At this time a deep blanket of grasses forms, supporting high populations of voles and shrews. These are the favoured food of short-eared owls, harriers and other predatory birds whose numbers increase accordingly. Without fenced-off plantations fewer of these birds would be able to breed and rear young. Although the plantations do add some species of interest, they are mostly things common elsewhere and often less interesting than what is lost. Afforestation is probably the greatest threat to the survival of attractive moorland scenery and its associated wildlife.

Ravenscar

has always been a by-product of the interplay between nature and people trying to earn a living.

The limestone belt

Along the south side of the high moors lies an arc of limestone. This is a relatively soft rock and weathers easily to form good, deep soils very different from the peaty uplands to the north. Gouging by glaciers has left spectacular vales, often with outcrops which are today the home of specialised plants clinging to the rock faces. Rocky ledges and fissures also provide secure vantage points on which kestrels nest.

In the valley floors run attractive streams which feed rivers, like the Rye and Dove. They carry many minerals dissolved in the water, which are derived from the limestone rocks of their catchments. These waters are very rich in aquatic invertebrates such as insect larvae and freshwater crustaceans. This is in contrast to the peaty streams on the moors to the north, whose waters are acid and deficient in nutrients, and support far fewer invertebrates and almost no aquatic plants.

The limestone streams offer diverse habitats for aquatic life. Many of them are fast-flowing: their cool, splashing waters dissolving plenty of oxygen from the air. This allows the survival of things like stonefly larvae which cannot tolerate low oxygen levels in the water. When they

melted, the glaciers which had formed the limestone valleys, left behind ridges and piles of boulders which create pools and calmer reaches, further diversifying the habitats available to aquatic life and offering homes for fish such as trout. Grayling are found in the River Rye; some say they were introduced by the monks at Riveaulx to add variety to Friday's monastic meals. Whatever their origins, grayling are very sensitive fish. They require clean river conditions and cannot tolerate water which becomes even moderately warm in the summer. These Yorkshire rivers are ideal because their waters come from high ground and remain cool as a result of evaporation during their splashing, tumbling progress from the hills. Conversely, many of the fish better adapted to slow-flowing, muddier conditions (for example tench and bream) are uncommon or absent from local waters.

Many of the most abundant invertebrates, so typical of the limestone streams, are young stages of various types of insect, such as midges and blackflies. When they emerge from the water in the summer, they can be so numerous as to cause considerable aggravation to visitors. However, they are also a rich source of food for insectivorous birds. These range from the elegant grey wagtails, which pick insects off stones along the rivers, to the swallows and spotted flycatchers that seize them in the air. Beside the rivers grow many alder trees, themselves a rich source of food (including insects) for birds and also for the fish in the water below.

The rich assortment of underwater food means that these streams are an ideal habitat for the dipper. This plump, dark brown bird, with its upturned tail and snow-white shirt front is a characteristic sight, bobbing up and down on a rock amidst the bubbling waters. Periodically it will plunge in and walk along the river bed, gripping rocks tightly with its feet, working its way along against the current. While submerged, the bird pokes its beak into clefts and under pebbles to collect invertebrates for food. During the breeding season, these may be taken back to the nest which is often in a hole below a bridge. Here three or four young are raised, sometimes as early as April. This leaves plenty of time to produce another family or even two, during the course of the summer.

Dippers are rarely seen away from water and make little attempt to hide. They are therefore easy to watch and a quiet vigil beside a clear fast-flowing stretch of river will usually be rewarded. Often the first indication of dippers is a loud 'zeet' call as the bird flashes by, fast and low over the water.

The pools and slower flowing reaches are used by kingfishers. They perch motionless on a branch above the water, waiting to spot small fish before diving in to catch them. Another fish feeder, the otter, was at one time common enough to be hunted regularly in these parts. But now this and other pressures have reduced its populations to scattered remnants which are rarely seen. Conversely, the smaller mink is becoming more abundant in Britain. An introduced species, the mink is able to thrive where otters once ruled, perhaps because it makes greater use of food sources such as rabbits and waterside birds and is less dependant upon fish. The mink is often active in daylight and is more frequently seen by visitors. Yorkshire is not yet a mink stronghold, but the species is spreading rapidly.

The slightly acid ground water which percolates down from the higher ground has dissolved away limestone rock in places to form small cave systems. Excavations in one of these, near Kirkbymoorside, yielded large numbers of teeth and bones from hyaenas, bison and even elephant. All were once part of the wildlife of this area, but during a warm period about 150,000 years ago, before the last Ice Age. At one time, such cave deposits were regarded as the victims of Noah's Flood,

Bog asphodel produces bright yellow flowers about 12 inches tall, on wet acid ground in July and August

and their occurrence in widely distributed places confirmation of the severity of the Deluge. It was the careful scientific study of the finds in Kirkdale Cave, made by the geologist William Buckland in the 1820s, that effectively challenged this notion and with it the accepted belief, based on Biblical scholarship, that the world was only 4,000 years old. Buckland's writings and reasoned analysis exercised a profound influence on the thinking of Charles Darwin, who was later to mount an even greater challenge to orthodox thought in one of the most important books ever written: *On the Origin of Species by Means of Natural Selection*. A few bones

Falling Foss near Whitby

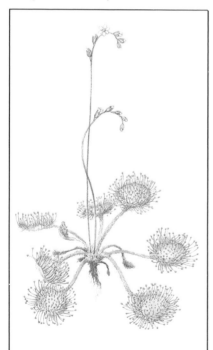

Sticky hairs on the sundew's long leaves trap insects. It is a typical inhabitant of acid bogs and produces a 4-inch-high flower stalk in summer.

and teeth that had lain quietly buried under the Yorkshire Moors thus proved to be an intellectual time-bomb!

The quiet upper reaches of the River Dove in Farndale are a fine and famous sight in April, being golden with the nodding heads of wild daffodils. A convenient riverside path allows enjoyment of these and close inspection of the river itself. To the south of the high ground sheltered humid woods are dominated by sessile oaks. This habitat is characteristic of moist western areas (such as Wales), but rare in eastern England. Consequently, certain species characteristic of western sessile oakwoods are unexpectedly found here in the north-east. For example, these woods are the stronghold for pied flycatchers. They are also home to sparrowhawks, wood warblers and many other more widespread woodland birds whose varied songs add much to the local attractions in early summer. This area is also near the northern limit for breeding lesser spotted woodpeckers in Britain. Fallow and roe deer are also found here.

The woodlands and south-facing soft grasslands provide a good habitat for many butterflies. However, apparently for climatic reasons, many familiar species common in southern England are either absent or close to their northern limit of distribution. The small skipper is an example; abundant further south, but absent to the north. Rare butterflies, such as the Duke of Burgundy fritillary, used to be found on the limestone grasslands but have suffered much from habitat loss. The white lesser hairstreak had its northern outpost here, but has everywhere suffered from the loss of elm trees (its larval food plant) in the 1970s due to Dutch elm disease.

In the woods and hedgerows, primroses and bluebells are a fine sight in the spring. The alkaline soils in limestone areas also support rare plants such as wood vetch. On the open limestone grasslands spotted and bee orchids can be seen in summer. These are typical of the many attractive flowers which are rapidly swamped by rank vegetation and scrub encroachment if there is too little grazing by sheep and rabbits to maintain the short turf in the face of natural succession by other plants. Within the region there are several local nature reserves giving special protection to particularly interesting wildlife communities.

Less popular than most of the local wildlife, the adder is widespread in the region. On the moors it probably feeds

A beck at Goathland

mainly on common lizards; around the hedgerows and woodland edges it will have greater access to mice and voles. Fear of adders is quite unjustified. They are shy animals and disappear quickly if they see people approaching. The adder is one of the few reptiles which live in the northern parts of Europe (even beyond the Arctic Circle!), and is tolerant of the cool, cloudy conditions on our uplands. It likes to bask in the morning and evening, but often retires to the shade if the sun gets too hot.

Adders are the only poisonous animals in Britain, but save this for their prey. They only bite people in self defence and are harmless if left alone. Their bite causes painful swelling (like a severe bee sting) but is only fatal in very exceptional circumstances. The probability of being killed by an adder has been wildly exaggerated. The average visitor to the countryside is far more likely to die from being struck by lightning or killed by a falling tree. Most probable of all, of course, is that none of these things will happen and you will not even see an adder! Male adders are boldly marked with a black zig-zag stripe along a creamy-white body. Females are heavier-looking and coloured in shades of brown. It is unusual for either to exceed 20 inches in length.

Grass snakes lack the zig-zag marking and are olive green with yellow neck patches. They are completely harmless and normally found in damp, lowland areas. They are close to their northen limit in this region. The slow worm superficially resembles a snake in having no legs. It is common, especially in the limestone areas, and is completely harmless except to the slugs and insects upon which it feeds. Slow worms are a beautiful bronze or chocolate brown.

The coast

Where the Cleveland Hills meet the sea, the spectacular scenery has been declared a 'Heritage Coast'. Here and to the south, the cliffs and sandy bays offer an attractive assortment of seashore habitats. In places, zonation of the seaweeds is evident, caused by some species being less tolerant than others of exposure at low tide. Where freshwater streams come down to the beach, bright green patches of sea lettuce grow prominently in the areas too salty for normal plants, but not salty enough for the brown and red seaweeds. Rock pools contain sea anemones, blennies, crabs and many attractive molluscs. Offshore, below the low water mark, the rocks provide hiding places for crabs and lobsters which are the basis for a local fishery. After heavy storms the strandline is littered with marine debris including starfish, 'mermaids purses' (egg cases of skate and dogfish) and seaweeds torn free from the rocks. In the dampness of the strandline debris are found millions of sandhoppers – tiny crustaceans that cannot tolerate the dry conditions of the open beach and live on particles of the decomposing debris cast up by the sea.

While rocky shores offer the most conspicuous signs of wildlife, sandy coasts also harbour a substantial variety of plants and animals most of which are hidden from sight. In the absence of seaweeds, which need to attach to rocks, animals have nowhere to shelter on a sandy shore. Consequently most bury themselves in the sand and will not be found without digging. Traces such as worm casts and burrow entries are a give-away to the bait diggers and cockle collectors who come to harvest the hidden hordes. The cockles (and other local molluscs) are sold as food on whelk and cockle stalls at Scarborough and the other seaside towns. Many birds come to reap the same harvest. Curlews and oyster catchers prod in the sand, seeking the shellfish and marine worms hiding there. Wading birds are most numerous in winter when harsh weather and frozen ground drives them off the moors. The sea does not freeze, so there is always water and soft sand in which to poke about for food, even in the worst winters.

Though scenically attractive, the cliffs along this coast are generally poor in terms of bird life. Perhaps this is because better nesting ledges are to be found not far away.

The great sea bird colonies of the Farne Islands to the north and Bempton Cliffs to the south are sufficiently close to act like magnets for most of the highly sociable species such as auks and kittiwakes. A few cormorants and fulmars breed at scattered sites along the coast; stonechats can be seen on the cliff tops and rock pipits on the shore below. Herring gulls are the commonest breeding sea birds. They are also an interesting sight, nesting among the chimneys of houses and hotels in coastal towns like Whitby, though their loud cries awaken many holidaymakers much earlier than their accustomed time.

Visitors wishing to see a spectacular seabird colony should use their OS maps to venture a few miles south of Scarborough to Bempton Cliffs. Here the sheer rockfaces support Britain's only mainland colony of gannets, the largest of our seabirds. Thousands of guillemots, kittiwakes and other cliff nesters are present in the nesting season, especially in June and July. The Bempton bird colonies were once notorious as the place where collectors would go by boat from Scarborough to shoot the birds for plumage to be used in ladies hats. Public outcry finally led to protective legislation for the birds. Today the cliffs are an RSPB

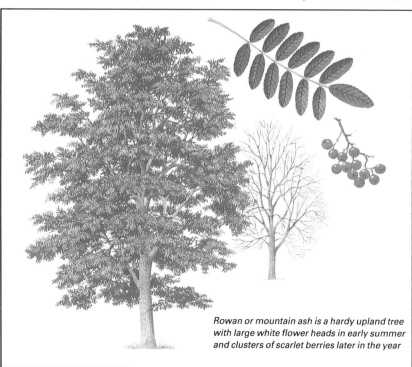

Rowan or mountain ash is a hardy upland tree with large white flower heads in early summer and clusters of scarlet berries later in the year

The River Rye

reserve with a small Visitors' Centre.

Many parts of the coast provide fine exposures of Jurassic rocks. A nature trail descends to the beach near Ravenscar and offers opportunities to see aspects of the local geology. The coast around Robin Hood's Bay is famous for its fossils: an interesting display of local ammonites can be seen in the museum at Whitby. There are also displays of jet – another special local material formed from fossilised conifer wood which was once very popular for carving into intricate brooches and necklaces.

The Vale of York

The glaciers which moulded the hard rocks of the higher ground worked a different kind of magic on the flatter areas to the south. Here they dumped a large assortment of geological debris derived from elsewhere. Large deposits of rich soils were laid down and now support the extensive areas of prosperous farmland which characterise the Vale of York. However, in smaller patches were deposited pockets of poor sandy soils which are less suitable for farming and now form areas of heathland such as Strensall and Skipwith Commons. Birch scrub and heather grow on the drier parts with breeding nightjars. Acid bogs develop in the poorly drained hollows. The latter support plants such as marsh gentian. Sundew and butterwort are also common, and could not survive on the better drained and alkaline soils roundabout.

Both compensate for the poor supply of nutrients in bog waters by trapping insects and digesting them. The wet pools are also ideal for colourful dragonflies and damselflies.

The River Ouse – collecting its tributaries from the moors to the north and Pennines to the west – flows placidly southwards through undulating farmland. Here are many copses and shelterbelts, linked by an extensive network of hedgerows. All shelter typical, though unremarkable wildlife communities. Yellowhammers, corn buntings and other finches are particularly abundant – especially in winter when they are joined by migrants including the brambling. The many hedgehogs seen dead on the roads in summer are testimony both to their own abundance and to that of the beetles and worms on which they feed in the adjacent rich grassy pastures.

Some of the low-lying fields beside the river are subject to frequent flooding. The wet conditions preclude many forms of development and regular inundation by nutrient-rich, silt bearing river water enhances growing conditions for the grass. The land has therefore been used mainly for grazing and hay crops rather than arable farming. These water meadows (like the 'ings' north of York) develop a very rich flora and also support large numbers of birds in the winter and on migration. The rising water attracts waterfowl and also brings worms and insect food close to the surface within reach of the prodding beaks of snipe and other wading birds. Wet areas such as these provide plenty of flying insects for many other birds, especially in summer. At night, bats exploit the same food source before returning to hollow trees or the house and church roofs of York to pass the day asleep.

Rooks also feed on the larger soil invertebrates, particularly worms and beetle larvae. Large flocks can be seen prodding in the pastures, and their rookeries are prominent in hedgerow trees. The birds begin to assemble and noisily refurbish their nests in early spring before the leaves open and hide their activities. Over much of southern Britain rooks seem to be declining in numbers, perhaps because their invertebrate food becomes less abundant in fields which are drained, treated with chemicals and otherwise encouraged to grow more crops and less wildlife. The lapwing also appears to be declining, perhaps for similar reasons. Both are still common on the rich, unspoilt farmland of Yorkshire.

Leisure Activities

Useful Names & Addresses

TRANSPORT

Motoring:
Automobile Association, Tel: (0904) 27698
R.A.C., Tel: (0532) 448556

Buses & Coaches:
Scarborough:
Scarborough & District, Tel: (0723) 375463
Primrose Valley, Tel: (0723) 512034
Wallace Arnold, Tel: (0723) 375522

Whitby:
United, Tel: (0947) 62146 & (0642) 210131
Howards Tours, Tel: (0947) 602317/ 602494

York:
United Coaches, Tel: (0904) 24161
West Yorkshire Roadcar, Tel: (0904) 24161

Thirsk:
United, Tel: (0325) 468771

Trains:
Malton, Tel: (0653) 697911; North Yorkshire Moors Railway, Tel: (0751) 72508; Talking Timetable, Tel: (0751) 73535; Tourist Information Centre, Tel: (0751) 73791. Scarborough, Tel: (0723) 373486; Whitby, Tel: (0947) 602453; York, Tel: (0904) 642155.

Boat Trips and Cruises:
Scarborough:
Local Information, Tel: (0723) 373333

York:
Castle Line, Tel: (0904) 702240
Hills, Tel: (0904) 23752
Ouse, Tel: (0904) 425433
White Rose, Tel: (0904) 28324

Whitby:
Local Information, Tel: (0907) 602674

Bicycle Hire
York:
Cycle Scene, Tel: (0904) 53286
Rent-It, Tel: (0904) 20173
Cycle Works, Tel: (0904) 26664

Other locations:
Thornton Dale 75310
Scarborough 365751

Car Hire:
Budget, Tel: (0904) 644919
Economy, Tel: (0904) 470009
Fitton, Tel: (0904) 426868
Godfrey Davis, Tel: (0904) 20394
Godfrey Davis, Station Tel: (0904) 59790
Kenning, Tel: (0904) 59328
Polar, Tel: (0904) 25371
Reynards, Tel: (0904) 24277

LEISURE ACTIVITIES

Activity Centres:
These centres offer facilities to non-residents:
Marine Activities, Robin Hood's Bay, Tel: (0947) 880496 for watersports.
Park House Outdoor Centre, Ingleby Cross Tel: (0609) 82571 for climbing, canoeing and caving.
Sutherland Lodge Activity Centre, Cropton. Tel: Lastingham 228 for pony trekking, canoeing, climbing and cycling.

Boat Hire, rowing and sailing:
Dinghy Sailing:
Scaling Dam, Tel: Guisborough (0287) 32522.

Rowing and Canoeing:
Sleights (Tel: (0947) 810329. Robin Hood's Bay, Tel: (0947) 880496; Osmotherley, (Tel: (0609) 82571; Cropton, Tel: (07515) 228.

Off-Shore Sailing:
Enquiries at local information centres and H.M. Coastguard. Tel: Scarborough (0723) 372323 and Whitby (0947) 602107.
Sailboarding & Surf-Skiing:
Robin Hood's Bay. Tel: (0947) 880496

Camping & Caravanning:
Cleveland Way Campsites:
Sutton Bank:
The Hambleton Inn, Sutton Bank, Thirsk. Tel: (0845) 597202.
Boltby:
High Paradise Farm, Boltby, Thirsk, Tel: (0845) 537353.
Osmotherley:
Chequers Farm, Osmotherley. Tel: (060983) 291; Park House Outdoor Centre, Ingleby Cross, Osmotherley. Tel: (060983) 571.
Bilsdale:
Beakhills Farm, Chopgate, Stokesley. Tel: (0642) 778368.
Kirkby-in-Cleveland:
Toft Hill Farm, Kirkby-in-Cleveland, Great Broughton. Tel: Stokesley (0642) 712469.

Great Broughton:
White Post Farm, Great Broughton, Stokesley. Tel: (0642) 778293.
Hawsker:
Northcliffe Caravan Park, High Hawsker, Whitby. Tel: (0937) 880477.
Scalby:
Beacon Cottage Farm, Barmoor Lane, Scalby, Scarborough. Tel: (0723) 870378.

Other sites:
Boroughbridge, Yorkhouse Caravans, Tel: (09012) 3190; Forestry Commission, Tel: Pickering (0751) 60212 or Lastingham (075 15) 591; Fylingdales, Grouse Hill, Tel: (0947) 880543; Goathland, Abbot's Farm, Tel: (0947) 86270; Goathland, Brow House Farm, Tel: (0947) 86274; Guisborough, Tocketts Mill Caravans, Tel: (0642) 468011; High Hawsker, Northcliffe & Seaview Caravans, Tel: (0947) 880477; Oswaldkirk, Golden Square, Tel: (04393) 269; Pickering, Black Bull, Tel: (0751) 72528; Pickering (Wrelton), Wayside, Tel: (0751) 72608; Riseborough (Pickering), The Lodge, Tel: (0751) 75189; Robin Hood's Bay, Middlewood Farm, Tel: (0947) 880414; Rosedale Abbey, Caravans & Camping, Tel: (07515) 272; Saltburn, Fern Farm Caravans, Tel: (0947) 840350; Scarborough, Jacob's Mount, Tel: (0723) 361178; Scawton (Rievaulx) Bungdale Head Farm, Tel: (0439) 70589; Slingsby, Robin Hood, Tel: (065 382) 391; Staintondale, Lowfield, Tel: (0723) 870574; Sutton-under-Whitestonecliffe, Cleavehill Caravans, Tel: (0845) 597229; Ugthorpe (Whitby), Burnt House, Tel: (0947) 840448; Vale of Pickering, Carr House Farm, Caravan Park, Allerston, Tel: (0723) 85280.

Fishing:
Full details of licences and permits, locations and clubs from: Yorkshire Water, 21 Park Square South, Leeds LS1 2QG. Tel: (0532) 440191.

River Rye and Tributaries:
R. Rye (Hawnby) Tickets from Hawnby Hotel, Hawnby, Tel: Bilsdale (043 96) 202; R. Septh (Laskill) Hawnby Hotel, Hawnby, Tel: Bilsdale (043 96) 202; R. Rye (Nunnington) Estate Office, Nunnington, Tel: Nunnington (043 95) 202 weekdays, Keepers Cottage, Nunnington, Tel: Nunnington 247 weekends; R. Seven (Normanby) Sun Inn, Normanby, Tel: Kirkbymoorside (0751) 31051; Costa Beck (Kirby Misperton) Lendales Farm, Kirby Misperton, Tel: Kirby Misperton (065 386) 220; Manor Farm, Kirby Misperton, Tel: Kirby Misperton (065 386) 251.

River Derwent and Tributaries:
Dalby Beck, Forestry Commission Information Centre, Low Dalby, Tel: Pickering (0751) 60295; R. Derwent (Hackness) Pritchards Tackle, Eastborough, Scarborough, Tel: Scarborough (0723) 374017 or Hackness Grange Hotel, Hackness, Tel: Scarborough (0723) 369966; R. Derwent (Yedingham) Providence Inn, Yedingham, Tel: (094 45) 231; R. Derwent (Marishes) Lendales Farm, Kirby Misperton, Tel: (065 386) 220; R. Derwent (Old Malton) Fitzwilliam Estate Office, Malton, Tel: (0653) 2849.

River Esk:
R. Esk (Danby) Tickets available Danby P.O; Duke of Wellington Inn, Danby, Whitby. R. Esk (Sleights, Whitby) Millbeck, The Carrs, Ruswarp; Whitby Angling Supplies, 5 Haggersgate, Whitby.

Lakes and Reservoirs:
Lake Arden, Keepers Cottage, Arden Hall, Bilsdale, Tel: (04396) 343; Cod Beck Reservoir, Rod licences and tickets from Osmotherley Post Office (closed Wed. & Sat. afternoon and all day Sunday) Tel: Osmotherley (060983) 201; Scaling Dam Reservoir, Fishing Lodge, Permit Issue Office, Scaling Dam; Lockwood Beck Reservoir, Fishing Lodge, Permit Office, Lockwood Beck; Lockwood Beck is controlled by the Northumbrian Water Authority. Anglers require the Authority's licence to fish there; Scarborough Mere, tickets from local tackle shops.

Gliding and Hang Gliding:
George Cayley Sailwing Club, Beverley, (Tel: (0482) 881661; Newcastle and Teesside Gliding Club, Stokesley, Tel: (0642) 778234; Northern Hang Gliding Centre, Scarborough, Tel: Sherburn (0944) 70333; Ouse Gliding Club, Tel: (090483) 694; Windsports Centre, Wombleton, Tel: Kirkbymoorside (0751) 32356; Yorkshire Gliding Club, Tel: (0845) 597237;

Golf:
Scarborough:
North Cliff Golf Club, Tel:(0723) 360786; South Cliff Golf Club, Tel: (0723) 360522; Ganton Golf Club, Tel: (0944) 70329
Whitby:
Whitby Golf Club, Tel: (0947) 602768; Raven Hall, Ravenscar Tel: (0723) 870353; Esk Leisure Centre, Ruswarp, Tel: (0947) 605954.
York:
Fulford, Tel: (0904) 412882; Pike Hills, Tel: (0904) 706566; York, Tel: (0904) 490304.

Horse Racing:
Thirsk (Flat meetings: April, July, September); Wetherby (National Hunt: September, May); York (Flat meetings: May, October).

Horse Riding:
Cropton, Tel: Lastingham (075 15) 509, 384 and 228; Boltby, Tel: Thirsk (0845) 537375; Carlton-in-Cleveland, Tel: Stokesley (0642) 701027; Hawnby, Tel: Bilsdale (043 96) 225 or 252; Helmsley, Tel: Helmsley (0439) 70355; Irton, Tel: Scarborough (0723) 863466; Locton, Tel: Pickering (0751) 60325; Over Silton, Tel: Osmotherley (060 983) 344; Pickering, Tel: Pickering (0751) 72982; Ravenscar, Tel: Scarborough (07023) 870470; Robin Hood's Bay, Tel: Whitby (0947) 880249; Rosedale, Tel: Lastingham (075 15) 619; Saltburn, Tel: Guisborough (02087) 22157; Skelton, Tel: Guisborough (02087) 50303; Sleights, Tel: Whitby (0947) 810450; Snainton, Tel: Scarborough (0723) 85218; Swainby, Tel: Stokesley (0642) 700550; Thornton Dale, Tel: Pickering (0751) 74297; Ugthorpe, Tel: Whitby (0947) 840086; York, Tel: York (0904) 769029

British Horse Society Regional Bridleways Officer: 12 Oakley Close, Guisborough. TS14 7NF.

Sports Centres and Indoor Swimming:
Ampleforth, Tel: Ampleforth (04393) 485; Guisborough, Tel: Guisborough (02087) 33311; Helmsley, Tel: Helmsley (0439) 70173; Loftus, Tel: Guisborough (02087) 42020; Pickering, Tel: Pickering (0751) 73351; Saltburn, Tel: Guisborough (02087) 23761; Scarborough, North Bay, Tel: Scarborough (07023) 37244; Ryndle Crescent, Tel: Scarborough (07023) 367137; Scarborough Sports Centre, Tel: Scarborough (07023) 360262; South Bay, Tel: Scarborough (07023) 374446; Thirsk, Tel: (0845) 22447; Whitby, Tel: Whitby (0947) 604640; York, Barbican, Tel: York (0904) 30266; Edmund Wilson, Tel: York (0904) 793031; Yearsley, Tel: York (0904) 22773;

Walking:
Enquiries about Guided Walks to Information Centres or Tel: (0439) 70657. There are also more than 30 Waymark Walks available for a few pence from local information centres and shops.

Youth Hostels:
Boggle Hole (94)(NZ 95-04) Tel: (0947) 880352; Helmsley (100)(SE 61-84) Tel: (0439) 70433; Lockton (94,100)SE 84-89) Tel: (0751) 60376; Malton (100)(SE 78-71) Tel: (0653) 692077; Osmotherley (99)(SE 45-97) Tel: (060983) 575; Scarborough (101)(TA 03-88) Tel: (0723) 361176; Westerdale (94)(NZ 66-06) Tel: (0287) 60469; Wheeldale (94,100)(SE 81-98) Tel: (0947) 86350; Whitby (94)(NZ 89-10) Tel: (0947) 602878; York (105)(SE 59-53) Tel: (0904) 653147.

PLACES TO VISIT

Abbeys, Minsters and Priories:
Byland Abbey, Tel: (034) 76614; Guisborough Priory, Tel: (0287) 38301; Kirkham Priory, Tel: (065381) 768; Newburg Priory, Tel:(03476) 435; Mount Grace Priory, Tel: (0609) 83249; Riveaulx Abbey, Tel: (04396) 228; Whitby Abbey, Tel: (0947) 603568; York Minster, Tel: (0904) 2442.

Cinemas:
York:
Odeon Film Centre, Tel: (0904) 23040.
Scarborough:
Futurist, Tel: (0723) 370742; Hollywood Plaza, Tel: (0723) 365119; Odeon, Tel: (0723) 361725; Royal Opera House, Tel: (0723) 369999.

Forests and Forest Trails:
Dalby Forest Drive, Tel: (0751) 72771 or (0751) 60295.

Historic Houses, Castles and Gardens:
Beningbrough Hall, Tel: (0904) 470715; Castle Howard, Tel: (065384) 333; Duncombe Park, Tel: (0493) 70213; Ebberston Hall, Tel: (0723) 88885516; Gilling Castle, Tel:(04393) 238; Helmsley Castle, Tel: (0439) 70442; Hovingham Hall, (consult local information office); Nunnington Hall, Tel: (04995) 283; Osgodby Hall, Tel: (0845) 597534; Pickering Castle, Tel: (0751) 74989; Rievaulx Terrace, Tel: 04396) 340; Scarborough Castle, Tel: (0723) 72451; Shandy Hall, Tel: (03476) 465; Sutton Park, Tel: (0347) 810249;

York:
Assembly Rooms, Tel: (0904) 59881; Clifford's Tower, Tel: (0904) 646940; Fairfax House, Tel: (0904) 55543; Guildhall, Tel: (0904) 5988l; Kings Manor, Tel: (0904) 59861; Merchant Adventurer's Hall, Tel: (0904) 54818; Merchant Taylor's Hall, Tel: (0904) 24889; Minster Library, Tel: (0904) 25308; St Anthony's Hall, Tel: (0904) 64315; St William's College, (0904) 34830; Treasurers House, Tel: (0904) 24247; York House, Tel: (0904) 86360.

Museums, Art Galleries and Exhibitions:
Aldborough Roman Town, Tel: (09012) 2768; Beck Isle Museum of Rural Life, Tel: (0751) 73653; Captain Cook's Museum, Great Ayton, Tel: (0642) 723268; Crescent Art Gallery, Scarborough, Tel: (0723) 374735; Eden Camp, Tel: (0653) 7777; Friargate Wax Museum, York, (Tel: (0904) 59775; Jorvik Viking Centre, York, Tel: (0904) 643211; Malton Museum, Tel: (0653) 2610; Model Railway, York, Tel: (0904) 30916; Levisham, St Mary's Museum of Church Art, Tel: (0274) 493116; National Railway Museum, York, (0904) 21261; Rotunda Archaeological Museum, Scarborough Tel: (0723) 374839; Ryedale Folk Museum, Hutton-le-Hole, Tel: (07515) 367; Sion Hill Hall, Thirsk, Tel: (0845) 587206; Sutcliffe Gallery, Photographs, Tel: (0947) 602239; Thirsk Museum, Tel: (0845) 22755; Whitby Museum and Art Gallery, Tel: (0947) 602908; Wood End Museum, Scarborough, Tel: (0723) 376326; York Art Gallery, Tel: (0904) 23834; York Castle Museum, Tel: (0904) 53611; York Mansion House, Tel: (0904) 5988l; Yorkshire Museum, York, Tel: (0904) 29475; Yorkshire Museum of Farming, York, Tel: (0904) 489966; York Photographic Gallery, Tel: (0904) 54724; York Story, Tel: (0904) 28632.

Theatres and Concerts:
Scarborough:
Floral Hall Theatre, Tel: (0723) 372185/360644/373039; Futurist Theatre, Tel: (0723) 370742; Royal Opera House, Tel: (0723) 369999; Spa Theatre, Tel: (0723) 365068; Stephen Joseph Theatre in the Round, Tel: (0723) 370541; YMCA Theatre, Tel: (0723) 374227.

Whitby:
Spa Theatre, Tel: (0947) 604855; Spa Pavilion, Tel: (0947) 604855.
York:
Arts Centre, Tel: (0904) 27129; Theatre Royal, Tel: (0904) 23568; Youth Theatre, (0904) 39707.

Tourist Information Centres

Boroughbridge* Tel: (09012) 3373; Danby Lodge National Park Centre, Tel: (0287) 60654; Guisborough, Tel: (0287) 33801; Helmsley* Tel: (0439) 70173; Hutton-le-Hole* Tel: (07515) 367; Malton, Tel:(0653) 600048; Moorland Centre, Tel: (0287) 60654; National Park Department, Tel: (0439) 70657; National Trust, Tel: (0904) 702021; National Trust Centre Tel: (0723) 870138; North York Moors Information Centre, Tel: (0287) 60654; Pickering* Tel: (0751) 73791; Scarborough* Tel: (0723) 373333; Sutton Bank* Tel: (0845) 597426; Thirsk* Tel: (0845) 22755; Whitby* Tel: (0947) 602674; York* Tel: (0904) 21756/21757 or (0904) 643700; Yorkshire and Humberside Tel: (0904) 707961

Other useful addresses and/or telephone numbers

BBC Radio York, Tel: (0904) 641351;
Dental Emergency, Tel: (0904) 30371;
Forestry Commission, Helmsley, Tel: (04392) 346;
Forestry Commission, Pickering, Tel: (0751) 72771;
Historic Buildings and Monuments Commission, Tel: (0904) 22902;
Ryedale District Council, Malton, Tel: (0653) 600666;
Weather: Pre-recorded Tel: (0898) 500418; Forecast Tel: (0642) 8091; 5-Day Forecast, Tel: (0898) 500430;
York District Hospital Tel: (0904) 31313;

Further useful information

Early Closing Days:
Wednesday: Great Ayton, Guisborough, Helmsley, Pickering, Robin Hood's Bay, Scarborough, Sleights, Staithes, Stokesley, Thirsk, Whitby, York, Middlesbrough.
Thursday: Kirkbymoorside, Malton, Ruswarp, Northallerton.
NOTE: Many shopkeepers do not observe an early closing day during the season.

Market Days:
Monday: Pickering, Thirsk.
Wednesday: Kirkbymoorside, Northallerton.
Thursday: Guisborough, Scarborough.
Friday: Helsmley.
Saturday: Malton, Guisborough.

Places of Interest

Aislaby (94,100) (SE 77-85)
The village is situated on the steep slopes of the River Esk near its mouth. Most of the houses were built from local stone for the men working at the nearby quarry. Stone from this quarry was used in the construction of Covent Garden Market, Old London Bridge and Whitby Pier.

Aldborough (99) (SE 40-66)
This village, with its fine Georgian houses, is a suburb of Boroughbridge ★ – but is in fact much older. The Romans chose the site as an administrative centre on the main route to the north which they called Isurium Brigantium. It was the base of the Ninth Legion and is thought to have been developed as a recreational centre. Aldborough's beautiful church, with its medieval carving of Daniel in the lions' den, is believed to be built on the site of a temple to the god Mercury.

After the Romans left Britain, Aldborough went into a long decline. The invading Anglo-Saxons and Vikings ignored the town and used York, which is nearer the sea, as the main centre for the region. The Normans also scorned Aldborough, deciding instead to develop Boroughbridge.

It was not until Georgian times, around the end of the eighteenth century, that there was any extensive re-building, creating the village as we see it today. The original Roman street pattern was used as a 'town plan'.

Evidence of the importance of Aldborough as a Roman centre was discovered as recently as 1852 when some buildings were uncovered in the Manor House gardens. There is now an excellent museum run by English Heritage with an exhibition of Roman finds. The museum also gives access to parts of the Roman wall surrounding the town and two well-preserved sections of mosaic floor (see **Tour 5**).

Ampleforth (100) (SE 58-78)
The visitor might wonder why Ampleforth Abbey is so complete, when many of Yorkshire's abbeys suffered badly during the Dissolution of the Monasteries ordered by Henry VIII. The answer is that this Benedictine abbey was founded by monks escaping from France after the Revolution who were given refuge by the Fairfax family. It was built between 1785 and 1790. The famous Roman Catholic school is part of the abbey and this section is closed to the general public. The abbey church, designed by Sir Giles Gilbert Scott and completed in 1961, contains some excellent wood carvings by a local man, Robert Thompson, who lived in Kilburn ★.

Visible across the plain is a wood hiding Gilling Castle. Over the centuries different incumbents have added to the castle in a

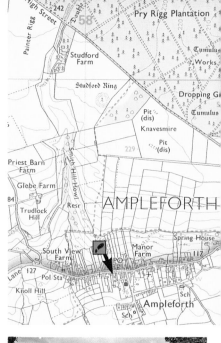

Gilling Castle

variety of architectural styles, including Elizabethan and Georgian. There is a fine example of Tudor stained glass in one room which was sold to William Randolph Hearst, but returned in 1932.

To the north of the village is the earthwork known as Studford Ring and there are also Bronze Age barrows on the moors. **Walk 9** starts from Ampleforth and there are also pleasant strolls in the area (see also **Tours 5 and 10**).

Appleton-le-Moors (94) (SE 73-87)
Until quite recent times the village was called Wood Appleton. It was the advent of the GPO which caused it to be renamed Appleton-le-Moors. A Roman farmstead has been discovered in the parish. Most of the existing buildings, and the current street plan, date from medieval times. From the air, or a large-scale Ordnance Survey map, the typical layout of a medieval village can be seen: there is a single main street with a row of houses on either side. Behind each row of houses is a back lane and beyond that the common fields. The Victorian church is modelled on the earliest type of French Gothic. There is also a medieval wayside cross.

was necessary, the building and carving blend unobtrusively into the old. The eminent writer on architecture, Nikolaus Pevsner, records that the work is completely satisfactory – an accolade indeed! It is an example of how restoration should be done, a new Norman church.

Barton-le-Willows (100) (SE 71-63)

This village to the east of the busy A64 was once a major stopping place for horse-drawn coaches travelling between York ★ and Scarborough ★ , and probably saw more traffic in the early nineteenth century than it does today. It looks over the River Derwent and nearby Howsham Hall ★ , where a short stroll is recommended. There have been several manor houses here, and one of the early owners in the thirteenth century endowed Kirkham Priory ★ which lies a mile or so to the north-east.

The village has some good Regency houses still remaining among more modern buildings. Its name is derived from the Old English word 'bar' for barley: 'willows' is probably a contraction of 'wool house'.

Battersby (93) (NZ 59-07)

This is a charming little village nestling at the southern end of Kildale. As with all place names ending in 'by' we can be sure that this was a Danish settlement. It was a form used for small farms or hamlets. Battersby Old Hall dates from late seventeenth century.

The short valley of Kildale was formed by the erosion caused by the River Leven which, finding its path to the sea blocked by glacial deposits, flowed inland instead. This break in the high escarpment that runs along the edge of the Moors for most of the western border, provided a convenient entry point for the railway engineers who constructed the line from Battersby Junction to Whitby ★ . Battersby Junction station is now a rather strange terminus, as the line to the west has been dismantled, so that trains to Whitby have to stop on their way from Middlesbrough and go into reverse in order to continue towards the coast.

The steep slopes of Ingleby Bank and Battersby Crag lie to the east. It is a difficult climb, deterring all but the very fit from clambering up to the Cleveland Way here for a splendid view of the Cleveland Plain. **Walk 2** shows a route from Ingleby Greenhow ★ to the top.

Forge Valley

Ayton (East and West) (101) (SE 98-84)

These two villages have no connection with Great Ayton ★ , on the opposite corner of the Moors close to Middlesbrough: they are near Scarborough ★ on the main road to Pickering ★ . The villages are separated by the River Derwent as it turns its back to the sea and flows inland towards York ★ having forced its way through the narrow Forge Valley. See the map on this page to plan strolls in Forge Valley. The bridge over the river was built with stone taken from the ruins of the fourteenth-century castle. The church in East Ayton, though rebuilt in the last century, still retains much of its original thirteenth-century construction.

Barton-le-Street (100) (SE 72-74)

Set on the north side of the Howardian Hills this village lies on one of the arteries which serve the Moors, the B1257. Barton-le-Street's most remarkable feature is its church. This was built during the Norman period and although it has seen the hand of Victorian workmen, the firm from Leeds who carried out the work did it in a most sympathetic manner. The repairs were carefully executed, and where new work

Beadlam and Nawton (100) (SE 65-84)

Though sited in separate parishes, these two villages are really one, and now share a common church. The remains of a large Roman villa were found near here recently and there are several ancient cruck-style cottages still standing in Beadlam. The cruck style may be derived from the early Norse method of house-building. A fine example can be seen at the Ryedale Folk Museum in Hutton-le-Hole ★.

Anyone interested in gardening who visits this region in late May should go to Nawton Tower to see the superb private garden that is open to the public on certain days at that time of the year. Visits can also be made by appointment at other times.

Beck Hole (94) (NZ 82-02)
This is an attractive hamlet set at the bottom of a wooded valley surrounded by harsh moorland. There is a short walk up Eller Beck to Thomason Foss ('foss' is the local world for waterfall).

Beck Hole

George Stephenson opened a regular railway line between Whitby ★ and Pickering ★ in 1836 using the steep 1-in-55 incline for the section between Beck Hole and Goathland ★. The incline was too steep for the locomotives and it was necessary to haul wagons up using a rope cable and water tank system. This eventually proved unsafe and the line was later re-routed by blasting a ledge along the side of the Eller Beck valley. This allowed

trains to be hauled by steam locomotives over the entire length of the line from Whitby to Pickering. It is now an attractive section of the preserved and active North Yorkshire Moors Railway ★ which runs from Grosmont ★ to Pickering. It is possible to walk the whole length of the original route and still see sections of the old line by the railway cottage at the foot of the incline. Though no touring centre – visitors should stay in Goathland up the hill – it is a pretty spot for ramblers and cyclists to pause for a rest (see **Tour 3**). The inn can boast that a member of the Royal Academy painted the sign.

Beggar's Bridge (see Glaisdale)

Beningbrough Hall (105) (SE 51-58)
This magnificent early eighteenth-century Baroque building was designed by the architect William Thornton, for John Bourchier, one of the signatories to the death warrant of Charles I. It stands in a delightful setting near the River Ouse some eight miles north-west of York ★ and is now in the care of the National Trust.

The brickwork is an unusual claret colour which is seen at its best early or late on a sunny day. The approach from the north along the lime tree avenue is extremely impressive. Beningbrough Hall has superb examples of woodwork by local carpenters and carvers. York was a centre of excellence for these crafts when the Hall was built and the skill still thrives in Kilburn ★ on the edge of the Moors.

Beningbrough Hall also houses part of the National Gallery collection of portraits covering the years 1688 to 1750. Included among these dignitaries are Pepys, Handel, Alexander Pope and Sir Robert Walpole.

In the laundry, which was added by the Victorians, there is a fascinating exhibition of how servants worked in the last century. **Tour 5** includes a visit to Beningbrough Hall.

Beningbrough

Bilsdale (see entry on Clay Bank)

Boroughbridge (99) (SE 39-66)
This town dating back to Norman times, is set on either side of the River Ure. Although Boroughbridge was by-passed in the 1960s, it marks an ideal bridging point and for many centuries prospered as an important staging post on the main route from York ★ to Edinburgh. Many coaching inns can still be seen: the Crown Inn had stables for more than a hundred horses. It is no wonder that the locals used to complain of the racket caused as the long-distance coaches arrived and departed.

Nearby Boroughbridge are the three ancient monoliths knowns as the 'Devil's Arrows'. Local legend has it that Old Nick flung them in anger at the town as a warning not to provoke his wrath. Less imaginatively, they can be considered as part of the complex of Neolithic and Early Bronze Age monuments which extend north for over eleven miles. There used to be four Devil's Arrows, but one of them was cut into pieces and used to make a bridge over a local stream. Recent research has shown that the stones were quarried at Knaresborough to the south-west. Experts believe they were floated down the river on rafts.

The Normans were the first to build a wooden bridge over the Ure (there does not seem to have been a stone structure until the sixteenth century). An incident on one of the early wooden bridges proved significant in the Battle of Boroughbridge fought during the Wars of the Roses in 1322. The Earl of Hereford had allied himself with Thomas, Earl of Lancaster against the king, Edward II. The turning point in the battle came when Hereford – attempting to cross the bridge – was killed by an enterprising soldier who thrust his spear up between the planks from underneath. Lancaster's end was more sedate: he was beheaded at Pontefract. Boroughbridge was the scene of another potential uprising in 1569 when Mary Queen of Scots tried to organise support to put her on the English throne.

From the early middle ages onwards there were several fairs and markets in the area, but only one remains active today. This is the June Barnaby Fair dating back to 1682, which attracts dealers in the trade of buying and selling horses from all over the North of England.

The town of Boroughbridge is a pleasant, and now peaceful, place to stay if touring either the Yorkshire Moors or the Yorkshire Dales to the west (see **Tour 5**).

Bossall (100) (SE 71-60)
This little village is part of the estate of Buttercrambe ★ east of York ★ . Bossall Hall is a fine Jacobean building next to the church of St Botolph. Most of the church is thirteenth century, although some original Norman work is still visible.

There was a thriving agricultural community here in the fourteenth century, but it is a silent place now in its lovely position above the Derwent valley.

Botton (see entry on Danby)

Boulby (94) (NZ 76-19)
Not in itself remarkable, this small collection of single storey houses should still be visited (see **Tour 1**). The long distance path of the Cleveland Way passes by, and this is the point where the cliffs soar to nearly 700 ft above the sea. These are the highest cliffs on the east coast of England and the view in either direction, or inland, is breathtaking. Half way down the cliff is the site of a former alum mine and works which is now an industrial trail. It is fascinating to learn how the ore was mined and processed using urine brought in vast quantities from the ale houses of London.

Bransdale (see entry on Cockayne; Walk 12 and Tour 7)

Bridestones (94) (SE 87-91)
These naturally weathered rocks have been sculpted into fantastic shapes by wind, water and ice over a period of 60,000 years. They are approached from a picnic site at Staindale on **Tour 8** (see map on this page). The path is clearly marked and it is very pleasant to walk through the forest and then onto open moorland to reach the stones. An excellent leaflet is available for a few pence from the Forestry Centre and local tourist shops.The name 'bridestone' has Norse origins meaning 'edge' or 'brink' stones. The spectacular shaping has oc-

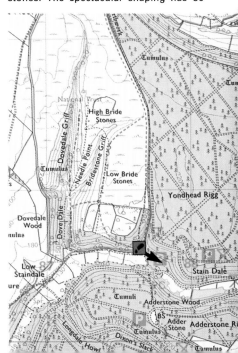

High Bridestones

curred because this particular Jurassic sandstone is layered, and the silica is not affected by the weather as much as the calcium.

Brompton (101) (SE 94-82)
Many motorists, intent on reaching or leaving Scarborough ★ with all haste, pass through this village without discovering its secret. In Brompton's charming church the Lakeland poet William Wordsworth married his beloved Mary Hutchinson in 1802. The surrounding countryside is where they did their courting while she lived at nearby Gallows Hill Farm. The village of Brompton itself is a pleasant place, with a stream and a pond.

Buttercrambe (105, 106) (SE 73-58)
Anyone travelling from Malton ★ to Stamford Bridge ★ should make a detour and cross the packhorse bridge to see this perfect example of an early Georgian Hall with a village clustered around the main gate (see **Tour 6**). As there has been no significant development since the village was planned, nothing has intruded on the original design – though the watermill is now a private house and no longer grinds corn. The Darley family, anti-Royalists in Charles I's reign, built the Hall and the village. There is a tradition that the Hall, with its splendid portico supported by massive pillars, was built on the site of a Saxon palace where Harold spent the night before the Battle of Stamford Bridge.

Byland Abbey (100) (SE 54-78)
The Abbey was founded by Cistercians in 1177 on the edge of the Hambleton Hills near the old drovers way. The monks moved to this site from an earlier one at Old Byland because Abbot Roger thought

Byland Abbey

it was too near Rievaulx. Apparently the bells were in conflict! Although many parts of the building are in ruins, it is possible to trace the floor plan in the foundations and to get an overall impression of its original size and grandeur. There is an excellent example of a geometric tiled floor in the chapel. This, together with the magnificent gatehouse and transcept, give an indication of Byland's importance. The church was the largest of the Cistercian order in England: far larger than Rievaulx ★ or Fountains.

It was here in Byland that Edward II was very nearly captured by a Scottish army in 1322 when they used the old drovers' path to launch a surprise attack. The king left the crown jewels and the Great Seal behind in his haste to escape.

Although the setting and overall effect is not as magnificent as nearby Rievaulx, this is a moving place and anyone interested in religious architecture will find much to enjoy with a detailed guidebook to the site (see **Tours 5 and 10**).

Captain Cook's Monument (93) (NZ 58-10)
High on Easby Moor, where James Cook

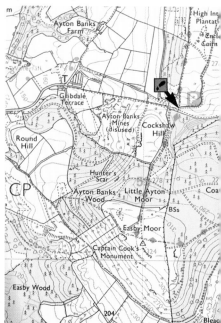

must have walked as a young boy, is a monolith erected in 1827 to his memory (see **Tour 1**). From here there is a panoramic view of Great Ayton ★ below, where Cook spent most of his childhood and where part of the school he attended is now a museum of his life. (The small map on this page shows the public footpath from the road to the monument.)

Carlton Bank (93) (NZ 51-02)
On the north-western edge of the Moors the road from Chop Gate ★ descends a steep bank with extensive views to the Cleveland Plain below. At the side of the road is the Three Lord's Stone which marks the spot where three manorial boundaries met. Many of the moorland stones were used for this purpose although' others were erected as 'way-markers' or to mark a burial place. (The map on this page shows a suggested short walk towards the top of nearby Cringle Moor where the view north and west is even more impressive).

The view from Carlton Bank

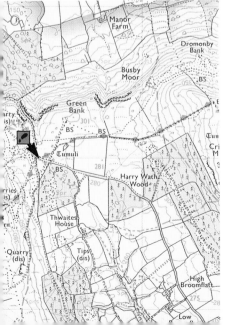

Carlton in Cleveland

Carlton in Cleveland (93) (NZ 50-04)
This is one of the little villages that cluster along the foot of the Cleveland Hills. Carlton sits astride a road that climbs into the moorland above, up a steep cliff escarpment: the view over the Cleveland Plain from the top is worth the climb for the energetic rambler or cyclist.

The village, like most in this part of the world, has its stream; but in Carlton it is hidden between the houses and is heard before it is seen. Some of the larger houses have very pretty gardens. The quarries above the village, where alum was mined in the seventeenth and eighteenth centuries, have now been colonised by heather and the ugly scars hidden. The rough moorland is in sharp contrast to the wooded Busby Park below.

Carlton in Cleveland was the home of the Colling brothers who, in the last century, bred the huge Ketten Ox which weighed no less than 270 stones at its death. The wretched beast is supposed to have lost weight in its last months due to a dislocated hip. The ox was taken to many local markets where it was the centre of attraction and it sired, for an appropriate fee, many offspring. Most of its weight, it must be said, was fat rather than meat which would not have endeared it to modern stockbreeders. The Blackwell Ox inn commemorates the animal.

Castle Howard (100) (SE 71-70)
'A palace, a town, a fortified city' – Horace Walpole's description of Castle Howard gives some impression of this magnificent example of the eighteenth century at its most lavish.

Chosen as the main location for the television series of Evelyn Waugh's *Brideshead Revisited*, the castle and the grounds are a 'must' for anyone travelling near Malton. Covering a total area of over 1000 acres, of which seventy are taken by the lake alone, the house is open to the public from late March to the end of October.

The designer of the house was Sir John Vanbrugh and it rivals his other great creation, Blenheim Palace. Vanbrugh's choice of Nicholas Hawksmoor, who had worked under Sir Christopher Wren architect of St Paul's Cathedral, was to prove inspired. Hawksmoor was the main archi-

41

Castle Howard

Hawksmoor's Mausoleum

tect for the two other buildings of note, the Mausoleum and the Pyramid. Vanbrugh's Great Hall is no less than seventy feet high, and a triumph.

A brief summary cannot really do justice to the structure, its contents, or the setting. Amongst the artistic collection are paintings by Gainsborough, Rubens and Holbein, stained glass by William Morris and furniture by Chippendale.

In the old stable block there is an imaginatively presented and extensive costume exhibition, showing how fashions have changed. The formal garden reflects the style in vogue in the eighteenth century.

Castle Howard has all the normal refreshment facilities that most stately homes now offer, in addition to a garden centre.

It is recommended that visitors allow at least half a day for visiting Castle Howard: one of the nation's greatest treasures and still lived in by the family who built it (see **Tours 4 and 7**).

Castleton

Castleton (94) (NZ 68-08)
This village lies on the edge of Esk Dale, clinging to the steep valley side at the northern tip of the long ridge that divides Westerdale from Danby Dale. A drive from here up to Hutton-le-Hole ★ provides glo-

rious views in all directions. **Tour 1** takes this route. The village takes its name from a long forgotten castle, now recorded as a 'motte' on OS maps.

This is where Robert de Brus, the first baron of this area, set up his residence. The de Brus family found the fertile glacial deposits that line the valley floor ideal farming land, and began a tradition which continues to this day. The sudden change from pasture to heather-covered moor is typical of the region.

Many roads reach Castleton from all directions. The railway station is on the BR line from Middlesbrough to Whitby ★ . A journey along this line as it clings to the valley side, crosses rushing streams or meanders through sleepy villages nestling in a patchwork of fields, is a most attractive way of seeing the area for the first time.

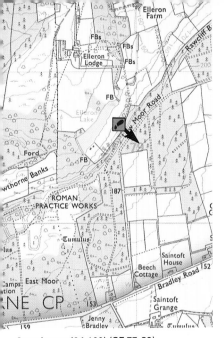

Chop Gate

which records the fact that it was the 'lock up' where the more unruly were incarcerated until they became sober.

The name Chop Gate – which locals pronounce as 'Chop Yat' – is supposedly derived from 'Chapman's Gate', a pedlar's gate, reflecting the fact that many paths crossed at this spot, and consequently pedlars congregated in the village. There is an excellent car park and picnic site for the modern traveller to stop and enjoy the pleasures of the village.

Cawthorne (94,100) (SE 77-89)

Just to the north of the hamlet of Cawthorne is a Roman campsite which caused considerable problems to archaeologists when it was first discovered. The layout of the four camps, the design of the foundations and the construction methods used, did not follow the patterns which the Romans used elsewhere. This raised some doubt as to whether the site had been Roman at all.

The most widely accepted theory is that these were training camps used by troops from Malton ★, which was the main fort for the area and the headquarters of the local legion. From pottery found at the site it is possible to date it at about AD110. A main Roman road across Ryedale ran near Cawthorne, over Wheeldale Moor and ended at an unknown site on the coast. The Romans were brilliant engineers but they had to teach their troops and local workers how to build: it appears that Cawthorne was, in effect, a training school.

There is a short walk to the camp from a nearby parking spot alongside the Cropton ★ to Newton-on-Rawcliffe road.

Chop Gate (100) (SE 55-99)

Most traffic hurries through Bilsdale, only ramblers and cyclists rest awhile here. The village of Chop Gate is a fine place for walking onto the surrounding Moors (see **Tour 9**).

Earlier visitors were the monks who regularly travelled between the abbeys on the northern edge of the Moors and Byland ★ or Rievaulx ★ in the south. The monks' way has left its traces above a sunken road near the village store. Later and less sedate visitors were the miners who came down to the village from their workings on the moors and got drunk on their earnings. Near the store is a building

Claxton (100) (SE 69-60)

This little village of less than 200 inhabitants still has a village post office. In 1807 a lead box containing a Viking hoard, including some intricate bracelets, was ploughed up in a local field. This find was particularly interesting, not because it was evidence of a Viking settlement here, but because the engraving on the bangles was oriental, indicating the extent of the trading network in those times.

Clay Bank (93) (NZ 57-03)

This steep incline is at the northern end of the long valley of Bilsdale that runs north from Helmsley ★ on the southern slopes of the Moors. The summit of Clay Bank, at 842 ft above sea level, gives extensive views over the Cleveland Plain and the northern Moors. There is a car park at the top for the weary cyclist to recover or for the motorist to enjoy the view.

By the fourteenth century monks were mining iron ore in the area and were extracting and working the metal. The limited extent of these early excavations did not change the face of the landscape as did the nineteenth-century miners in their quest for minerals.

There is an interesting tradition concerning the name 'Bilsdale'. After 1066 the countryside around York rose in revolt three times against the Conqueror. On the third occasion, William himself came north to gain control once and for all. His plan was to quell the locals and leave carefully chosen barons behind to keep the peace.

Whilst returning from Teesside, William was caught and delayed on the moors near Helmsley for three days in a 'roak', a thick mist. The king was in a foul temper at the delay and swore long and loud. Afterwards the locals are supposed to have named the spot 'King Billy's Dale' or Bilsdale. The story may be apocryphal, but it is interesting that there is still a saying in Yorkshire that a foul-mouthed man 'swears like Billy Norman!'

Cockayne (94,100) (SE 62-98)
This is the dead-end of Bransdale so far as the motorist is concerned, though the beginning of some marvellous moorland walks for the rambler. The collection of

Cockayne

houses and the church that make up this hamlet are situated on either side of the valley road as it sweeps round in a gradual curve. It is possible to drive up from Helmsley ★ and to return via Kirkbymoorside ★ in a great loop. This makes a pleasant drive and is featured in **Tour 7**. Any motorist or cyclist should make the detour to see, within a relatively short space of time, all the varied aspects of the Moors: farmland, bleak moorland and rushing streams. There are several old stone landmarks, or waymarks, which led travellers off the moorland and down the valley to Helmsley. The rambler can sometimes keep on course using these today – but never venture on the Moors without taking adequate maps.

Between Helmsley and Cockayne, at Carlton Grange, is the remains of a watercourse that was designed to bring fresh water to the town. Nearby at East Moors ★ is a little church where there is a suggested short walk (see entry on East Moors).

Commondale (94) (NZ 66-10)
There is much evidence of Early Man in the form of flints and burial grounds in this area of the Moors, especially on the higher reaches.

The dale was farmed from Norman times, and this use of the land continues today. The moorland was mined in the last century, for alum and iron ore, but this work ceased long ago. The railway line to Whitby ★ from Middlesbrough enters the

Moors proper here and there is a lonely row of railway cottages in the middle of nowhere, built when the line was somewhat busier than it is now. More recent mining has left the useful legacy of a quarry, which has been turned into a scout centre.

Cook's Monument (see Captain Cook's Monument)

Coxwold (100) (SE 53-77)
This charming village on the borders of the Hambleton Hills is a microcosm of the history of the North Yorkshire area. The name itself is a legacy of an early Viking settlement.

The Augustinian priory at Newburgh, founded in 1145, and the nearby abbey of Byland ★ are part of a chain of religious buildings which once encircled the Moors. After the Dissolution of the Monasteries in the 1530s, Henry VIII gave Newburgh Priory to his chaplain, Anthony Bellasis, who began its transformation into a country house. Consequently little remains of the original, and the architecture reflects the hands of various owners through the ages.

The presence of Oliver Cromwell is felt

Newburgh Priory

Shandy Hall

very strongly at Newburgh. The priory was the home of his daughter, Mary, who married a local landowner, Earl Fauconberg. The house, as well as supposedly containing Cromwell's body snatched from the gallows by his daughter to prevent mutilation, has many of his relics including a screw top pen.

The priory has had gardens from the time of its inception. The main feature of these is topiary; a range of yew trees cut into the shape of birds and dogs with, as the main feature, a splendid coronet by the main drive. There is also an extensive water garden and an avenue of trees planted by royalty.

The almshouses and well-built cottages of the village indicate the wealth and importance of Coxwold in the seventeenth century. The village church, St Michael's, is built in the Perpendicular style with an unusual octagonal tower: the interior has work by Grinling Gibbons. The churchyard contains the grave of the eighteenth-century novelist Laurence Sterne, whose house on the other side of the street — Shandy Hall — has an exhibition of his books and is open to the public. There is also an attractive and peaceful walled garden. To visit Coxwold see **Tours 5 and 10.**

Cropton (94,100) (SE 75-89)

This is a pleasant village on the south side of the Moors north of Pickering ★ , built on the point of a promontory with a commanding view of Rosedale ★ . It is not surprising that Cropton was the site of a castle, and the large motte indicates that this was a sizeable structure. The ditch and part of the ramparts are well preserved.

William Scoresby, the arctic explorer and whaler, was born in Cropton and used to sail from Whitby ★ with a crew of village men for up to ten months at a time! He once sailed to within 510 miles of the North Pole; the furthest north a sailing ship had ever been.

Most of the land round the village is farmed. To the north east lies the forest of Newton Dale ★ .

Dalby Forest Drive (see Low Dalby and Tour 8)

Dalehouse (94) (NZ 77-17)

This is a minute village between Whitby ★ and Loftus ★ . Like its near neighbour, Staithes ★ , it has declined as its original commercial purpose has been lost. Some of the houses are typical miners' cottages built when ironstone extraction was still important. Dalehouse once had an active watermill, which is now a private house.

The Dales

The 'dales' of the North Yorkshire Moors are not to be confused with the Yorkshire Dales, which is an area of wide valleys and high peaks to the west forming part of the Pennine Chain. Our dales, which are relatively narrow, run mainly north-south. Only the River Esk runs west-east into the sea at Whitby ★ . The intervening high ridges or 'riggs' were used by Early Man and most of the riggs now have a road running their length. A drive along one of these is an intensive lesson in geography. Towards the end of the Ice Age the meltwater from the moorland snowfields was unable to reach the North Sea because of the solid ice along the coast, and was trapped in a huge lake in the present-day Vale of Pickering. This gradually drained away, leaving behind swamps, or carrs, which were not fully drained and turned over to agricultural use until two centuries ago.

Danby (94) (NZ 70-08)

Visitors should first call at the well-equipped National Park Centre. This contains a wealth of information about the locality and there are frequent film shows and exhibitions about the Park. The Lodge is a pleasant building, surrounded by thirteen acres of fields, woods and gardens by the side of the river. It has the usual picnic and play areas (see **Tour 1**).

Danby Castle, the remains of the palace fortress of the Latimer family, was built in the fourteenth century. According to tradition, it was once the home of Catherine Parr who, as all schoolchildren know, was Henry VIII's last and surviving wife. This was the manorial centre for the region, and the farm which was once the manor house has a room that is used to settle any local

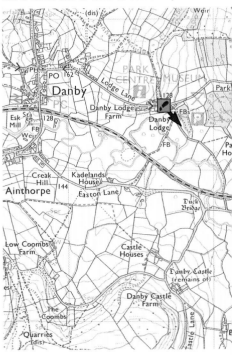

Danby Castle

The National Park Centre

grazing disputes to this day.

One of the many packhorse bridges that cross the River Esk is the narrow and much photographed Duck Bridge which is shown on the map on this page. It is an easy stroll from the National Park Centre to this attractive spot.

The village of Danby has the usual inn and shops, with open moorland on the higher slopes. It was the home of Canon Atkinson whose book 'Forty Years in a Moorland Parish' is a minor classic of English social history. South of Danby, at Danby Botton village, is a community centre for the handicapped which sells craft gifts and refreshments to help cover its running costs.

Devil's Arrows (see Boroughbridge)

Easington (94) (NZ 74-17)
A hamlet on the coast, near the high cliffs at Boulby ★ , which are the highest on the east coast of England. The views over the sea and the Moors are unequalled on a fine day. The Victorian church of Easington contains some fine Norman carvings.

Easingwold (100) (SE 53-69)
The town of Easingwold straddles the main road from Thirsk ★ to York ★ , the A19, and suffers from the heavy traffic passing through its centre. The east side, however, is surprisingly quiet and has some superb Georgian houses with a fine avenue of trees down the main street. These are indicative of how the town developed rapidly in the eighteenth century,

when it became a staging post for coaches from York to Edinburgh. Most of the inns were also built during this period.

The name 'Easingwold' is said to derive from an early tribal group, the Esingas, who occupied the area before the Roman invasion. The Domesday Book records that the village belonged to a Northumbrian Earl. The local populace were active in the opposition to the Normans and suffered badly during the genocidal 'Harrowing of the North' ordered by William the Conqueror. Unfortunately the town was also on the main route south from Scotland, and marauding Scottish armies frequently put the farms and houses to the torch in the thirteenth and fourteenth centuries.

East Moors (100) (SE 60-90)
The traveller on the country road leading north from Helmsley ★ to Bransdale could easily pass through the parish of East Moors without realising that it even existed. A telephone box on the right side of the road indicates that there must be some form of habitation in the woods. Hidden behind some large rhododendron bushes is the peaceful and attractive little church of East Moors, with its minute nave and beautiful stained glass window. Next to the church is a house, and that is East Moors!

The area is so attractive that it has been chosen for one of the suggested short walks. The map on this page gives a general impression of the terrain, with the footpaths clearly marked. One of these tracks gives a fine view from the edge of the woods over moorland to the north (see **Tour 10**).

East Moors

The River Esk near Egton Bridge

Ebberston Hall

Ebberston (101) (SE 89-82)
The village of Ebberston was three separate hamlets in Norman times. The church was built in the twelfth century and is well worth a visit. One part of the village was moved 'lock stock and barrel' in 1718 by the local MP. He had built Ebberston Hall as his country home, and felt that the village spoilt the view from his drawing room across the plain to the Wolds. The architecture of Ebberston Hall has been compared to a miniature Castle Howard. One of the builder's less successful features was a stream which ran under the house in order to feed the lake and water gardens. Not surprisingly this made the house excessively damp and the stream had to be diverted. The Hall is now open to the public.

Egton (94) (NZ 80-06)
In the seventeenth century this large, windswept upland village was a Roman Catholic stronghold. In 1679 its 83 year old priest, Father Postgate, was martyred for his faith. Later, William of Orange granted the village a Royal Market Charter and for many years Egton was famous for its fairs and markets. Today, the annual Gooseberry Fair in August attracts the most attention.

Egton Bridge (94) (NZ 80-05)
This is a very pretty village lying on either side of a wooded valley, with the River Esk rushing over a weir at the bottom. As Egton Bridge is a stop on the railway line from Middlesbrough to Whitby ★ ramblers often alight here and walk up the valley to Leaholm to catch a train home. The 1930s metal bridge replaced the old stone structure which was swept away by floods.

Ellerburn (100) (SE 84-84)
This picturesque hamlet near Thornton Dale ★ is notable for both its church and its churchmen. St Hilda's retains some pre-Conquest features: the woodwork and the font are also interesting. Although many of the churches around the Moors seem to have had eccentric vicars, Ellerburn has had more than its share. In the last century, one incumbent regularly conducted services with water pouring off his clothes having fallen into the stream on his way to the church. The reason for his clumsiness is best guessed at. One of his predecessors, in the previous century, was caught red-handed in the worthy, if foolhardy, enterprise of stealing stones from the local quarry to rebuild the church.

There is a camping site in Ellerburn, and there can be fewer more attractive places to pitch tent. Sitting by the stream, it is difficult to imagine that not so long ago the clear waters were polluted with effluent from the now closed paper mills further up stream.

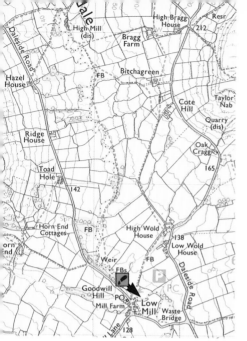

Farndale

Farndale (see map on this page to plan a stroll in Farndale; also the entry on Gillamoor)

Fat Betty (see entries on Ralph's Cross and
Rosedale Head)

Forge Valley (see Ayton)

Fylingdales (see Fylingthorpe)

Fylingthorpe (94) (NZ 94-04)
Its name indicates Norse origins: the 'thorpe' ending means that this is a secondary settlement of the original village of Fyling. The Cleveland Way passes Fylingthorpe which lies in an elevated position above Robin Hood's Bay ★ Boggle Hole Youth Hostel serves walkers, who pass the Old Hall built by the Cholmley family in the seventeenth century on their way to the hostel.

On the Moors inland, but not visible from the village, are the domes of the Ballistic Missile Early Warning Radar System which has made the name of Fylingdales known throughout the world. The station is located on Ministry of Defence property.

'Early Warning' is also the reason for Lilla's Cross, which lies on the prehistoric moorland track known as 'Old Wife's Trod'. In AD 626 there was an assassination attempt on King Edwin. The attempt failed because one of his attendants threw himself in the way of the assailant's dagger and was killed instead. A grateful king buried his saviour, Lilla, under a Bronze Age howe and erected a cross, Lilla's Cross.

Gillamoor (94,100) (SE 68-89)
This is an ideal place to stop for a first view of Farndale, best known for the profusion of wild daffodils which cover the valley in spring. Not long ago traders used to come and cut or dig up the flowers in their thousands, but now it is a local nature reserve and picking is illegal. Some would have us believe that the poet William Wordsworth came here when he was courting his future wife from the village of Brompton ★ and that this is what really inspired his poem 'Daffodils'.

At the famous 'surprise view' by the church, there is a thoughtfully provided bench where visitors can sit to enjoy the vista. In an extraordinary feat of devotion and stamina, a stonemason built the church single-handed in 1802. The village green has an unusual sundial with four faces.

In the early eighteenth century a local engineer decided that the villagers could do with fresh drinking water, so he built an aqueduct to carry the water from a spring high up on the moors. The neighbouring villagers from Fadmoor objected and it took several arguments before the local squire decreed that both villages could use the water. **Tours 7, 9 and 10** pass through Gillamoor.

Gilling Castle (see Ampleforth)

Glaisdale (94) (NZ 77-05)
The village is now a peaceful place but it was not always so. From early times Glaisdale was an important trading centre

Beggar's Bridge

village. A caravan and camping site is located near the church. A regular bus service from Whitby ★ and Pickering ★ passes through, or visitors can arrive in style by steam-hauled train on the North Yorkshire Moors Railway ★.

One of the most spectacular local waterfalls 'The Mallyan Spout' is covered in **Walk 5**. Two others are in the recommended short walk from Beck Hole ★. A remarkably well-preserved section of Roman road is visible on Wheeldale Moor to the south-west of the village. This is also featured in **Walk 5**, but can be reached by road (see **Tour 8**). There is evidence of early Bronze Age Man on the high ground of Two Howes Moor to the south-west. This burial site may have been a wayside grave beside a track from one village to another, and does not necessarily indicate a permanent settlement.

Goathland village reflects the open aspect of the surrounding moors. A wide village green runs nearly its whole length with scattered houses on either side. The sheep which roam freely keep the grass well cropped.

Goldsborough (94) (NZ 83-14)
This windswept spot was where the Romans chose to construct a look-out station, one of a chain of signal stations along the coast. The station was discovered in 1918 and the grisly remains of skeletons suggests that there had been a battle between the defenders and the Picts which the Romans had lost. The rough earthwork defences can still be seen.

Great Ayton (93) (NZ 56-11)
Captain Cook spent much of his childhood in this small town (see **Tour 1**). It is an attractive place of old houses and open

The obelisk marking Cook's childhood home

as can be deduced from the many stone causeways built at the time when goods were carried by pannier ponies. A drive up the quiet valley, which has several delightful places to picnic, will give a good view of these old tracks on the right hand side of the dale. In the mid-nineteenth century there were three blast furnaces in Glaisdale. (See **Walk 7 and Tours 1 and 3**).

Near the village, where the road to Egton ★ crosses the River Esk, is the much-painted and photographed Beggar's Bridge (see the map on this page for some possible strolls). It is said that this high, single arch footbridge was built by a local man who was once prevented from visiting his sweetheart because the river was in flood. When he became a rich man he built the bridge so that no other suitor would have the same problem.

Goathland (94) (NZ 83-01)
Goathland is set on the north-eastern edge of the Moors and is an ideal touring centre (see **Tour 8**). There are several good hotels and guest houses, and Wheeldale Lodge Youth Hostel is situated just outside the

The Roman Road on Wheeldale Moor

grassy areas, which is bisected by the River Leven. The Quakers have left their legacy here – not only in some fine houses, but also in the public school founded in 1842. The school which Captain Cook attended for five years (1736-1741) is now a museum of his life.

Anyone wanting to see the cottage in Marton where he was born would have to travel some distance, as in 1934 the Australians took the cottage to Melbourne in return for some stones from Point Hicks in Victoria, the place where Cook landed after sailing half-way round the world. These stones are in the form of an obelisk erected on the site of the cottage. Some mischievous locals maintain that the original cottage had already been demolished and there just happened to be another cottage on the same site. It is difficult to pin down Captain Cook – he is one of those individuals who inhabit the never-never land between history and myth.

On Easby Moor behind the town is the monument to his memory (see Cook's Monument ★) and from here and the prominent Roseberry Topping ★ there are marvellous views in all directions. The unusual shape of Roseberry Topping with its exposed western flanks is due to mining subsidence. Early prints show the peak as a perfect conical shape.

Great Edstone (100) (SE 70-84)
Just south of Kirkbymoorside ★ is a little hill, about 120 ft high, which rises steeply out of the flat
plain around. It is an obvious place to build a village in what was a very swampy area until quite recently. There was a settlement on this hill site from a very early date, and the church has a pre-Conquest sundial not dissimilar to the more famous one at Kirkdale ★ . Though not far away from the busy A170 which is full with holiday traffic in summer, this is a place that is hardly ever visited by strangers to Yorkshire. Great Edstone is a very pleasant backwater and an excellent place from which to enjoy a panoramic view of Ryedale, the Wolds and the edge of the Moors.

Grosmont (94) (NZ 82-05)
This is the northern terminus of the North Yorkshire Moors Railway ★ , connecting with the BR line from Middlesbrough to Whitby ★ . It is a railway junction, a river junction, a road junction and has a ford and a bridge to cross the River Esk. The first impression for the traveller alighting from the train is industrial. Spoils of disused mines and worked out quarries, and begrimed Victorian workers' houses are all that remains of a once vital industry. At its height, in the mid-nineteenth century, the Grosmont seam was supplying 100,000 tons of ironstone a year to the furnaces of the Tyne.

Grosmont takes its name from the abbey

Grosmont

founded in AD 1200 by monks from Grandimont in Normandy on a site where Priory Farm stands today. Little remains of the abbey now except its name, the stones having been used by local builders.

A suggested day's outing is to walk along the old railway track of George Stephenson's original line via Beck Hole ★ and to catch the train back from Goathland ★ . There is a trail booklet obtainable from the station showing this route. Most people come to Grosmont to see the preserved locomotives, either in action hauling trains to Pickering ★ , or at rest in the engine sheds which can be reached through a foot tunnel alongside the main railway tunnel. Grosmont is also included in **Tour 3**.

Guisborough (94) (NZ 61-15)
Guisborough was once the capital of Cleveland. It is now a suburb of sprawling Teesside. However, it should be visited to see the ruins of the Augustinian priory founded in the twelfth century by Robert de Brus. It is believed that the de Brus cenotaph, in the parish church, was given by Margaret Tudor, the daughter of Henry VII.

The main street of the town, with its trees and old houses, is interesting and there is a local Art Gallery and Museum. **Walk 8** begins in Guisborough.

The secret of alum production is said to have been brought to this country by the local Challenor family, who laid the foundation for the expansion of the mining industry in North Yorkshire. Many old alum mines can be seen on the coast and on the Moors. There is a tradition that an Italian alum processor was smuggled into Britain by the Challenors who were thus able to break the monopoly which had previously been enjoyed by the Pope. The family were, apparently, excommunicated for this outrage.

Hackness (94,101) (SE 97-90)
The attractive village of Hackness has grown up at the really delightful spot where Lowdale Beck and the River Derwent meet. The fine Georgian Hall, set in spacious grounds, is not open to the public. There are glorious views around

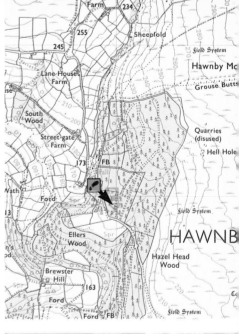

here: down the twisting Derwent towards Forge Valley and the fan of pretty dales which radiate from the spot. As well as Forge Valley – named after an eighteenth-century ironworks – Wykeham Forest and Broxa Forest nearby have clearly marked walks and nature trails. For the more energetic, a sixteen mile trail starts at Reasty Bank car park.

St Hilda of Whitby established a nunnery in this peaceful place in AD 680. Alas the tranquility was not to last: the nunnery was sacked by marauding Danes in AD 867. In the church there is a cross with a poignant inscription made by the terrified nuns before violence destroyed their world: 'O Aethelburga... may thy Houses ever be mindful of thee and love thee, most loving Mother... Abbess Aethelburga pray ye for us!'

Hambleton Down (100) (SE 51-83)
This is a flat area of land just to the north of Sutton Bank ★ , the steep climb on the Thirsk ★ to Helsmley ★ road. There was once a famous racecourse here. York ★ , Wetherby ★ and Ripon meetings are still held, but in its day Hambleton was more famous than any of these. Gold cups were presented by Queen Anne and King George I, and the air was noisy with all the bustle of high life and low life that is an important race meeting. Now the area is only used for training racehorses. Walkers on the Cleveland Way in the early morning can be surprised by the pounding hoofs of horses hidden by the mist.

Harwood Dale (94,101) (SE 96-95)
This small hamlet lies in open countryside at the bottom of a steep slope leading up to Reasty Bank. From the Forestry Commission car park on the top of the hill there is an excellent view of the eastern section of the Moors. There was once a Jacobean chapel, built by Sir Thomas and Lady Hoby, but now this is only a sad ruin.

Hawnby (100) (SE 54-89)
This remote and pretty village lies on a spur overlooking the River Rye. Some 800 years ago the Abbot of Byland and the

Hawnby

Hawnby Moor

Prioress of Arden chose this as a suitable spot to meet and settle the differences between their two houses. The Church of All Saints was restored in the Victorian period but many interesting features can still be seen. Earlier, fourteenth-century repair work suggests that it may have been damaged by marauding Scots. The map on this page shows a pleasant place for a stroll or a picnic to the north of the village. See also **Tour 9**.

Haxby (105) (SE 60-57)
The monks of York Minster put seven farmers into Haxby 'to till the soil' in 1086. Today this early Viking settlement is fast becoming a dormitory town for York ★ . Haxby was once a centre for brick and tile-making. The quarries dug at that time have become the large ponds which are a feature of the place. Surprisingly it was only in the middle of the fourteenth century that the first chapel was built here, in spite of a succession of pleas from the inhabitants to be given their own place of worship. It was not until some coffins were swept away down the flooded River Foss

that the religious authorities relented and allowed a chapel to be built.

The River Foss is now a much more peaceful stream. The Ebor Way, a path that follows the river from York, provides a pleasant riverside walk to the east of the town.

Helmsley (100) (SE 61-84)

This is an attractive, prosperous town on the north bank of the River Rye with a large market square and a good selection of hotels. There is also a camping site nearby at Beadlam ★ (see **Tours 7,9 and 10**).

At the end of the last Ice Age, some 15,000 years ago, the area was on the northern shore of a large meltwater lake over thirty miles long and ten miles wide. As the waters gradually drained southwards they left a marshland behind, some of which was first drained by the monks who started to build monasteries and dig irrigation and drainage canals in the thirteenth century. The fertile land on the edge of the marshes was ideal for crops and Byland ★ is a site where the monks undertook extensive drainage work.

Helmsley Castle, now in the care of English Heritage, remained intact until the Civil War in the middle of the seventeenth century. It was captured for the Parliamentarians by Fairfax and put out of action, but only after a three month siege. It stands in

Helmsley Castle

Duncombe Park

an imposing position at the eastern end of Duncombe Park.

The gardens and mansion of Duncombe Park were constructed in 1713 for the local landowners, the Duncombe family. In the grounds are two temples set above a bend in the River Rye: originally they were planned as the start of a long terrace which was to extend all the way up to an identical pair of temples at Rievaulx ★. A collection of early photographs illustrating the activities of the family in the late nineteenth century is on display in the Ionic temple at Rievaulx. There is a private entrance to the grounds of Duncombe from the A170 near Sproxton through a pair of fine wrought iron gates erected in 1806 in memory of Nelson's victory at Trafalgar.

Although the town looks neat and tidy today, it was as recently as 1870 that an indignant vicar preached against the local landlords for allowing open sewers and for fouling the streams with the smelly effluent from bleaching and dyeing. He also extolled the virtues of washing with soap. His sermons were not in vain because the Fevershams (the head of the Duncombe family had been created Lord Feversham in 1826) put money into correcting the problems, and also set up a village school and a public library.

The town is an ideal centre for seeing the western half of the Moors and the Ryedale plain. The headquarters of the North York Moors National Park is housed in the old vicarage in Bondgate. The Cleveland Way starts in Helmsley: the long distance footpath which skirts the west, north and east moors to end at Filey on the coast.

High Hawsker (94) (NZ 92-07)

Stop in this village on the A171 near Robin Hood's Bay ★ to look at the pre-Conquest stone cross with its knotwork and bird figures. The cross is a fine example of Norse craftsmanship.

Across the fields towards the sea are Hawsker Bottoms — a valley running down to the sea. This is bisected by the long distance path, the Cleveland Way, and by the disused railway line from Whitby ★ to Scarborough ★.

Hole of Horcum (100) (85-93)

This dramatic legacy of erosion by 'spring sapping' is understandably popular: there are panoramic views over the Moors and the valley below. Hang gliders soar from its edges, as the steepness of the incline and the strong upcurrents create ideal conditions for the sport. There are also several interesting prehistoric earthworks a little way south towards Levisham ★.

It is very easy to reach Hole of Horcum from Whitby ★ or Pickering ★ and the car park can become very crowded. But it is only necessary to go a little way down one of the many tracks in the valley to leave the noise and bustle behind (see **Walk 6 and**

A walk near Hole of Horcum

Tours 2 and 3). At the foot of the steep hill by the A169 is the isolated Saltergate Inn★, once a refreshment stop for traders carrying salt from Whitby to Pickering along the ancient track known as Salter's Way.

As with many natural features on the Moors there is an associated legend. Wade – the giant who is also credited with building Pickering Castle mound – is supposed to have scooped out the Hole of Horcum to throw earth at a rival. The mound of earth he threw is Blakey Topping to the east!

***

Hovingham (100) SE 66-75)
Hovingham Spa, as some inhabitants prefer to call the village, lays claim to being one of the prettiest villages in Ryedale. It can trace its history back to Roman times and excavations have unearthed evidence of a significant Roman villa and other buildings. Coins covering

Village houses in Hovingham

Hovingham Park

the period from AD 90 to AD 330 have been found. In Victorian times an enterprising entrepreneur tried to revive the use of the spring that attracted the Romans here and set up a spa which would rival Harrogate.

The Parish Church of All Saints has one of the few Saxon towers in Yorkshire and many other interesting features. The magnificent Hall, built in the Palladian style, has been the home of the Worsley family since the eighteenth century. The Duchess of Kent is a Worsley and was married in York Minster.

Hovingham expanded greatly in Georgian times. There is a Georgian quality about the village, with its wide, tree-lined streets, spacious gardens and fine buildings (see **Tours 4, 6 and 7; and Walk 11**).

***

Howsham (100) (SE 73-62)
South of the main road from York ★ to Malton ★, the River Derwent has carved a gentle valley. A little way north of Howsham, Augustinian Canons built Kirkham Priory ★. What attracted them to the spot, no doubt encouraged Sir William Bamburgh to build the fine Hall which lies by the river's edge in verdant fields (see map). The aristocracy, like their tenants, regarded deserted monastic buildings as a useful source of worked stone, and the Hall (which was built between 1612 and 1615) used material from Kirkham Priory. The east front of Howsham Hall was rebuilt in the early eighteenth century. Later alterations to the fabric were made by Nathaniel Cholmley.

The mellow stone of Howsham village is especially pleasant in the gentle light of a summer's evening. Near the stream is a splendid Gothic revival watermill. This pretty location has been chosen for a suggested short walk (see map). Also see **Tour 4**.

Huntington (105) (SE 62-56)
Unlike Haxby ★ to the west, this large
village is now joined to York ★. There are
records which indicate that the village was
rebuilt extensively in the fourteenth century by merchants from York who had
pasturing rights for their stock. The old
brick Manor House next to the River Foss
was rebuilt in 1850, but the older houses in
the centre still give a separate feeling of
identity to the village.

Hutton-le-Hole (94,100) (SE 70-89)
Situated just north of the main A170 between Helmsley ★ and Pickering ★, this is
a delightful village built in the local soft
brown stone. Hutton-le-Hole was once an
important Quaker centre, and many of its
solid yeoman houses have Quaker associations. Hutton Beck flows through the centre of the large green which is kept tidy by
the ubiquitous sheep.

The Ryedale Folk Museum is now recognised as one of the best of its kind in the
country and attracts thousands of visitors
each year. One of the Museum's most

The Ryedale Folk Museum

exciting features are the sixteenth century
cruck houses which have been rescued
from demolition, restored to their original
condition and rebuilt in the grounds. Later
buildings have also been painstakingly
rebuilt, and it is fascinating to see how
building methods developed over the centuries. See the map on this page to locate
the museum and to plan a stroll around the
village, as well as **Tours 7 and 10**.

Ingleby Greenhow (93) (NZ 58-06)
Lying on the edge of the Cleveland plain,
within a curve of the high moors, this
interesting village is protected on three
sides. It is built at the foot of the steep
Ingleby Incline where, in the last century,
wagons of iron ore were lowered from the
summit by a cable attached to a stationary
steam engine. These loaded wagons had
been hauled by steam locomotives across
the bleak moorland from the mines at
Rosedale ★. Today this is a tranquil place,
and it is hard now to imagine the noise of
steam escaping from valves, the clattering
of trucks and the oaths of railway workers
which once filled the air. Visitors can still
trace the route of the line and see the ruins
of the engine house. **Walk 2** begins in
Ingleby Greenhow.

Ingleby Manor, has a legend associated
with it. An early owner of the manor – a
local noble called Foulis – had the misfor-
tune to help Harold win at Stamford
Bridge ★ only to be on the losing side after
the long treck south to Hastings. Somehow
he, and the Saxon claimant to the English
throne, escaped and fled to Scotland
where they were both given refuge. His

The Norman church in Ingleby Greenhow

Hutton-le-Hole

descendants remained in Scotland until 1606 when, as the two kingdoms were united, King James restored the family to the Manor.

Because of the high slopes behind Ingleby Greenhow some parts of the village receive little sunlight and have been nicknamed 'midnight' by the locals.

Kilburn (100) (SE 51-79)

This typical Moors village – with streams running in front of the houses, so that the front path crosses a bridge up to the front door – is famous for two things.

The first of these is the highly visible Kilburn White Horse on the escarpment above the village. It is 95 metres long and 69 metres high and was designed in 1857 by a local schoolmaster who had been impressed by the chalk figures on the South Downs. He enrolled his pupils to dig to his plan in a sort of nineteenth-century community project (see the map on this page).

Kilburn's second claim to fame is that the village is a centre for excellent hand-made furniture. The workshops of Robert Thompson, whose own work can be recognised by his signature of a carved mouse, are still active. Examples of the 'mouseman's' superb carving can be seen in York Minster and St Paul's Cathedral in London, as well as in several local churches.

The name of Kilburn is interesting as the 'burn' suggests that the Vikings did not settle here and the original name was not changed to 'Kilbeck'. The ancient tradition of an annual feast is still maintained in Kilburn. The mayor and mayoress (a man dressed as a woman) still demand forfeits from villagers who commit misdemeanours.

The White Horse

Kildale (94) (NZ 60-09)

The village lies on the Middlesbrough to Whitby ★ railway line – one of the few in the area to escape the Beeching Axe. There is a 'motte' near the station: the remains of an early fortification built on a mound. On the edge of Coate Moor to the north is Bankside Farm which was constructed in the style of a Norse long house. It is interesting to compare this with the replica in the Jorvik Centre in York ★ . The long distance Cleveland Way drops down briefly from the moor above Kildale ★ before rising up to Coate Moor.

Kirkbymoorside (94,100) (SE 69-86)

This is a town with two distinct parts: there is an attractive old market town to the north and a modern estate to the south. The town is now by-passed and traffic between Helmsley ★ and Scarborough ★ does not disturb the locals. Among the many buildings worthy of note is the Market Hall, which has a market place on the ground floor and a meeting room on the first – a typical arrangement. Since the thirteenth century there has been a market every Wednesday in Kirkbymoorside. The town also became an important staging point for the York ★ stagecoach. Both these facts explain the large number of inns – many of which are of great antiquity.

George Villiers – the notorious second Duke of Buckingham – is said to have died in Buckingham House. The death of this famous intriguer and debaucher is said to have followed a riotous hunting party and prompted his enemies to write some doggerel: 'In the worst inn's worst room, With mat half hung, The floors of plaster, And the roofs of dung!'

At the top of the hill behind the church are the remains of the castle built by the de Stuteville family from which there are splendid views over the town. To the north of the town are the crumbling walls of a later 'castle' – in fact it was probably a hunting lodge built by the Nevilles.

Kirkbymoorside's Town Brass Band has won many national awards for its playing.

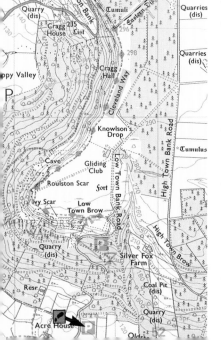

Particularly in the summer months when there is a local event of some kind, the sound of music is an added bonus for visitors to this bustling market town. All visitors to the Moors should make a point of seeing Kirkbymoorside (see **Tours 9 and 10**).

Kirk Dale (100) (SE 67-85)

About a mile to the west of Kirkbymoorside ★ is Kirk Dale. This is the site of St Gregory's Minster which can trace its history back to the seventh century. It lies in an attractive setting, away from any other buildings, by a stream which can be crossed at a ford. This is a charming place for a stroll (see map).

The Minster is said to have been founded by a monk from Lindisfarne, the island off the Northumbrian coast, who came south to spread Christianity and build places of worship. Saxon remains still exist, notably the famous sundial above the main door in the porch. The proud inscription on this wonderful device that has measured the hours for more than 800 years reads 'Orm, Gamel's son, bought St Gregory's Minster when it was ruined and fallen down and he caused it to be built anew from the ground in the days of Edward and in the days of Tosti the Earl. This is the day's sun marker at each hour. Haworth made me and Band – priests'.

Nearby is Kirk Dale Cave where, during quarrying work in the early nineteenth century, the remains of prehistoric animals were discovered. These relics from a warmer time included bones from mammoth, rhinoceros, lion and hyena.

Kirk Hammerton (105) (SE 46-55)

Just off the main York ★ to Harrogate road is the quiet village of Kirk Hammerton. The interesting church dates from Saxon times. Although the ever-industrious Victorians added to the church, they left the south-west alone and this viewpoint gives a good impression of what the building must have looked like originally. It would have been a large church by Saxon standards and is recorded as such in the Domesday Book.

An amusing feature of the church is the special pew designed for the squire, which has its own stove for use on cold days.

Kirkham Priory (100) (SE 73-65)

Though a ruin, and not as well preserved as Rievaulx ★ which had the same architect, this priory founded by Augustinians in the twelfth century should be visited if only to see the gatehouse with its heraldic shields.

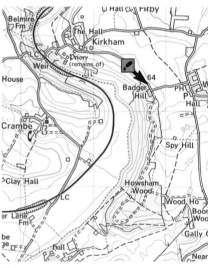

Kirkham

The Priory

Lastingham

The setting is magnificent. The Priory stands on the eastern slopes of the valley of the River Derwent near a weir. **Walk 10** goes by this beautiful spot or there is a stroll (see the entry on Howsham). Travellers by rail between York ★ and Scarborough ★ will see the abbey across the river south of Malton ★ ; the nearest railway station. It is possible to walk from nearby Low Hutton, a distance of four miles, along the river bank to Malton.

Langton (100) (SE 79-67)
This estate village, three miles south of Malton ★ , has won many competitions to find the prettiest village. It is a neat, well-maintained hamlet dominated by the gate to the Hall. This imposing entrance bears the crest of the Norcliffe family who did much to improve the Wolds and turn the area over to pasture.

The tranquil atmosphere of Langton is typical of this part of Yorkshire.

Lastingham (94,100) (SE 72-90)
This is one of the most beautiful villages on the Moors, lying in a peaceful hollow on the ridge between Rosedale and Farndale. St Cedd chose this position for his monastery which was built in AD 660 probably on the site where St Mary's Church now stands. An outbreak of plague in AD 664 resulted in the death of Bishop Cedd and several of his brethren, and it is recorded that he was buried in the monastery he loved.

St Mary's Church

Although the monastery continued to flourish after Cedd's death, in the ninth century it was destroyed by the Danes. Between 1078 and 1088. Stephen of Whitby founded a new monastery on the same site; the well-preserved crypt of his Norman church can still be seen.

Leavening (100) (SE 78-63)
An unspoilt stone-built village, situated at the foot of the long ridge that rises suddenly to start the Wolds. It is an area rich in tumuli and prehistoric sites.

The village, which is a pleasant place to stop for a rest, is reached by a side turning on the Norton to Kirkham ★ road.

Levisham (94,100) (SE 83-90)
This pretty village is set in a remote, narrow valley reached from the Whitby ★ road, north of Pickering ★ (see **Tours 2 and 3**). The railway station on the North Yorkshire Moors Railway ★ is a favourite alighting point for ramblers, who either explore the surrounding countryside, moorland and forest, to return from the same station, or walk down narrow Newton Dale to the market town of Pickering.

Visitors should walk down from the little one-street village, with its long green, to the watermill and the church. The pre-Conquest carvings in the church are certainly worth the climb.

Levisham Moor is peppered with earthworks and tumuli, which have given rich pickings to the local archaeological society. The fruits of their excavations are on display in the Rotunda Archaeological Museum in Scarborough ★ . To the northeast of the village is the remarkable Hole of Horcum ★ , a dramatic bowl in the moors (see **Walk 6**).

Lilla's Cross (see Fylingthorpe)

Littlebeck (94) (NZ 88-04)
The stream that flows from the Falling Foss waterfall down May Beck twists its way through a deep gorge. A ford crosses here with a very steep road up either bank. There is a small hamlet at this crossing,

Littlebeck

with cottages built in local stone. One of the steep ways up from Littlebeck has the telling name 'Lousy Hill Lane'.

This is a quiet, pleasant place for a stroll, and a footpath from Littlebeck goes along one side of the stream to May Beck ★. The map on this page shows a shorter walk to Falling Foss (see **Tour 8**).

Lockton (94,100) (SE 84-89)
This long village lies on the way to Newton Dale ★ from the main Pickering ★ to Whitby ★ road. The village is built in the local limestone and has a shop or two as well as a youth hostel. Although rebuilt over the years, parts of the church indicate its thirteenth-century origins.

Lockton is a more pleasant place to stop and explore the Hole of Horcum ★ (see **Walk 6**) than the car park on the main road above Saltergate Inn ★ (see **Tours 2 and 3**).

Loftus (and its environs) (94) (NZ 71-18)
This long village is set on a ridge in the north-eastern corner of the area covered

by this guide. Since the closing of the mines at Liverton, unemployment has been a problem in Loftus which is essentially an industrial settlement. Although the village is not pretty like many of the Moors villages, and not somewhere which tourists would normally visit, it has a long and interesting history.

As with so many settlements on or around the Moors, the early development had to do with the Church. Loftus lies on the ancient way that ran from the religious settlement on the island of Lindisfarne off the Northumbrian coast, to the abbey at Whitby. The local inhabitants built their church in Liverton, a hamlet to the west, in the twelfth century. The church remains completely unaltered and can be reached either by a wooded path from Loftus, or down a track from the roadside as you enter Liverton village from Loftus. There are remarkable carvings of dragons and foliage, somewhat in the style of work at Ripon. The church is an unexpected gem, and well worth a visit. At Handale the Cistercians constructed a priory, further evidence of the religious importance of the area, but the stones have long-since been used to build farmhouses.

On the coast at Skinningrove, dominated by the potash works today, there is a record in 1607 of the capture of a supposed merman by local fishermen. He went on display until he escaped to return to the sea, and seems to have been a hit with the local girls.

Like Whitby ★ and Scarborough ★ further along the coast, Loftus has been shelled from the sea – in this case not by the German fleet in the First World War, but by Paul Jones during the American War of Independence. In the early days of the Industrial Revolution an entrepreneur, Patrick Waddell, planned and began extensive engineering works to link Teesside by rail with the mines in the dales and on the local moors. Loftus could have become a major centre, but Waddell's plans were thwarted by pressure from local Quakers who supported George Stephenson. The only legacy is Paddy Waddell's Bridge, now isolated on Danby High Moor. As it was, Loftus came to depend almost totally on the alum works and mining – and they have gone now.

It is difficult to imagine it today, but until the 1914-1918 War the whole countryside around Loftus was thickly wooded. The trees were felled as part of the war effort, and only a few remain in some small dales as a reminder. The restoration of woods would improve what is otherwise a rather bleak landscape.

Low Dalby (94,100) (SE 85-87)
This is a Forestry Commission village built to house the forest workers. Since the opening of the toll drive through the woods (see **Tour 8**) and the general development of the forest as a tourist attraction,

it now has an Information Centre. The houses are neat and well-maintained, one of them offers bed and breakfast. The Centre sells a good selection of guide books to the forest and stocks several leaflets on the special nature trails that have been created for the rambler.

The warden is always happy to offer advice and is a mine of information on what to see during the different seasons of the year.

Lythe (94) (NZ 84-13)

This little village was once a centre of the alum industry. St Oswald's church, although modern, has some interesting Viking relics from an earlier church on the same site. Inland from the village stretch Mulgrave Woods which contain the remains of ruined castles. These are entered from the main road through a gate half way up the hill: a notice on the gate gives details of times when the woods are open to the public.

There is a camping site here and a few shops as well as a public house. There is a lovely view back along the beach at Sandsend ★ to Whitby ★ from the top of the steep 1-in-4 hill into the village – (see **Tour 1**).

Malton (100) (SE 78-71)

The modern town of Malton was built near to the site of Roman Derventio. The interesting museum in the market square displays much evidence of the Roman presence in the area. The Roman camp – thought to date from the first century AD – covered some eight acres. The Normans used the Roman foundations to build their fortification when they came north, almost a thousand years later. This castle witnessed a fierce battle when the Lord of Malton proclaimed his support for the king of Scotland, who had designs on Northumberland. However, the Archbishop of York gathered the northern barony and defeated the Scots.

The River Derwent at Malton

Malton lies on the River Derwent and has several pleasant riverside walks. St Mary's church incorporates part of the Gilbertine Priory that once stood here (circa 1150). Much of the town's development was Georgian, and there are some large houses set around the market square, and several traditional coaching inns. Situated on the boundary between the East Riding and the North Riding, Malton has always been an important agricultural market. To the north of the town is the separate village of Old Malton, where the whole atmosphere is quieter and very different.

With Castle Howard ★ Kirkham Priory ★ , the Wolds and attractive Ryedale nearby, Malton – or its suburb over the river, Norton – makes a convenient place to stay and explore the surrounding countryside. (See **Tours 4, 6 and 7, and Walk 10**).

The Information Centre can provide suggested places to stay as well as useful leaflets on places to visit.

Marston Moor (105) (SE 49-53)

This moor's claim to fame lies not in any geographical feature, or an attractive setting, being on a rather dull flat area of farmland, but to the major battle which was fought here in the Civil War. See the general introduction at the beginning of the guide for an account of the bloody engagement which was fought during a summer storm.

May Beck (94) (NZ 89-02)

This is an attractive area of mixed farmland, woods and moorland to the south of Whitby ★ on the edge of Fylingdales moor. It is easily reached from the A171 Whitby to Scarborough ★ road.

In 1973 the North York Moors National Park created a nature trail here, with the aim of showing the various uses of land in the region, and the conflicts that might arise between different needs. There is a marked-out walk which takes about three hours gentle walking to complete, looking at all the points of interest. A shorter walk takes about an hour. A leaflet and a booklet giving full details are on sale at local shops and information centres. See **Tour 8** and the entry on Littlebeck ★ for further suggested strolls and a map.

May Beck

Middleton (94,100) (SE 78-85)
On mile west of Pickering ★ on the A170 is
this mainly Georgian village. The Vikings
liked the location so much that they made
a permanent settlement here. Some of the
houses are of cruck construction and very
old indeed, although modern brickwork
hides much of the original structure.

The church can trace its history back to
Viking times and although extensively
rebuilt in the thirteenth century, the tower
and the west doorway are considerably
earlier.

Moor Monkton (105) (SE 50-56)
Like its neighbour Nun Monkton ★ , a little
way upriver, this village lies at the end of a
road: a dead-end created by the River
Ouse. But unlike its sister to the north, it is
not set around a village green but spread
out along the banks of the river.

The manor of the Red House forms a
central point for this community which lies
between the Ouse and its tributary the
Nidd. This rather isolated building is now a
preparatory school and was once the home
of Sir Henry Slingsby, a leading Royalist.
The Jacobean chapel that he built in the
grounds is a fine example of the architecture of this period. It is sometimes possible
to see over the chapel by enquiring at the
school office.

Mount Grace Priory (99) (SE 45-98)
This fine example of a Carthusian monast-
ery was founded in 1398 at the bottom of
the high slope leading up to the moors
above Osmotherley ★ . The ruins of the
Priory are clearly visible from the busy
Thirsk ★ to Teesside dual carriageway (see
Tour 9).

The monks of Mount Grace lived in complete solitude in cells, seeing each other
only in the chapel and on religious festivals. The administration of the monastery
was left to lay brethren. Twenty-one of the
small cells can be seen today with their
tiny individual gardens and workrooms.

It is very rare to find a Carthusian
monastery in such a good state of preservation. Mount Grace is now in the care of
English Heritage.

Mulgrave Woods (see Sandsend)

Nether Poppleton (see Upper Poppleton)

Nether Silton (see entry for Over Silton)

Newburgh Priory (see Coxwold)

New Earswick (105) (SE 61-55)
The important influence of the Quakers in
the region is mentioned in other parts of

this guide book. In York ★ their presence is
seen, not only in the confectionery busi-
nesses of Rowntree and Terry, but in the
model village of New Earswick built in
1902 under the auspices of the Joseph
Rowntree Trust. Though improvements
have been carried out over the years to
take account of changing life styles, the
advanced thinking that went into the original design is still obvious. The gabled
Tudor-style houses were given light, airy
living rooms, individual approaches and
garden walls. They were set in curving
avenues and groves. It was a time when
pleasant, sanitary housing at a reasonable
price was unique in Britain – nor were the
houses restricted to employees of the company. The village remains under the management of the Trust and is a tribute to the
foresight and humanitarian approach of
the first chairman.

Newgate Bank (100) (SE 56-89)
There is a vantage point here on the B1257
north of Helmsley ★ , just before it enters
Bilsdale stretching to the north. There is a
picnic site, maintained by the Forestry
Commission, from which there are marvellous views of Bilsdale and the Hambleton
Hills. Behind there is a footpath through
the forest up Riccal Bank to some contro-
versial modern sculptures. It is possible to
continue along this path and return to
Helmsley.

Bilsdale

Newton Dale (100) (SE 81-91)
The narrow, twisting valley of Newton Dale
was formed by the meltwater coming off
the moor towards the end of the Ice Age. It
has been calculated that the shallowest
depth of snow on the moors was 200 ft
above the present ground level, so a considerable force must have been exerted as
this flowed off the high ground and into
the lake that once covered the whole of the
Ryedale plain. Part of the floor of Newton
Dale became a bog, Fen Bog, which still
existed when the railway line from Whitby ★ to Pickering ★ was being constructed
in 1836 – George Stephenson was able to
make a firm base for the track using a
mixture of heather saplings and sheep
hides. The line has been saved from the
fate of other discarded sections of track by

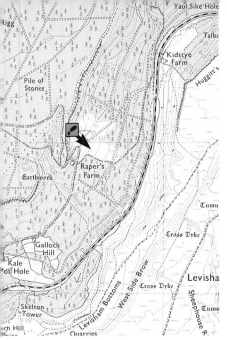

the North Yorkshire Moors Railway Trust who purchased it from British Rail in 1967.

The bog is now a nature reserve and the Forestry Commission has planted conifers on the western slopes. This area was farmed intensively until shortly after the First World War. There are several pleasant short walks in the woods. One way of reaching them is to catch the train to Newton Dale Halt, leaving the car at Levisham ★ , and to walk along the valley side or follow the ancient way past Scarhill Howe, to return to the car.

To the east of the area is the unusual Hole of Horcum ★ (see **Walk 6 and Tours 2 and 3**), much favoured by the hang-gliding fraternity. There are several earthworks and tumuli marked on OS maps of the area, indicating that the high ground above the dale was settled in the Bronze Age, or possibly earlier. To the west is a cave where the bones of prehistoric animals have been found.

Newton-on-Ouse (100,105) (51-60)
This impressive village abuts the grounds of Beningbrough Hall. Many of the villagers were at one time servants at the great house. The church, with its tall spire, has been a well-known landmark for those travelling by boat along the River Ouse for four centuries, as it can be seen for several miles.

In the eighteenth and nineteenth centuries there was a considerable amount of additional river traffic at weekends, as boats came from neighbouring villages and York ★ to discharge their day trippers. These people came to enjoy the village fairs that were held on the green. Reports at the time indicate that some of the more staid inhabitants objected to the noise and 'immoral behaviour'. In the nineteenth

century the Whitsuntide Newton Feast was a major annual event with a brass band that marched through the village. There was also a keenly contested cricket match with the villagers of Nun Monkton ★ from across the river. Access between the villages was easier then as there was a footbridge. Now the nearest means of crossing by foot or vehicle is the toll bridge at Aldwark to the north.

North Yorkshire Moors Railway
The original railway line from Whitby ★ to Pickering ★ – with coaches and wagons hauled by horses – was designed and developed by George Stephenson in 1836. Several major engineering problems had to be overcome as the line was being developed. A tunnel was blasted through the rock at Grosmont ★ ; there was a steep incline at Beck Hole ★ where a novel cable and water mechanism was used to haul and lower wagons and coaches up and down the slope; and the line as it entered Newton Dale ★ on its final leg to Pickering had to traverse a bog. Trees, heather and sheep fleeces and hides were sunk into the bog to make a firm foundation.

The line opened in 1836 with much festivity in the towns and villages. Some experts maintain that it was only the third railway in the world to carry passengers. Stephenson's costs were roughly double his original estimate. The section at Beck Hole had to be abandoned after several mishaps with the cable system. A new route was blasted out of the rocky ledge into Goathland ★ , with a long embankment at Esk Valley near Grosmont at the start of a gradual incline up to the highest point. This enabled steam locomotives to haul traffic (mainly freight) over the whole route by 1847.

In 1965 British Rail closed the line and it would have rapidly fallen into disuse had not a preservation society been formed in 1967. Local councils and individuals gave help and funds which enabled the line to be reopened in 1973. The society has several locomotives, mostly steam, with a few restored diesel engines from with-

Goathland

drawn classes. The daily timetable indicates the method of locomotion so that passengers who are not in a hurry can choose which method, ancient or modern, is going to haul their train. At Grosmont there is a locomotive works reached through a special foot tunnel, where engines in various stages of restoration can be seen.

The route from Grosmont to Pickering is one of the most attractive ways of seeing this part of the Moors, and the line goes through many sections which cannot be reached by car. An excursion on the North Yorkshire Moors Railway is highly recommended for all visitors whether they are train enthusiasts or not.

Nun Monkton (105) (SE 50-57)

Any visit to Beningbrough Hall on the other side of the River Ouse should be combined with a stop at this charming village with its old duckponds, large green and decorated maypole. According to one legend, a hermit, Monechtone, who was slain by the Vikings, gave his name to this and its sister village of Moor Monkton ★ . See the map on this page to plan a stroll.

Nunnington Hall (100) (SE 67-79)

This interesting Tudor mansion is owned by The National Trust. It lies in an attractive position surrounded by gardens on the banks of the River Rye, about 2 ½ miles north of Hovingham ★ and 4 ½ miles south-east of Helmsley ★ . There is a beautiful seventeenth-century arched bridge across the river by Nunnington Hall, linking it to the village.

There is a persistent tradition that the Hall was built on the site of a nunnery suppressed for 'immorality' in the thirteenth century. The ghost of a young woman is said to roam in the orchard.

One of the manor's first owners was a Robert Huikes, the physician to both Henry VIII and Queen Elizabeth I. He had the unenviable task of telling the Queen that she would be unable to bear children.

Viscount Preston, a close friend of Charles II, and his ambassador to the court of the French king, Louis XIV, modified and extended the structure in the seventeenth century. He is buried in the thirteenth-century church across the river. The design and the internal decor of the rooms mainly reflect this period, and they are in an excellent state of preservation. In the attic

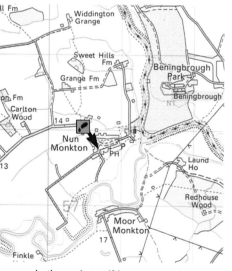

In the early twelfth century an important Norman nobleman founded a nunnery here and made his daughter the prioress. After the Dissolution this was given by Henry VIII to a close friend of his, John Neville, who demolished the building and erected a Hall in the grounds. When Henry died his surviving wife, Catherine Parr, married John Neville and lived here. The only part of the nunnery thought to have survived intact is the chapel which, it has been suggested, was incorporated into St Mary's, the parish church. St Mary's also has a splendid window designed by William Morris.

Nunnington Hall

the Trust has housed a fascinating collection of model rooms, with fittings, decorations and furnishings representing different styles and periods. This is an interesting way to obtain a bird's eye view of English domestic styles through the centuries. To visit Nunnington Hall see **Tours 6, 7 and 10**. To plan a stroll, see the map on this page.

Old Byland (100) (SE 54-85)
It is as if time has stood still in this sleepy, quiet place close to Byland Abbey ★ and Rievaulx ★. Perhaps this phenomenon can be attributed to the fact that the Anglo-Danish sundial on the east wall of the church tower was fitted upside down. Its Latin inscription reads: 'Sumerledan Huscarl made me'.

Osmotherley (99) (SE 45-97)
This is a large village which was once an important market town. It stands half way up the western side of the Moors, below the old Drover's Way that once knew the tread of cattle from as far afield as the Scottish Highlands on their way to the markets of the south. The Drover's Way is now part of the long distance Cleveland Way footpath. The Youth Hostel to the north of the village provides a modern counterpart to the old drovers resting place at the Chequer's Inn, just to the south

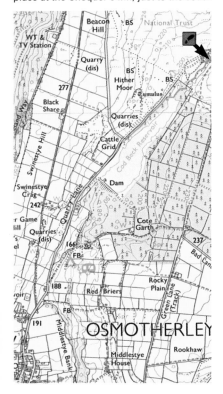

on the edge of the Moors (see **Tour 9**).
No visitor to the area should fail to see Mount Grace Priory ★ which is now in the care of The National Trust. This is the best preserved example of a Carthusian monastery in the country and was built in the fourteenth century. One of the cells has been laid out in its original state, to enable visitors to understand the austere, closed lives the monks led.

The church in Osmotherley has many interesting features from all periods including a rare 'bear hog-back' gravestone showing Norse influence. Normal 'hog-back' graves are great slabs of stone fashioned like a long, low house: in the Osmotherley variant a bear holds each gable end. Close-by, in the village centre, there is a market cross and a stone table. Opposite is the Methodist Chapel which claims to be one of the oldest in the country. John Wesley held an open-air meeting around the stone table and the chapel was built shortly afterwards in 1754.

There is a good selection of shops and inns in Osmotherley including the 'Queen Catherine' named after Catherine Parr, who lived nearby. Occasionally low-flying RAF aircraft disturb the tranquility of what otherwise is a peaceful, pretty moorside town (see map).

Oswaldkirk (100) (SE 62-78)
It is very easy to miss the village entering from Ampleforth ★, as the main road goes left up the hill towards Helmsley ★. The whole of Oswaldkirk is built on the side of a steep wooded hill which means that no garden appears to be level and the church roof is almost at the level of the road surface. The name 'Oswaldkirk' indicates a pre-Conquest church: according to tradition a monastery was founded here in the ninth century, but the building was never completed for some reason. One of the manors of Oswaldkirk was once owned by Sir William Pickering whose son – 'a brave, wise, comely English gentleman' – wooed Good Queen Bess herself!

Over (and Nether) Silton (99) (SE 45-93)
To the east of the busy Thirsk ★ to Teesside dual carriageway, nestling below the hills which lead up onto the Moors, are two sister villages where time seems to have stood still. Because of the lie of the land and the way the lanes meander, this is not a through route to anywhere. Both Over Silton and Nether Silton are charming. The houses are completely original, with no shops, garages or other modern conveniences to spoil the stillness. There is a lonely forest drive to a picnic site in the woods above Over Silton. For the person who wants to get away from it all, this is the place. Not a mile away to the west, traffic hurtles on its way along the A19 – but you would never know it.

Pickering (100) (SE 79-84)

Pickering is known as the 'Gateway to the Moors'. The street map gives an overall impression of the town (see also **Tour 8**). The town stands at a crossroads. To the north is moorland and Whitby ★ , to the east Dalby Forest and Scarborough ★ . South lies the gentle Vale of Pickering and to the west a succession of moorland villages and Helmsley ★ . As well as the four main roads, this is also the southern terminus of **The North Yorkshire Moors Railway ★ (3** which provides a relaxing means of transport to the eastern section of the Moors.

Pickering has always been an important crossroads and there is evidence that there was a settlement on the site from the very earliest period. The name of the town has a legend associated with it which is echoed in its coat of arms. In 270 BC – a suspiciously exact date – the local tribal king is supposed to have lost a ring. This was subsequently recovered from the inside of a large pike that had been caught in the

Pickering

river and the king was in the process of devouring – hence the name of 'Pike-ring'.

The town of Pickering was chosen by William the Conqueror to be the site of one of his Yorkshire castles. The early structure was a simple motte and bailey castle, but the wooden keep had been replaced in stone by the twelfth century. Robert the Bruce of Scotland attacked Pick-

Pickering

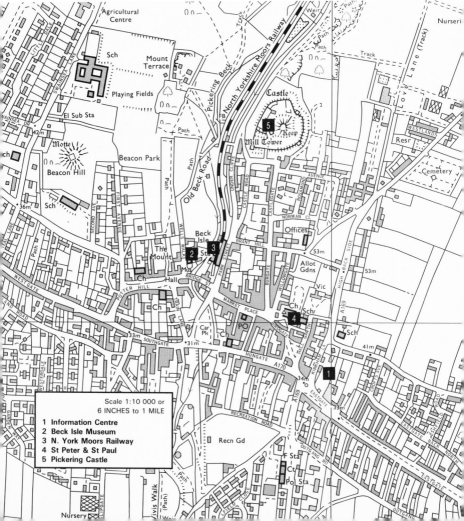

Scale 1:10 000 or
6 INCHES to 1 MILE

1 Information Centre
2 Beck Isle Museum
3 N. York Moors Railway
4 St Peter & St Paul
5 Pickering Castle

ering Castle (5) on one of his forays south. It is believed that Richard II was imprisoned there before being taken to Pontefract where he suffered his painful and ignominious death.

Although the castle suffered at the hands of Parliamentarian troops in the Civil War, more damage was caused by a local landowner using a section of the ramparts to build himself a home in the fifteenth century and the fact that the Royalists took the lead from the roof to make shot with which to defend Scarborough. The building is now maintained under the auspices of English Heritage: the circle of walls and the towers still remaining, enable visitors to visualise how this formidable castle must have looked in its prime.

A walk around the town and the market square will reveal a wide variety of architectural styles, from the early small cottages typical of the Moors, to some well-built Georgian houses, many constructed by Quakers. One particularly fine Regency house is now **The Beck Isle Museum of Rural Life (2)**. The museum has many interesting displays: each room being devoted to a particular theme including a printer's shop, a cobbler's and an inn. There is also a collection of the superb photographic work of Sydney Smith who recorded the lives and faces of bygone Ryedale. It was once the home of the Marshall family who started an agricultural college on the site in the last century.

The church of **St Peter and St Paul (4)** is hemmed in by houses in the market square. It is built on the site where a Saxon church once stood. The church is of particular interest to Americans because of three connections with the USA. There is a memorial to a local man, Robert King, who was chosen by George Washington to survey the new city of Washington DC in 1800, which explains why there are two maps of the city in the church. In 1924 the Statesman F.B. Kellog, who was then American Ambassador to the Court of St James, installed a plaque to commemorate the joint efforts of the two nations to defeat the Kaiser. He was the principal negotiator of the 'Kellog Pact' – a multilateral treaty to outlaw war – and was awarded the Nobel Peace Prize in 1929. The third feature of particular interest to Americans is the chancel panelling, which is a memorial to an American soldier whose ancestors came from the locality, and who died in the 1914-1918 War.

The most famous feature of the St Peter and St Paul Church are its magnificent fifteenth-century frescos. These were only rediscovered in the middle of the last century, having been whitewashed over by fanatical iconoclasts. The paintings have now been restored and include lively scenes of St George slaying the Dragon, as well as Biblical scenes and more sombre events such as the martyrdom of Thomas a Becket.

Pickering has a wide range of shops and

A mural in the Church of St Peter & St Paul

hotels, typical of a bustling market town. It is a good centre from which to explore the region, by rail or by car.

Port Mulgrave (94) (NZ 79-17)

This is a slightly melancholy place which has outlived its original purpose. Port Mulgrave was built in the last century when there was a thriving industry exploiting the rich iron-ore deposits inland. The harbour, unlike others along this coastline, is not a natural feature formed by a river eroding the soft clays and shales which form most of the cliffs here: it was blasted out of the rocks at the edge of the sea. The ore was transported by a railway line that descended to the waiting ships through a tunnel from the high ground above. As a village that was hastily built to house the miners and the harbour workers and their families, it has none of the attraction of Staithes ★ . But Port Mulgrave is interesting none the less as an example of an Industrial Revolution village. There are good views in both directions from the cliff tops: north towards the high cliffs near Boulby ★ and south to Whitby ★ .

Ralph's Cross (94) (NZ 67-02)

High on Westerdale Moor, 1409 ft above sea level, is a point where several old ways meet. Some of these are still only footpaths, but four are now tarmacadam roads, leading respectively to Castleton ★ and Westerdale End to the north and to Hutton-le-Hole ★ and Rosedale ★ in the south (see **Tour 9**). At this crossroads is an old waymark, Ralph's Cross, which has been chosen as the emblem of The North

Ralph's Cross

York Moors National Park. Many of the waymark stones were erected to guide travellers across the moorland in olden days. An ancient custom is that anyone passing the monument should leave a coin in the top for 'poor pilgrims'. There are other crosses in the area, including the evocatively named 'Fat Betty' (See also the entry on Rosedale Head).

Ravenscar (94) (NZ 98-01)

This is a beauty spot that is often visited by tourists from Scarborough ★ or Whitby ★ (see **Tour 2**). It is a cliff some 600 ft above sea level, and being on a promontory has views both north to Robin Hood's Bay ★ and south towards Hayburn Wyke. The Romans erected one of their signal stations here as part of the coastal warning system.

In the eighteenth century a local entrepreneur planned to build a resort at Ravenscar to rival Scarborough. Had he succeeded the natural beauty of the area would have been spoiled. This enterprise failed but – as with other sections of the cliffs along this coastline – alum was discovered and mined. The open cast works are still visible at the foot of the cliff. This has become a favourite place for fossil hunters and geologists, and dinosaur footprints have been found near here.

The National Trust has a tourist office and information centre at the end of the road by the entrance to the Raven Hall Hotel. A signposted geological trail starts at the centre.

Rievaulx (100) (SE 57-85)

You will not forget your first sight of Rievaulx. The ruins of the Cistercian monastery, founded by Walter l'Espec in 1131, are quite magnificent. Also of outstanding interest are the gardens of the Terrace and the village (See **Tours 9 and 10**).

The first thing visitors notice about the abbey is that, because of the direction of the valley, it lies almost north to south, instead of the normal east to west orientation. The ruins, maintained by English Heritage, are kept to a high standard, and the plaques giving information about the layout of the abbey and its associated buildings, are clear and instructive. The nave is Norman, with magnificent arches, whilst the rest of the structure is a fine example of Early English architecture. It is fascinating to see how an abbey worked, as there are part buildings or complete foundations for all the main rooms and outhouses. This includes a remarkably large infirmary, possibly needed because the valley was damp, and rheumatic and respiratory ailments must have been common. At its height, an estimated 650 monks and lay brothers were housed in Rievaulx. Over the years there have been many reports of hauntings, generally explained by the mists rising from the River Rye and the wind moaning through the ruined arches.

The Terrace was intended to be a place to have a picnic at the end of a drive along the riverside at a time when 'ruins' had become fashionable. They were laid out in the eighteenth century by the Duncombe family, and are now looked after by the National Trust. The Terrace is reached through a rather unprepossessing gate on the B1257 at the top of the hill. A short walk from the National Trust shop suddenly opens out onto splendid lawns and wooded slopes, with two Greek temples at either end of a horseshoe terrace. Below, in the valley, there are glimpses of the Abbey ruins through gaps in the trees. The Ionic temple contains an interesting history of the Duncombe family (Lord Feversham) illustrated by early Victorian photographs, and a collection of furniture and china. The Tuscan temple at the far end of the lawns is decorated with ornate Italian plasterwork.

The charming village, with its thatched cottages, grew up on the hillside by the Abbey. It is sad to reflect that these houses were all built after the Dissolution of the Monasteries, with stones pillaged from the Abbey itself.

Rievaulx Abbey

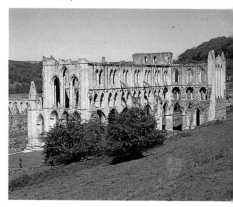

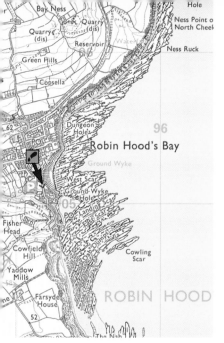

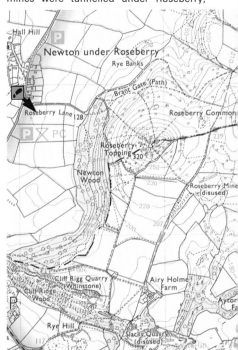

Robin Hood's Bay

Robin Hood's Bay (94) (NZ 95-05)

This well-preserved and enchanting fishing village occupies an idyllic position with spectacular views over a wide bay. The general impression walking down from the car park – access is on foot only – is of a jumble of tiled roofs. The houses huddle together, with narrow streets and passages climbing up and down the steep hillside. There are steps everywhere in Robin Hood's Bay. A feature of many of the houses is the 'coffin window' at first floor level: no doubt used for furniture as well as for the more macabre purpose to which they owe their name. Every twist and turn reveals a different aspect, with new sights to interest the eye: perhaps this is why artists love the location.

The village was once a fishing port, and one of the many theories about its name is that the legendary outlaw Robin Hood was chased here and escaped arrest by disguising himself as a local fisherman. Certainly, as early as 1538 the settlement was known by its present name.

The view from the cliff tops is one of the best on the East Coast – especially over the bay to the south towards the 600 ft Old Peak at Ravenscar ★ . There is a good beach, which is safe for bathing, and a rocky shoreline: an interesting place to explore. It is possible, but only on a falling tide, to walk the length of the shore to Ravenscar, but anyone attempting this should be careful to keep an eye on the sea. A safer route is along the clearly marked Cleveland Way on dry land. There is a fascinating geological trail, detailed in an information sheet sold locally, which is an interesting way of having a walk with a 'purpose'. See the map on this page.

The sea has always been part of life in the village, both as provider and enemy. Once, more than a hundred fishing boats and even some whalers, sailed from Robin Hood's Bay. It was also a notorious centre for smuggling, with a thriving illicit trade in contraband brandy.

But the sea also takes from those who depend on it. Many of the village men were lost at sea over the centuries, others were lost to the press gangs who prized them for their seamanship. The sea has also claimed the land itself: the original main street disappeared in 1780, and whole houses were often swept away. In recent times a sea wall has been built as a protection against the terrible North Sea storms.

Roseberry Topping (93) (NZ 57-12)

This unusual conical hill, the site of an ancient beacon, is clearly visible from the Thirsk ★ to Teesside main road, on the western edge of the Moors. The peak rises up dramatically, 1051 ft above sea level, to give glorious views in all directions. Until the end of the eighteenth century the hill was conical in shape, and prints from that time show an unblemished hill. Ironstone mines were tunnelled under Roseberry,

Roseberry Topping

and due to subsidence the whole of the west face collapsed. Apart from the obvious effect on the hill itself, the west side is now rather unstable, and the village of Newton under Roseberry has suffered from rock falls, especially after heavy rain.

For the fit there is a short, but steep, track to the summit from the village on the plain far below (see map). It is well worth the effort.

Rosedale and Rosedale Abbey (94,100) (SE 72-95)

Rosedale is a narrow, wooded valley which runs north-south for about eight miles to the south of the Cleveland Hills which form the backbone of the Moors. The principal village is Rosedale Abbey, a very pretty hamlet with the remains of a twelfth-century priory beside the church. From monastic times iron has been mined in the area, and that is the clue to the large number of deserted and derelict cottages which characterise Rosedale. In the nineteenth century this was a 'Klondike' settlement. The population rose from 548 in 1851 to 2839 in 1871 – by 1961 it had dropped to a sad 286 souls.

Visitors today are hard-pressed to imagine the furious mining activity for iron ore that was carried on here in the last century. Initially the ore was carried in horse-drawn wagons to Pickering ★ to be transported by railway to Whitby ★ . Later, a specially constructed railway line was built across the moors to Cleveland, with a summit of 1300 ft and a steep, cable-operated incline at Battersby ★ . The locomotives stayed all their working lives on the Moors, as there was no route down to lower ground. At its peak, the Rosedale line carried 1000 tons of ore a day. Part of the disused railway line is one of many of the long distance footpaths which criss-cross the region. Details of many of these walks can be obtained from the local tourist information centres.

Tourism is a vital industry for Rosedale now. There is a well-equipped camping site at Rosedale Abbey as well as the usual hostelries. It is an excellent location for exploring this section of the Moors, which are easily within walking reach. There are two 'waymark' walks, but one of the most fascinating rambles is to visit the old iron-works on the hill above the village, and to

walk along the old disused railway track, imagining the busy steam locomotives hauling their wagons of iron ore on the start of the tortuous journey across bleak moorland, to Ingleby Incline. Both Rosedale and Ingleby Incline, the start and finish of the railway, are starting points for **Walks 4 and 2**. Also see **Tour 3**.

Rosedale Head (94) (NZ 67-01)

This high point of the Moors, nearly 1400 ft above sea level, provides spectacular views in all directions. It is accessible by car, cycle and on foot, being at the junction of four roads and two footpaths. At this point stands Ralph's Cross ★ , one of the many ancient crosses that dot the Moors and were once used as waymarks for the horseman or foot traveller.

From here, on a clear day, it is possible to obtain a picture of the geography of the whole Moors – Eskdale to the north, running across nearly the whole width from east to west, and the southern dales running parallel with each other north to south: Rosedale, Farndale, Bransdale, and, hidden to the west behind Bilsdale Moor, Bilsdale itself (see **Tour 9**).

A waymark

To the north-east from the vantage point of Rosedale Head is Whitby ★ and the North Sea. Sometimes it is even possible to see York Minster forty miles away to the south. If it is near the end of a hot Summer's day and there is a dark smudge above the sea, you would be well-advised to get onto the lower ground of Danby Dale or Westerdale to the north, as soon as possible. To be caught on the high moors in the thick 'roak' as it moves inland is a dangerous and frightening experience.

Runswick Bay (94) (NZ 80-16)

This is one of several delightful little villages on the coast between Boulby ★ and Scarborough ★ . Unlike Staithes ★ and

Runswick Bay

Robin Hood's Bay ★ , there is no real street system: the cottages are connected by passages and steep steps. The soil and its sheltered position make Runswick Bay a gardener's paradise. The sandy beach is both safe and attractive: at the far end of the sands is the quaintly named Hob Hole, caused by a combination of natural erosion and mining for jet. There is a local legend that a goblin lived by the stream which runs into the sea at this point. This benevolent fairy had the power to cure children's illnesses.

The cliffs here take a terrible battering from the North Sea and the weather, and are quite unstable. In 1682 an earlier village sank completely into the sea in a cliff slide caused by heavy rain. Luckily the inhabitants were warned and taken on board a ship off-shore: no lives were lost in what otherwise would have been a major tragedy.

St Gregory's Minster (see Kirkdale)

Saltergate (94,100) (SE 85-94)
The old track used for centuries by the salt traders is knows as 'Saltergate'. The area between Lockton High Moor and Lockton Low Moor has become known as Saltergate Moor, and it is also the name of a famous inn on the main Pickering ★ to Whitby ★ Road which lies just below the steep incline that leads up to the Hole of Horcum ★ (see **Walk 6 and Tours 2 and 3**). Salt was once panned at the coast and carried by packhorse, or men, along the Salters Way across Fylingdales Moor to the market in Pickering. Saltergate Inn is now a busy public house in the summer as walkers from the Moors, or motorists out for a day's drive, find it a convenient and pleasant place to stop. The inn must have been an equally welcome sight for the weary travellers of earlier centuries.

Salton (100) (SE 71-80)
A typical village in Ryedale on the River Dove, Salton lies south-west of Kirkbymoorside ★ and Pickering ★ . There is a pleasant village green surrounded by brick-built houses; there was once a sulphur spring here. The main attraction is the

fine Norman Church of St John of Beverley which has many superb features and was once a place of pilgrimage. The church was attacked and burnt by marauding Scots in 1138 and again in 1322: there are still marks on the walls caused by the conflagration.

High tide at Sandsend

Sandsend (94) (NZ 86-12)
This settlement – as might be guessed – lies at the end of the sandy beach which stretches down to Whitby ★ from the north. It is a small village separated from its neighbour not only by the magnificent sands, but by a golf course which is open to the general public. The houses of Sandsend are clustered in the lee of a steep hill. A small stream enters the sea at this point, having flowed through the verdant Mulgrave Woods. This is one of the few natural woods that escaped being cleared as part of the war effort during the First World War. There is an old motte and bailey in Mulgrave Woods known as Wade's Castle; a second castle was once the home of Peter de Mauley, a henchman of King John. The third, more modern castle is near Sandsend Beck, and was built during the Stuart Restoration in the latter part of the seventeenth century. St Oswald's church, just outside the village, has some interesting Viking relics.

Scarborough (101) (TA 03-88) (see both **Tours 2 and 8**)
Scarborough is a beautiful seaside resort, with two magnificent sandy bays separated by a headland plateau which rises some 300 ft above sea level. Late Bronze Age Man temporarily occupied the headland, but it was a thousand years later that the Romans built a signal station as part of their early warning system for policing the coastline against the first English raiders. The remains of the signal station can still be seen, although the eastern perimeter wall has fallen into the sea.

Later, the Vikings colonised Scarborough – and gave it its name. The sagas tell of Thorgils Skarthi, a Scandinavian sea captain and raider, who made it his place – which translates as something like 'Scarthi's burgh'. The headland also played its part in the tumultuous events leading up to

SCARBOROUGH

Scale 1:10 000
or 6 INCHES to 1 MILE

1 Information Centre
2 Gardens
3 Art Gallery
4 Rotunda Museum
5 Castle
6 Spa
7 Church of St Martin
8 Valley Park
9 Natural History Museum

the Norman Conquest. The combined forces of Harald of Norway and Tostig, Lord of the Manor of Falsgrave (and Harold of England's brother), built a huge bonfire on the headland. They hurled brands of fire down into the town, forcing the submission of the inhabitants before moving off towards their defeat at Stamford Bridge. After the Norman conquest a castle was built on the headland. Today the formidable ruined keep which dominates the skyline, and the stone curtain wall, are visible reminders of the great Norman and medieval castle which has played a significant role in national politics through the centuries. The royal court stayed here whilst on tour. The great west wall of the keep was shattered by the Parliamentarian artillery in the Civil War, when control of the royal port and castle was essential to the outcome of the war. George Fox, the Quaker, was a political prisoner confined in one of the towers for over a year. The barracks built to house the garrison established after the 1745 Rebellion, and part of the curtain wall, were destroyed by the German bombardment of Scarborough on 16 December 1914. 'Remember Scarborough – Enlist Now! became a rallying cry in the Great War.

Standing on the approach road to the **castle (5)** is the Parish Church of St Mary founded in the mid-twelfth century. Originally a small building, it was greatly enlarged in the following centuries to meet the needs of the community. Its proximity to the castle was exploited in the Civil War when the Parliamentarian forces stationed a battery in the grounds during the 1644-45 siege. The return fire from the Royalists in the castle badly damaged the church, and the ruined chancel remains a silent testimony to that bitter struggle.

The graveyard contains an impressive range of headstones and tombs. Among them, in the separate eastern section, is the grave of the author Anne Brontë. Anne, already in poor health, had come to Scarborough to take the sea air and was staying at her favourite lodgings, No 2 The Cliff. It was here she died, only twenty-nine years old, in 1849.

Beneath the castle, to the south, the hillside has been terraced since medieval times when Scarborough was an important fishing and trading port. In the eighteenth century many of these streets were the fashionable addresses of shipowners and master mariners. Some, like Princess Street, have retained much of their Georgian character. Humbler fishermen's cottages cluster around the alleys and steps leading to the harbour.

The harbour consists of three piers: the East Pier, a great arm of stone reaching out to withstand the full blast of the North Sea; the older middle or Vincent's Pier capped with the lighthouse; and the West Pier, where all the business activity of running the port is centred. The harbour was the commercial and industrial heart of the

South Sands Scarborough

town. Ship-building yards constructed large ocean-going vessels. At the time of its closure, the Tindall yard employed the young Edward Harland who went on to found the Harland and Wolff shipping company.

In the herring season craft of every description – trawlers, yawls, drifters, smacks and cobles – jostled in the harbour so that it was possible to cross from one pier to another stepping from one deck to the next. The inner harbour still houses a diminished fishing fleet which keeps the fish market and stalls supplied with fresh cod and haddock, crabs, lobsters and all manner of shellfish. European traders can unload cargoes of timber and potatoes at the deep berth.

The Scarborough lifeboat is situated near the entrance to the West Pier. Since the first lifeboat in 1801, over 400 lives have been saved. The outer harbour, though fundamentally a harbour of refuge for distressed shipping, now resounds with the expensive jangle of luxury yachts at their moorings.

Stretching out beyond the harbour are the golden sands of the South Bay. The earliest illustration of sea-bathing in Britain depicts Scarborough, in an engraving of 1735. As part of the health cure the men bathed naked and the women used bathing machines – these were little boxes on wheels which were pulled out to sea allowing the occupants to undress, bathe and redress in complete privacy.

In 'the season', eighty years ago, the beach was a hive of activity. Jockey carriages and bathing machines lined up waiting for custom. These were a rich variety of side-shows ranging from photographers, phrenologists, sand modellers, and strong man acts, to daily performances by minstrel bands and the Pierrots. Amusement arcades have never looked back since the first 'penny in the slot' machines appeared at the funfair which opened in 1903. Now they compete for business with ice-cream parlours, rock shops, fish and chip shops, souvenirs, an ice-skating rink, waxworks and even hologram shows.

Nestling in the valley beneath the cliff bridge, only yards from the sea, stands the **Rotunda Museum (4)**. It is a small architectural gem, acknowledged to be one of the finest surviving Georgian purpose-built museums. The Upper Galleries are lined with elegant curved mahogany glazed display cabinets. The architect thoughtfully provided a 'Moveable Stage' to allow visitors a better view of the local antiquities and exotic curiosities – collected by Scarborough sea captains – which fill the upper cases. William Smith, the 'father of English geology', influenced the museum design. A geological section of the rock strata from the River Humber to the River Tees, drawn by his nephew John Phillips, covers the parapet wall of the Upper Gallery.

The atmosphere changes at the far end of the South Bay: from the razzamatazz of arcadia, to the refined aura of spa life. Tourism began with the discovery – by a respectable housewife in the 1620s – of the medicinal qualities of the spring waters which bubbled up at the base of the cliff, staining the rocks red. By the turn of the century, a large proportion of the nobility and gentry of England had taken the waters. Doctors claimed marvellous cures for asthma, consumption, deafness, madness, rheumatism, convulsions, worms, palsy, apoplexy, epilepsy, vertigo, jaundice, leprosy, scurvy, hectic fevers, windiness, unpleasant humour, stomach disorders through intemperance and, last but not least, hypochondria!

The transition from a fashionable health spa, to a cultural centre with a reputation for fine music and theatre, to a modern conference and entertainments complex, has involved many changes, many buildings and as many architects. Originally the spa buildings were rustic – the waters were taken 'al fresco' from cisterns separated from the sea by a wooden staith.

Sir Joseph Paxton was commissioned to produce a 'grand design' for the spa in the 1850s. Unfortunately his Grand Hall was burnt down in 1876. It was quickly replaced by the present hall, designed by Verity and Hunt. The **spa buildings (6)** now provide suites of rooms, restaurants, cafes, open air balconies and a bandstand. Recently a major programme of restoration and refurbishment has revamped the splendid opulence of the Victorian buildings, creating excellent conference and entertainment facilities.

'224 steps avoided for the price of 1d' (one old penny) was the boast of the first incline cliff tramway in England, adjoining the spa complex. Opened in 1875, this counter-balanced cable-hauled hydraulic tramway carried parties of eager holidaymakers onto the beach, and elegantly dressed promenaders or concert-goers to the spa from their luxury hotels on the Esplanade above.

The promenade continues past the spa to the outdoor bathing pool which opened in 1915. Above, the cliff sides have been landscaped and terraced to create some of Scarborough's most beautiful gardens –

among them the Italian Gardens (with a statue of Mercury), the Holbeck Gardens and Clock Tower, Shuttleworth Gardens (with a Blind Garden), and the Esplanade Gardens.

The Esplanade itself commands the most glorious sea views. It is hardly surprising that it became the site for luxury hotels. The Crown Hotel was the first of many, its imposing facade conspicuous in the Regency-style terrace. Catering for every amenity that the rich and fashionable on holiday required, it opened in 1844-45 amidst a blaze of national advertising which attracted an international clientele. Today's visitors can promenade on the Esplanade showing off the latest trends in fashion, as Victorian holidaymakers once strolled in the 'Church Parade'.

Tucked away behind the Esplanade and the Prince of Wales Terrace is the **Church of St Martin (7)**. Here, lovers of Pre-Raphaelite art can enjoy wonderful examples of the work of William Morris, Burne-Jones, Ford Madox Brown and Gabriel Dante Rossetti.

Development of the South Cliff and access from the town was made easier by the construction of two iron bridges. The Cliff, or Spa Bridge, was the first to open in 1827. An elegant pedestrian bridge, it is dwarfed at its northern end by the awesome proportions of the Grand Hotel. Described as the 'Grandest of The Grands', the hotel was designed by Cuthbert Broderick and fitted out with the most up-to-date furnishings and equipment when it opened in 1867. On the corner of St Nicholas Street stands the Royal Hotel, among the first large seaside hotels in the north of England and site of the Long Rooms, the fashionable entertainments centre of Georgian spa society. The second bridge spanning the **Valley (8)** came from York where it was originally intended to cross the River Ouse. The iron girders were re-erected as Scarborough's Valley Bridge in 1865.

At the northern end of Valley Bridge, to the west, is the famous Stephen Joseph Theatre in the Round, home to Alan Ayckbourn, one of Britain's most popular and prolific contemporary playwrights. To the east is the Crescent with its fine terraces and detached villas. Londesborough Lodge was the seaside villa of the first Lord Londesborough. His son, the first Earl, inherited the estate and an immense fortune and became one of Scarborough's most generous benefactors, a patron of sports and arts. His friendship with the Prince of Wales led to three royal visits between 1869-71, when one mile of red carpet was laid between the Lodge and the spa!

Lady Ida, Lord Londesborough's daughter, was chosen by Sir George Sitwell, then residing at Wood End, next-door-but-one, to become his wife. Edith, the eldest of their children was born at Wood End. Now a **Natural History**

Fishing boats in the harbour

Museum (9), writings and photographs of the famous literary trio – Edith, Osbert and Sacheverell – are on display. Between Londesborough Lodge and Wood End stands the **Art Gallery (3),** one of the finest of the houses in the Crescent, built in the Italianate style in 1835.

The railway station stands in the town centre, little changed since the 1880s. When the first train – with the 'Railway King' George Hudson aboard – steamed into the station on 7 July 1845, it signalled the end of expensive long-distance travel by coach and carriage and put Scarborough on the tourist map. The delights of a seaside holiday were now available to people living in the industrialised towns of West Yorkshire and the Midlands. Although high class visitors travelling first class continued to come for the season, 'specials' brought in thousands of excursionists and day trippers.

Opposite the railway station is the Victoria Hotel, birthplace of the legendary Hollywood star, Charles Laughton. As a boy he had taken inspiration from the Pierrots and his first amateur appearance in Scarborough was in Hobson's Choice in 1923. His films were later shown next door at Scarborough's Odeon – a typical example of the unmistakable architecture of the Odeon picture house empire of Oscar Deutsch which opened in 1936.

The North Bay is the least commercialised stretch of Scarborough's coastline. No trace survives of the Victorian pleasure pier which strutted out into the sea providing entertainment and refreshments for promenaders in the Saloon Pavilion. It was smashed to pieces by a stormy sea in 1905. Rows of tall houses and hotels overlook the bay. Every year residents and visitors crowd to the Scarborough Cricket Club ground for the Cricket Festival. It was inspired by Lord Londesborough, and has been held in the same place every September for at least a century.

At the northern end of the Bay **gardens (2),** theatres and pleasure grounds provide attractions for all the family. Peasholm Park is an artificial lake embellished in oriental style with bridges, cascading waterfalls, a pagoda and a floating bandstand. Peasholm Glen is a botanist's delight, planted with many rare and exotic species of trees and shrubs.

The majestic marine promenade, which stretches from the Corner in the North Bay to the spa in the South Bay, provides two and a half miles of incomparable views. The construction of the Foreshore Road in the South Bay was the first stage. When proposals were put forward to landscape the cliff and build a carriage road in the North Bay, there was a public outcry. However, development went ahead and Clarence Gardens and the Royal Albert Drive were both officially opened in 1890. The final stage came with the construction of Marine Drive – this link road round the foot of the Castle headland was a massive feat of civil engineering which took over ten years to complete in 1908. The little Toll House near the entrance to the east pier stands as a reminder that visitors once had to pay to enjoy this magnificent promenade.

Scawton (100) (SE 54-83)
On Scawton Moor, in the Hambleton Hills to the west of Helmsley ★ , is the small village of Scawton. The church here was built by monks from Old Byland ★ in 1146; much of their original work is still visible, including the splendid south doorway. The church bell is the 'lesser bell' from Byland which is said to be the oldest church bell in England, while the Hare Inn claims to be the smallest in Yorkshire. In the church is a memorial plaque dedicated to some French airmen who died when their bomber crashed nearby in the Second World War.

During the Middle Ages the manor, and nearby Hag Hall, was owned by the Malebiche family. They forfeited it for a time in 1190 for taking part in the terrible massacre of the Jews in York ★ .

Seave Green (93) (NZ 56-00)
It is very easy to pass through this village on the B1257 whilst driving up Bilsdale (**Tour 9**), but take the time to turn up by the sign to St Hilda's Church to find a most attractive little hamlet, with a ford and a

St Hilda's Church

stream. The map on this page shows a suggested short walk to some ancient earthworks and the church in which there is a very early font.

Shandy Hall (see Coxwold)

Sheriff Hutton (100) SE 65-66)
The ruins of the great castle can be seen from far to the south: they dominate the village of Sheriff Hutton today as they have dominated its life through the centuries. The earlier castle was built by Ansketil Bulmer, steward of the Norman Nigel Fossard between 1119 and 1129. He was a Sheriff and gave the village its name. The imposing earthworks of the first castle can still be seen at Church End.

In 1382 John Neville built a magnificent new castle. The structure has been systematically pillaged for building materials for many generations, but two towers and enough of the original structure remain to give visitors some idea of its past glory. The castle has seen some of the most important figures in the pageant of English history: the Earls of Westmorland; Richard, Earl of Warwick; Richard III; Thomas Howard, Duke of Norfolk and many others. Part of the castle is on farmland, but can be visited by asking at the farmhouse and making a small donation to a charity.

The church of St Helen and Holy Cross is a repository of much of Sheriff Hutton's glorious history. Among its monuments is the famous effigy of Edward, Prince of Wales, the son of Richard III who was doomed to die before he reached manhood.

The village has many interesting features. There are cruck houses and small cottages around its three greens, built with stone pillaged from the castle. To visit Sheriff Hutton see **Tours 6 and 7**).

Sinnington (94,100) (SE 74-85)
Fortunately this village, which lies between Pickering ★ and Kirkbymoorside ★, is by-passed by the busy A170 – so holiday traffic rarely ventures here. It is a fascinating place, with a rich history dating from the Viking period and many fine buildings. The village has a curious packhorse bridge as well as the imposing structure which spans the River Seven. The stone buildings around the wide green are full of interest, while up the hill by Nun's Walk are the Church of All Saints and the medieval Hall. The ancient Sinnington Hunt, which was founded by 1745, meets at the village green, before setting out into the surrounding countryside. This tradition is reflected in the fox which adorns the village maypole.

Skelton (105) (SE 57-56)
Four miles north-west of York ★ is this large village with its perfectly preserved thirteenth-century parish church. The church is said to have been built out of stone 'left overs' not needed for York Minster; it is an architectural gem measuring only 44 ft by 33 ft. Because of the connection with York Minster, although it is All Saints' Parish Church, locals still refer to it as 'Little St Peter's'.

About 1 ½ miles north of the village, is the thirty-seven acre Moorlands Nature Reserve. This is run by the Yorkshire Naturalist Trust, which has planted many trees and shrubs in the reserve to provide colour in the early summer as well as a breeding ground for a wide variety of birds and wild animals. There is an Information Centre on the site of the Nature Reserve, or further details can be obtained from their office, at 20 Castlegate in York.

Sleights (94) (NZ 86-07)
This is a small town rather than a village, which straddles the main Whitby ★ to Pickering ★ road on the northern edge of the Moors.

The River Esk defines the border on the north and steep Blue Bank is the natural border to the south. Drivers crossing the bridge over the Esk, as the road from Whitby descends to the valley bottom, might like to reflect that a previous bridge was washed away in the exceptional floods of 1930.

The town is not attractive in the way that most other moorland towns are, but it is a good centre in which to stay to explore this part of the Moors. Very quickly visitors can be either fishing in the attractive Esk Dale (with salmon in the river at the right time of year); striding over the Moors, or exploring the tranquil paths around Littlebeck ★.

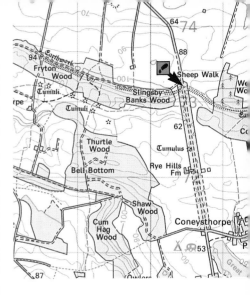

The old tradition of the Whitby 'penny hedge' began with an incident which occurred near here, when a hermit was murdered by a local man. The villagers' difficult penance, which their successors still dutifully perform, was to build a hedge in the mud at low tide on Whitby beach, the day before Ascension.

Slingsby (100) (SE 69-75)

The limestone-built village of Slingsby is set on the edge of the gently rising ground which forms one of the boundaries of Castle Howard ★. To the north is Slingsby Carr, a local name for a swampy region. The remains of a prehistoric settlement have been uncovered in a local field. Slingsby is featured in **Tours 4 and 6** and the map on this page shows a good place for a stroll to the south of the village.

Slingsby consists of a main street with a church, a village green with a maypole and what appear to be the ruins of a castle or manor house. This is in fact an unfinished building which was intended to be the country home of Sir Charles Cavendish, 'a dwarf, a soldier, a mathemetician, a poet and a philosopher'. Building started in 1642 but was never completed due to the Civil War.

In the church is a monument to Sir William Wyvill, who killed a monster that was terrorising the region. According to legend, the intrepid Wyvill 'with his dog, did kill a monstrous serpent that lived and preyed on passengers on the road to Malton'. The curious may wish to discover the monster's lair which locals have identified as a disued gravel pit. Yorkshire has several tales of serpents being slain by

Slingsby Manor

commoners and gentry: myths which are fertile ground for both folklorists and psychologists. However, no-one has ever explained the old coffin unearthed on the Moors which bore the inscription 'snake killer'.

Spaunton (94,100) (SE 72-89)

This sparsely populated village lies due south of Lastingham ★ and was once part of a manorial estate that included its neighbouring village. The fact that the field layout reflected the Roman style of farming led archaeologists to investigate possible burial sites. At the turn of the century a Roman grave was discovered and the artefacts are now on display in the Yorkshire Museum in York ★.

In 1960, a dig uncovered the foundations of a large medieval Hall. The manor of Spaunton grew to be very large and prosperous under the care of various shrewd abbots from St Mary's Abbey in York, to whom the lands were granted by William the Conqueror.

After the Dissolution of the Monasteries the new owner sold off the estate in parcels to several freeholders, whose descendants have common land rights and still hold a court once a year to decide on local ownership and boundary problems.

Spaunton today is a very quiet place indeed, and gives no idea of the large number of houses that once existed in the location.

Staithes (94) (NZ 78-18)

It is an artist's dream: an old seaside town clustered round the harbour in a narrow inlet, surrounded by high cliffs on three sides. In Staithes each new corner reveals another interesting prospect. Motorists will approach Staithes from the main road at the top of the hill. But those who walk along the Cleveland Way, and wind their way down the cliffside to the sea's edge, have the best view of this charming place.

Staithes

Until recently, Danish customs, a legacy of the Viking invasion, were strong here, and women wore bonnets as part of their normal everyday dress. Staithes can claim connections with Captain Cook as he was apprenticed to a draper whose shop was near the harbour. The actual shop was swept away by the sea along with several other buildings near the shoreline. Behind the little beach is 'The Cod and Lobster', a pleasant inn which was rebuilt as recently as 1953, predecessors having been destroyed by the sea no less than three times. On a calm day it is difficult to imagine the fury of a North Sea storm when great waves are channelled up the inlet, crashing over the sea wall onto the houses.

There used to be what must have been an exhilarating railway journey from Loftus ★ to Scarborough ★ which ran near to the cliff edge along the coast. There was a viaduct at Staithes to carry the line over the gorge. Because of the Tay Bridge disaster — when in high winds the bridge broke and a train fell into the river — great care was taken to stress the structure to withstand high winds. If the wind reached a dangerous speed, a bell would ring and no trains were allowed to cross the viaduct. However, like many modern burglar alarms, the bell was too sensitive and was often tripped, causing much annoyance to local inhabitants. The only sounds now are the sea and the gulls.

Stamford Bridge (105,106) (SE 71-55)
Most schoolchildren can remember the date of 1066, when Harold was defeated by William at Hastings. Some will also know that the defeat was in part due to the fact that Harold had twice marched the length of the country with his army. He was on the south coast waiting for the expected invasion from Normandy, when his treacherous brother claimed the throne and joined forces with a Viking army which had designs on northern England. Harold rushed north and met the foe at Stamford Bridge winning a remarkable victory. The stone bridge on the main road into the town is built on the site of the wooden bridge which was the centre of the bloody battle. From here, the defeated, and greatly depleted, Vikings sailed back down

the river to the sea.

Another even more vicious battle was fought here in 1453 between the opposing factions in the War of the Roses. The first in that bloody campaign for the English Crown.

The modern town of Stamford Bridge lies on the main York ★ to Bridlington road, the A166. There is a large camping site and a useful collection of shops and hotels.

Stockton on the Forest (105,106) (SE 65-55)
This is an attractive village about four miles north-east of York ★ on the old Roman road to Malton ★ : the new trunk road passes to the north. Stockton on the Forest was a Saxon settlement, and is recorded in the Domesday book under the name of Stocthun. It is difficult to visualise now, but this whole area was densely wooded in medieval times, hence the 'on the Forest'. This was part of the Royal Forest of Galtres which was reserved for hunting.

The village is no longer compact, but modern developments are not too intrusive, and blend well with the older Georgian architecture. The sporting and other attractions which this region held for the nobility in the early part of the eighteenth century led to a building boom, and most villages in the area have a 'Hall'. Stockton's is no longer in private hands, and is now a school at the south end of the village.

Stonegrave (100) (SE 65-77)
On the B1257, half way between Hovingham ★ and Helmsley ★ , is a village which most traffic passes through. This is the 'Staningagrave' which Pope Paul I asked King Eadbert of Northumbria to restore to its rightful owners and the service of God (there was a monastery there in AD 757, which had been misappropriated together with the religious houses at Jarrow and Coxwold ★). Today only the great Saxon cross of the monastery remains. This is preserved in the Church of the Holy Trinity. The ecclesiastical authorities seem to have had other problems in Stonegrave. In the mid-thirteenth century Simon de Stonegrave was regularly excommunicated for taking Church dues. The respected critic and art historian Herbert Read lived in Stonegrave, which is a pretty village well worth visiting.

Studford Ring (see Ampleforth)

Sutton-on-the Forest and Sutton Park (100) (SE 58-64)
The village is situated about eight miles north of York ★ (see **Tours 4 and 5**) on the B1363. The great Georgian house of Sutton Park has extensive gardens, reputed to

Sutton Park

have been designed by Capability Brown. The house and gardens, though open to the public, are privately owned. The plasterwork of Sutton Park is an outstanding example of eighteenth-century workmanship, and there is also a marvellous collection of porcelain. As well as the colourful gardens – creatively utilising the original terraces – there is a shady wooded area with a pleasant walk.

The garden has been designed so that there is always something of interest in bloom. It is one of those places where you come away full of ideas to transform your own garden.

Sutton Bank (100) (SE 51-82)

Large signs warn motorists towing caravans to avoid this hill: the road climbs 500 ft in half a mile. There is a large Information Centre at the top of Sutton Bank with spacious car parks. This lies close to the old Drovers' Way that was used to drive cattle from Scotland to the market towns of England two centuries ago. Nowadays the travellers along the edge of the escarpment are likely to be walkers on the Cleveland Way, the long distance path from Helmsley ★ to Scarborough ★ via the northern Moors. The view from the top of Sutton Bank is one of the finest in England and on a clear day it is possible to see the Pennines, more than thirty miles away. Far below is Gormire Lake which though on a nature trail, can only be reached by a steep

Gormire Lake

descent (and subsequent steep climb!) The Lake appears to have no inlet or outlet, and the water is believed to drain through a tunnel. Surrounded by trees, with a strangely still surface. Gormire is a rather eerie place. One legend tells of how an angel went to homesteads along the lower reaches of the ridge asking for water. No-one would meet his request until he found a couple who shared their last drop with him. Having quenched his thirst, he caused a chasm to open, that drowned the other houses, and provided his benefactors with an unlimited supply of water.

Sutton-Under-Whitestonecliffe (100) (SE 48-82)

The village lies nearly two miles away from Sutton Bank. In Sutton-under-Whitestonecliffe there is a workshop for woodcarving and hand-made furniture. The master carpenter uses a beaver as his symbol. To the south of the village, down a side road on **Tour 10**, is Osgodby Hall. It is a perfect example of a Jacobean House, and should be visited by anyone interested in domestic architecture.

Swainby (93) (NZ 47-02)

Like many of the other mining villages in this area, Swainby has now returned to the calm and peace it had enjoyed for centuries. It is difficult to imagine the noise and traffic caused by the mining industry during its peak in the nineteenth century: In 1880 nearly 70,000 tons of iron ore were dug out of the local mine.

The first recorded village was built for estate workers in the middle ages, the 'swains'; although Roman coins have been found in Swainby suggesting an earlier settlement. The medieval village was located near the church and the castle; but when the population was decimated by the plague, a new village was reconstructed where present-day Swainby now stands. The settlement is effectively cut in two by the river which flows down the middle of a long green, with bridges joining the two parts together.

Swainby has had two remarkable inhabitants among its farming folk: Elisabeth Harland, who died of old age at 105, the year Napoleon was beaten back at the gates of Moscow, and one Harry Cooper, reputedly 8 ft 6 ins tall, who was exhibited at Barnum's Show in America.

Terrington (100) (SE 67-70)

This little village lies on a ridge in the Howardian Hills. It is not on any major through route and is a very peaceful place, with mainly Georgian and Early Victorian houses. Although there are very few older buildings, there are records of a village existing on the site long before the Norman Conquest. The name 'Terrington' in Old English indicates some connection with sorcery. In the seventeenth century the village was a notorious centre for witchcraft, and folklorists have found remnants of pagan religion in the local Plough Monday garland dance. In the churchyard is the grave of one of the country's leading botanists, Richard Spruce. There is only one public house in Terrington, The Bay Horse: two less than at the end of the last century.

Thornton Dale

Thirsk (99) (SE 43-82)
Visitors in search of James Herriot's 'Darrowby', which was modelled on Thirsk, will find a working, functioning town, whose long history as an important market centre and a coaching stop has given it a very special character. But although the town itself makes few concessions to tourists – and is all the more interesting for that – there is a great deal to see in Thirsk.

Cod Beck runs through the centre of the town, separating the original Saxon settlement of Old Thirsk from New Thirsk with its wonderful cobbled marketplace and eighteenth-century coaching inns. The beautiful parish church of St Mary stands in meadowland by the beck. Built in the Perpendicular style, it dates from the fifteenth century. St Mary's has an 80 ft tower and contains some fine woodwork and interesting glass.

In the eighteenth century Thirsk was an important centre for coining. The little racecourse is one of the earliest in England – some say the earliest – and is still well attended. Thomas Lord, founder of the famous Lord's Cricket Ground in London, was born in Kirkgate. His house is now the Thirsk Museum and it contains a wealth of cricket memorabilia as well as exhibits of life and industry in the area.

Thirsk is an excellent centre from which to explore both the Moors and the Dales (see **Tour 10**). Communications are good and there is plenty of accommodation. Visitors will enjoy the Monday market when they will see the liveliest face of this fine old town.

Thornton Dale (100) (SE 83-82)
It is not surprising that many people choose to retire to this beautiful village just over two miles east of Pickering ★ . Although the busy A170 brings many visitors during the holiday season, Thornton Dale has so many places of interest and so much history that, somehow, it retains its charm. There are broad fields above and below the village, which has Thornton Beck running through its centre. There was an important fulling mill in the early fourteenth century, owned by Lord Latimer. He it was who married Lucy de Tweng, whose five husbands in rapid succession and other proclivities anticipated Hollywood by 600 years.

Much of Thornton Dale's attraction comes from its complicated shape: it is a fascinating jumble of streams and paths and thatched houses. The pattern of the village is medieval – the result of manorial division – but most of the building is from later periods. The almshouses are seventeenth century, while many of the houses in the village centre are Georgian.

In the village church is the grave of Matthew Grimes who guarded Napoleon Bonaparte on St Helena, his island prison. The village green still has wooden stocks – although they are no longer used for punishing petty criminals – and a market cross. As most of the village lies to the south of the A170, it does not give the impression of being on a major road. A short stroll south of the green into quiet streets, with views over the Vale of Pickering, and it is easy to forget the lorries and cars hurrying to and from Scarborough ★ . Most of the attractive area to the north-east is owned by the Forestry Commission, and they have laid out several nature trails of the Dalby Forest drive. The drive can be entered, via a toll, to the north of the village. Also see **Tours 2 and 8**.

Upper Poppleton (and Nether Poppleton) (105) (SE 55-54)
The old village has now been swallowed up by encroaching York ★ . One of the best ways to view Poppleton is from the River Ouse. On a fine day it makes a pleasant outing to row upstream from one of the many places hiring boats at the landing stages to the north-west of York. Those who are not keen oarsmen can approach the village from the A59.

Points of interest to look out for are the cottages and Poppleton Hall, with its exceptionally long stable, in Nether Poppleton. This is also the site of The Fox Inn which still has a river sign indicating its presence and access via a narrow path from the landing stage: a legacy of days when river traffic was much greater. The inn was once a sixteenth-century farmhouse, though little remains of the original building. Upper Poppleton has retained its village green and maypole.

Warthill (105.106) (SE 67-55)
It is a pity that this hamlet did not keep its

ancient and more attractive name of Ward-hills or Wardille, for it is in fact a pretty, Georgian village with houses clustered round a village green and duckpond. Warthill is situated half-way between two arterial roads, the A64 and the A166, to the east of York ★ , and has not suffered the fate of random development that has befallen some of those villages which lie on main roads.

King Harold is supposed to have walked to the top of the hill to look at the forces of his brother, Tostig and Harald Haardraade from Norway, the evening before his victorious battle at Stamford Bridge ★ .

Wass (100) (SE 55-79)

Next to Byland Abbey ★ , at the bottom of the steep rise towards Helmsley ★ , is the pleasant village of Wass. It was built with stones taken from the Abbey after the Dissolution of Monasteries. It was fairly normal for villagers to plunder building materials from institutions which had no clear ownership: it is sad to reflect on what the abbey might have looked like had it not been scavenged.

The Wombwell Arms is the local hostelry, named after the lords of the manor. One of the family took part in the ill-fated Charge of the Light Brigade during the Crimean War.

Welburn (100) (SE 72-67)

The pretty countryside around Welburn has been chosen for one of the suggested short walks (see map), which gives a glorious view over the grounds of Castle Howard ★ . The village, like many others in this region, has a wide village green. The oak tree was planted at the time of the wedding of Edward VII, then Prince of Wales, to Princess Alexandra. There is another connection with royalty: the local

inn was renamed The Crown and Cushion to commemorate the coronation of Queen Victoria in 1837. The church of Welburn was erected by the owners of Castle Howard in 1865.

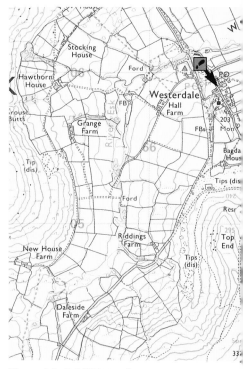

Westerdale (94) (NZ 66-05)

This village on the north-western corner of the Moors houses one of the chain of youth hostels that welcome the walker and the cyclist in these parts (see **Tour 9**). The hostel is a pleasant building which was originally a Victorian shooting lodge.

The road to the north-west skirts bleak Hograh Moor, where much evidence of Bronze Age settlement has been discovered. Across the valley to the north of the village are a series of dyke defences. To cross Great Hograh Moor on foot take the path known as Skinner Howe Cross Road, near the disused quarry to the left of the road about half a mile beyond the youth hostel. The area is used for grouse shooting, so take care in the season. This path joins a tarmac road near Baysdale Abbey, now a private farmhouse. The monks were attracted here by the sheltered position and by the profusion of juniper bushes: the wood is ideal kindling and the juniper berries have medicinal and other uses. The enigmatic Knights Templar had associations with Westerdale in the Middle Ages.

This is a rather lonely village, but the youth hostel does make it a good place for the visitor who wants solitude. See map on this page for planning short strolls.

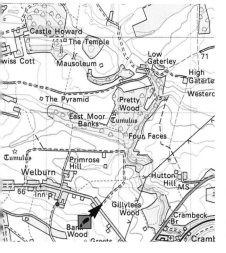

Westow (100) (SE 75-65)
To the east of Kirkham Priory ★ is Westow, a small village of grey stone cottages, (see **Tours 4 and 6**). In the area are several farms that were originally established by the monks to provide both produce and revenue for the abbey. There is a superb eighteenth-century Hall, which is still in private hands. It is an excellent example of the plain Georgian style. The church, which is a mile from the village, was extensively modernised in the last century, but the font is Norman. The stone outside the church, with a carving of the crucifixion, has holes in it which are said to have held lights to guide travellers and pilgrims towards Kirkham Priory.

Wetherby (105) (SE 40-48)
This town is known to all who travel north up the A1, as the point where the road turns sharp right to avoid the town ahead. In the not-too-distant past traffic went straight on through the town, causing considerable noise and congestion in the narrow high street. Now a modern by-pass is being built to replace the first by-pass, and Wetherby should become even quieter.

The old market square is typical of many towns in this region, and is full of life and incident on market day. There is a fine Market Hall and a little 'shambles' or street of butchers. A covered stone arcade running parallel to the shambles was built enabling some stallholders to remain dry when it rained.

Wetherby is a pleasant town with many interesting buildings, particularly in the centre near the River Wharfe. There is an Information Centre and several hotels, in addition to the famous racecourse. The locals are understandably proud of their Brass Band which has produced at least one notable musician.

Whitby (94) (NZ 89-10) (See **Tours 1,2 and 3**)
Whitby – a little harbour town on the Yorkshire coast, isolated from the rest of England over centuries by miles of almost trackless moorland and often inclement weather – has always reached out eagerly across the seas. There were times in its history when its name was known throughout the western world. It has always been a close-knit, mutually supportive community, forever battling against the elements and the unkind blows of economic change: ready for any new venture, however hazardous.

The town's civic motto, – 'we were and we are' – befits a community of survivors who have seen one industry after another rise and flourish only to collapse amid much hardship. Some relics of Whitby's history are still around for all to see; others must be sought in its museums and archives.

Stand first in the ruins of the great

The jaw bone of a whale

Benedictine abbey (4) on the East Cliff, which still dominates the town as in times past. In late Roman times there was almost certainly one of the chain of coastal watch-towers here. Three successive abbeys were built on the site. The first was founded by St Hilda in AD 657, no more than a humble group of cells and chapels, yet home for Caedmon, the 'father of English poetry', whose modern monument stands nearby. In AD 664 the abbey's fame resounded throughout Christendom as the site of the Synod which reconciled the Roman and Celtic Churches.

The Anglo-Saxon abbey was destroyed in Viking raids in AD 867 and now only a few traces of it, and of the second abbey founded soon after the Norman Conquest, can be found. The third abbey still partly standing, was built in stages from the thirteenth to the fifteenth centuries. It dominated the area not only visually and spiritually, but also economically as holder of a large and wealthy manor.

In the shadow of the abbey grew up a fishing and trading community round the mouth of the River Esk below. To serve this community the parish church of **St Mary (5)**, begun in the twelfth century, was built near the abbey. It still serves the people of Whitby today and much of the interior has not changed since Whitby craftsmen fitted it out in the eighteenth century with box-pews and galleries. Round it stand the eroded grave-stones of Whitby's dead.

With the dissolution of the abbey by Henry VIII in 1539 came the third great building still standing on this headland: the 'Abbey House', seat of the Cholmley family, Lords of the Manor of Whitby, who took over the lands, wealth and prerogatives of the abbey and built their mansion from its stones. One of them held Scarborough Castle for the king in the Civil War and there must have been many resolute Whitby men in the starving garrison which finally yielded. Another Cholmley took Whitby stonemasons overseas to build the harbour at Tangiers in North Africa, dowry of Charles II's queen. The skills of its masons can be seen wherever one looks in Whitby's narrow streets, and in sixteenth-century Bagdale Hall across the river.

Go down into Church Street, the backbone of old Whitby, by the 199 'Church Steps': it is easy to imagine you are in the eighteenth century, from which much of it dates. Fronting the market-place is the fine Market Hall erected by Nathaniel Cholmley in 1788. By then Whitby had become a 'boom-town', drawing-in manpower from all around for its first industries: alum-mining, shipping and ship-building. To house this growing population in the narrow valley, the long plots or 'tofts' of the earlier townsfolk were quickly crammed with rows of humble dwellings served by narrow alleyways off the main streets. Many, such as New Way Ghaut, Argument's Yard and Linskill Square, are still to be seen despite the clearances of the 1950s.

Alum-mining and refining, 'Britain's first chemical industry', lasted from the late sixteenth to the mid-nineteenth century in conditions of alternate boom and bust. Vast quantities of alum were used by the Yorkshire woollen industry in the process of dyeing wool. Millions of tons of rock were dug out by hand. It was then burned and processed to extract the alum in atrocious conditions of heat and fumes, often at starvation wages. Yet it has left little trace other than re-shaping the coastline and landscape at nearby Saltwick and Kettleness.

Further along Church Street are two significant buildings, the Friends' Meeting House (Quakers), built in 1813 to replace a former one built in 1676, and the Seamens' Hospital founded in 1670, but with a nineteenth-century facade by Sir George Gilbert Scott. In the eighteenth century the Quakers were very strong in Whitby and included many of the great merchant and shipowning families. Their influence was felt in every sphere, especially in the choice of ship's captains.

By the end of the seventeenth century a considerable shipping trade was based in Whitby – some 100 ships – originally to service the alum industry. Soon this figure was doubled and by 1776 there were 250 ships employing 2000 men, a number which was not to vary greatly right up to the 1920s. From the eighteenth century Whitby-built ships, many of them the fam-

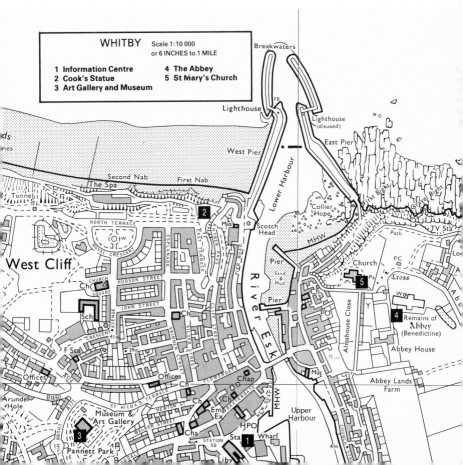

ous Whitby collier-brigs or 'cats', were carrying the bulk of the coal-trade from the Tyne to London. They were also plying across the North Sea, far into the Baltic, over the Atlantic to the American colonies and, as army transports, to every British campaign overseas. By the end of the century Whitby was the sixth largest port in England in terms of ship registrations.

The builders, owners and suppliers of that shipping made huge fortunes. They lived at first in the substantial old townhouses still to be seen in Church Street, Grape Lane, Flowergate, Baxtergate and Haggersgate. Later they built the noble

Dracula
Bram Stoker (1847-1912) was secretary and adviser to the great actor Sir Henry Irving. An Irishman who had travelled widely in Britain and abroad, he wrote various novels but none as famous as Dracula which was published in 1897. Many writers – including Goethe, Baudelaire, Southey and Byron – had explored the ancient belief that blood-sucking demons can inhabit the bodies of the dead and prey upon the living: somehow it was Count Dracula who captured the imagination of the world. Stoker borrowed the name from a fifteenth-century Balkan nobleman whose hideous cruelty and blood lust earned him the title 'dracul', or devil. Many film-makers have portrayed Count Dracula, none as successfully as F.W.Murnau in his 1922 film Nosferatu illustrated here.

When the schooner Demeter ran ashore at Whitby during a terrible storm all those years ago, Dracula took the form of a great dog and jumped ashore. Walks on the East Cliff at Whitby have never been quite the same since....

Georgian terraces of Bagdale and St Hilda's Terrace or mansions outside the town. Though some have been demolished, examples such as Airy Hill, Larpool Hall and Newton House are still to be seen. The fine chapel of St Ninian in Baxtergate is of the same period.

At the other end of the scale there were the inevitable widows, orphans and broken men of the shipping industry. For them an insurance scheme was started in 1670, reinforced by Act of Parliament in 1747, by which the shipowners had to pay a fixed sum for each sailor per month of voyage. This was used for small monetary grants and for providing homes in the Seamens' Hospital. The records are still extant.

Shipbuilding continued into the age of steam and did not finally cease till 1902 when the need was for ships larger than could be built in Whitby. The eighteenth-century 'cats' were excellent ships: strongly-built, shallow-draught and roomy, designed to carry bulk cargoes and land them if necessary on open beaches. They were thus well-suited for long voyages to unknown lands. In such ships Captain James Cook RN, the great explorer, learned seamanship and navigation plying up and down the North Sea: first as apprentice, then as seaman and finally as mate in the employ of John Walker of Whitby before entering the Royal Navy. All four of his famous ships were built in Whitby. **Cook's Statue (2)** stands now on the West Cliff looking out to sea. The house of his employer, John Walker, in Grape Lane, in which Cook himself lived as an apprentice, is now the Captain Cook Memorial Museum.

Cook was not the only explorer from the area. At the same period Captain Constantine Phipps of Mulgrave Castle near Whitby was endeavouring to find a north-west passage to the Orient. Soon after this the great whaling captain William Scoresby was to explore the Arctic Seas.

From 1753 to 1837 Whitby was a centre of the whaling industry. Every year ships set out for the Arctic; some were lost but others returned with rich loads of whale-oil, whale-bone, blubber and seals. The town had to suffer the appalling stench of blubber being rendered down along the riverside – but it represented jobs and wages while it lasted. This industry died in its turn and its sole memento is the arch of whale jawbones erected on the West Cliff, with a plaque recounting the industry's history. There were two celebrated whaling captains, the Scoresbys father and son – the latter was also a world-famous scientist in the field of magnetism.

Whitby harbour, formed by the mouth of the Esk, was never an easy one to enter: but it was the only refuge in a storm between the Tees and the Humber. Over the centuries the piers at its entrance have been re-built and extended many times, as can easily be seen. To join the east and west sides a bridge has always been

Whitby fish is unbeatable

needed which could open to allow shipping to pass. The present one is a swing bridge, but there were several earlier lifting bridges dating back to at least 1327.

With the dwindling of Britain's merchant navy the jobs of hundreds of Whitby men have vanished, but there is still a little North Sea cargo trade bringing timber from Scandinavia and steel from Holland. The fishing industry also goes on. As far back as the Middle Ages it supplied quantities of herring to the abbey. The great days of the herring industry were the nineteenth and early twentieth century. Then, fleets of vessels came in from Scotland filling the harbour from side to side, and keeping the lassies busy gutting and packing the fish on the quayside. Those days have gone forever, but there are still keelboats and cobles active in the fishing trade. A new yachting marina represents another seafaring venture. All these forms of marine activity mean there is no reduction in the age-old need for lifeboats. The latest can be seen on the river; older ones can be found in the Lifeboat Museum.

Just as the whaling industry was dying, the Whitby jet industry was starting – though jet beads have been found in Bronze Age burials. With support from

The harbour

Queen Victoria after the death of Prince Albert, jet jewellery for mourning became all the rage. Soon hundreds of Whitby workmen were engaged in mining the black fossilised wood and carving it to produce a flood of exquisite jewels and ornaments. This trade in turn collapsed early in the 20th century with a change in taste, though there are still old pieces to be found in antique ships and there is a trickle of new production.

In the mid-nineteenth century, with the coming of the railway, what had been small-scale entertainment of a few gentry became a mass holiday trade. Great areas of the West Side were developed to provide hotels and boarding-houses, and Whitby boomed as a holiday resort for northern cities. But in this respect also tastes have changed. A few of the great hotels remain but the modern tourist industry – still one of Whitby's mainstays – is one of small hotels, holiday flats and cottages, and day visitors.

As well as seeking employment on the seas Whitby men have always been willing to work inland if opportunity offers. In the nineteenth century it was the ironstone industry of Cleveland; more recently the steel and chemical industries of Middlesbrough; now the potash mining at Boulby, just up the coast.

A visit to the **Art Gallery and Museum (3)** in Pannett Park will reveal the pictures and artefacts and archives which bring to life the whole history of the area from the age of the dinosaurs to the present day: the ancient abbey; the alum, shipping, whaling, the jet and potash industries; Cook, Phipps and the Scoresbys; the merchants and shipbuilders of the eighteenth century; scenes of old Whitby; and the exotic objects brought back from every continent by generations of Whitby seamen.

Whorlton (93) (NZ 48-02)
Little remains of the old village which was once an important settlement. It lies above Swainby ★ on the northern edge of the Moors where they meet the Cleveland Plain. The Romans are thought to have had an outpost in this commanding position – certainly Roman coins have been discovered nearby.

The village of Whorlton is recorded in the Domesday Book, and the Normans built a motte and bailey castle here in the twelfth century when Robert de Meynell controlled the region. An effigy carved in bog oak in the parish church is said to represent one of his descendants: Sir Nicholas de Meynell, who fought in Edward I's compaigns against the Welsh. The hillside was heavily wooded in the Middle Ages and hunting rights were granted to Nicholas de Meynell in 1269.

The castle is worth visiting. It has a superb Gate House, still decorated with a coat of arms. The castle grounds originally extended over four acres and included large fish ponds to provide food. The building suffered during the Civil War, and the marks of Roundhead cannon fire can still be seen on the walls.

After the Black Death in the fourteenth century most of the village was deserted and the new settlement of Swainby grew up half a mile to the west. This explains the isolated Church of the Holy Cross, the only building to survive the ravages of time.

On the Moors above the village are six sharp peaks which remained exposed during the Ice Age. This makes the plant fossil remains particularly interesting to experts. Both the church and the castle are fascinating places to visit (see **Tour 9**).

Wombleton (100) (SE 67-83)
This village, which is situated in the Vale of Pickering, is reached from a side road to the south of Beadlam ★ halfway between Helmsley ★ and Kirkbymoorside ★ . The single street and field pattern – clearly visible on large-scale OS maps – indicate its medieval origins. Several buildings, including the Plough Inn, are of cruck construction. During the last war there was a military airfield close to the village.

York (105) (SE 59-51) (See **Tours 4, 5 and 6**)

York

A walk around the city
York is a chequerboard of eight successive cities, intermingled above ground and piled layer on layer beneath, like the tiers of a rich cake: excavate almost anywhere within its walls, and you cut through twenty centuries of history. At the foundation lies Roman Eboracum, military headquarters of Roman Britain; next comes Anglo-Saxon Eoforwic, ecclesiastical capital of the Christian North; then prosperous Viking Jorvik, which became proud medieval York, second city of Plantagenet England. Above again lies Tudor and Stuart York, the 'metropolis of the North', torn between Royalist and Parliamentarian; and then fashionable Georgian York, with its races, assemblies and opulent town mansions. Then, very near the surface, comes the workaday Victorian city of railways and chocolate works; and finally busy modern York, which has assured its present and future by preserving so much of its past.

The strata of York's history are most strikingly seen near the **Anglian Tower (2)**, where this tour begins: here the bank of the city wall has been cut away to reveal four successive layers of ramparts, medieval on Norman on Viking on Roman. The Anglian Tower itself, built of rough masonry to plug a gap in the Roman wall, belongs to the obscure centuries between Romans and Vikings, and is the only surviving fortification of this period in England.

Much more impressive is the nearby Multiangular Tower, at the western corner of the Roman defences, which still stands to its full height. It was altered in medieval times, the division between the neat Roman masonry and the more haphazard later additions being clearly visible. The tower was originally raised by the Roman general Constantius in about AD 300, soon after he had suppressed a British independence movement: seven more such bastions once lined the river front of the fortress, a show of strength doubtless intended to overawe recalcitrant Britons (whose settlement lay on the opposite bank) with the unconquerable might of Rome.

The external face of the tower can be seen by passing through an adjacent door into the grounds of **St Mary's Abbey (3)**, now the Museum Gardens. St Mary's was one of the largest and wealthiest Benedictine monasteries of the North, and some shadow of its magnificence survives in the ruined west end of its church, built during the thirteenth century and originally 360 feet long, or nearly three quarters of the size of the Minster. Every four years it forms a dramatic backdrop for the famous York Mystery Plays. The timber framed monastic guest house still stands by the river, and portions of the monks' living quarters can be seen in the basement of the Georgian **Yorkshire Museum (4)** – which also houses a fascinating collection of Prehistoric, Roman and Viking finds. Behind the museum (and accessible via a passage near the city wall) is red-brick and stone **King's Manor (5)** with its quiet courtyards and Elizabethan interiors. Once the residence of the abbots of St Mary's, under

Lendal Bridge

Henry VIII it became the headquarters of the King's Council in the North.

Leaving the Museum Gardens by the main entrance, the west front of the Minster (see introduction) immediately dominates the skyline. On the way, a short detour down Blake Street reaches the **Assembly Rooms (6)** designed by the aristocratic architect Lord Burlington in 1730. Its cavernous Classical interior witnessed the glittering entertainments of fashionable Georgian York, notorious for its unscrupulous heiress hunters. By the **Minster (7)**, turn left into narrow **High Petergate (8)**, and ascend the city wall at medieval **Bootham Bar (9)**, the north-west gate of the city. Its windows look out onto the **Art Gallery (10)** and down Bootham, a street which owes its Georgian character to rebuilding after the great Civil War siege of 1644.

The section of wall beginning here is the most impressive in York, with panoramic views of the Minster and its attendant buildings, notably the Minster Library, a former thirteenth-century chapel packed with ancient books and documents. At the turning of the wall, Rowntree's cocoa and chocolate works, a major York employer since Victorian times, can be clearly seen in the distance. Then the wall (now fronted by a deep dry ditch) continues along Lord Mayor's Walk to **Monk Bar (11)**, the north-east gate, topped by menacing sculptured figures eternally hurling stones at would-be attackers.

Thereafter the defences extend (via a much less spectacular section) to Peasholme Green — once the site of a marshy pool, unsuitable for wall-building and in any case impenetrable to assault — and they resume again at the Red Tower in **Foss Islands Road (12)**. It is therefore better

to descend at Monk Bar into Goodramgate, one of York's Scandinavian 'gatas' (or streets) named after a Viking resident called Guthrum. After passing a lane named Ogleforth ('the owls' ford') Goodramgate opens to the right onto a sudden close-up view of the east end of the Minster, with **St William's College (13)** opposite. The largest timber-framed building in York, this mainly fifteenth-century hall once housed the twenty-eight chantry priests who served the Minster's lesser altars. Beyond it is the **Treasurer's House (14)**, a dignified seventeenth-century gabled mansion, giving the impression of having been transported from some rural estate.

After the gap, Goodramgate continues past Our Lady's Row, the oldest occupied houses in the city. These were built for the fourteenth-century priests of Holy Trinity Goodramgate, which hides immediately behind them in its little churchyard. One of York's lesser-known treasures, its outer shell is medieval, but it is most memorable for its charming 'Prayer Book' interior, jam-packed with high Stuart and Georgian box-pews and dominated by a two decker pulpit: generally such fittings were swept away by Victorian 'restorers'.

Goodramgate finally emerges into King's Square, the centre of the ancient city and probably the site of its Viking royal palace, home of the notorious Erik Bloodaxe and other rulers of Scandinavian Jorvik. In later times it became the focus of the market district, and a turn left here reveals the **Shambles (15)**, York's most famous thoroughfare. Here the city butchers had their 'shammels', or meat-counters. The jumbled timber-framed houses lean over to almost touch across the street. Today the Shambles is full of souvenir shops, but immediately behind it York's bustling vegetable and general market still cheerfully and noisily operates six days a week, as it has done here for over 700 years.

On the far side of the market runs broad Parliament Street, site of York's great annual fairs until the 1920s. Almost opposite the lane from the market stand three tall painted brick houses, with ominous cracks between them — they were built across the inadequately-filled Roman defensive ditch, and over the centuries have settled into it.

Parliament Street ends at the church of All Saints Pavement, with its graceful lantern tower: this is the parish church of York's ancient trade guilds, whose ceremonial services continue to be held here. A few hundred yards beyond it, on Piccadilly, is the splendid medieval **Merchant Adventurers' Hall (16)**, still the home of the largest and richest of the guilds, whose prosperity sprang from trading Yorkshire wool for Baltic furs and French wine. The hall backs onto Fossgate, which leads after a longish walk to **Walmgate Bar (17)**, the south-east gate of the city and the only one to retain its barbican or outer gate, still

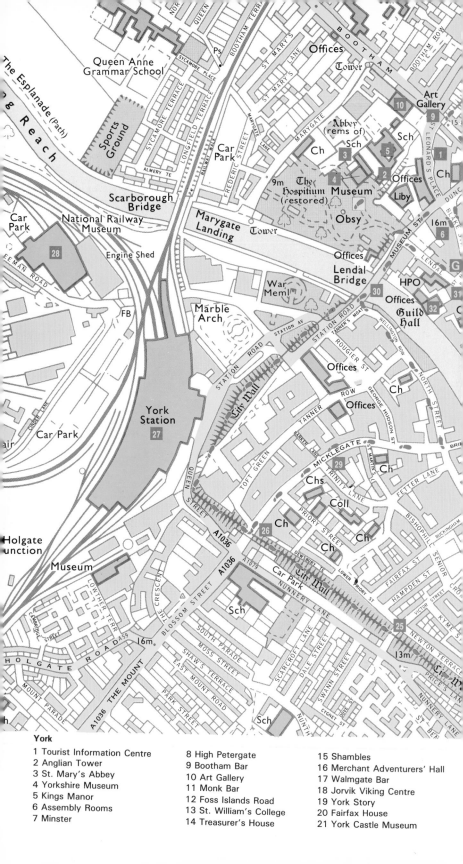

York

1 Tourist Information Centre
2 Anglian Tower
3 St. Mary's Abbey
4 Yorkshire Museum
5 Kings Manor
6 Assembly Rooms
7 Minster

8 High Petergate
9 Bootham Bar
10 Art Gallery
11 Monk Bar
12 Foss Islands Road
13 St. William's College
14 Treasurer's House

15 Shambles
16 Merchant Adventurers' Hall
17 Walmgate Bar
18 Jorvik Viking Centre
19 York Story
20 Fairfax House
21 York Castle Museum

Layerthorpe

22 Clifford's Tower
23 Baile Hill
24 Skeldergate Bridge
25 Victoria Bar
26 Micklegate Bar
27 Station
28 National Railway Museum

29 Micklegate
30 Lendal Bridge
31 Mansion House
32 Guildhall
33 Stonegate
Additional sites of interest
A Fishergate Bar

B Friargate Wax Museum
C Merchant Taylors' Hall
D Ouse Bridge
E St. Andrewgate
F St. Anthony's Hall
G St. Helen's Square
H University of York

SCALE 1:7 000 or 9 INCHES to 1 MILE

pitted with the bullet scars of the Civil War siege.

Immediately adjacent to All Saints Church, off Coppergate, is an area which epitomises York's many-layered history – a brand-new shopping centre, built above one of the city's most ancient trading streets. Excavations for the new Coppergate centre revealed the remarkably well-preserved remains of Scandinavian houses and workshops, the manufacturing core of Viking Jorvik: these are now imaginatively displayed beneath the complex in the **Jorvik Viking Centre (18)**, where visitors are borne in 'time-cars' through the sights, sounds and even smells of the Viking town.

Nor is this the only attraction of the area, for just beyond is the **York Story (19)**, an audio-visual display within the old church of St Mary Castlegate. In Castlegate itself is **Fairfax House (20)**, a noble Georgian town house with a wealth of fine furniture and interiors. Castlegate leads to another great York star, the **Castle Museum (21)**, housed in two vast Georgian blocks once used as prisons. Dick Turpin the highwayman was held in the condemned cell here, but the principal attractions are two complete streets of fully-stocked Georgian and Victorian shops, rescued from demolition and re-erected within the museum.

Protected on three sides by the rivers Ouse and Foss, York's castle was once one of the key fortresses of the North, and its most spectacular survival is **Clifford's Tower (22)**: this was begun in the 1240s as the keep or chief strongpoint of the castle, its four-leafed clover shape being unique in Britain. It stands on a precipitous steep-sided mound first raised by William the Conqueror in 1068-9, and is the fourth successive keep on the site. Within one of its predecessors, in 1190, the entire Jewish population of York committed suicide to avoid falling into the hands of anti-semitic local 'crusaders'.

The Conqueror did not deem one castle sufficient to control the unruly York citizens, who were only too happy to welcome raiding parties of their Scandinavian cousins. To close the Ouse against Viking longships he built a second stronghold on the opposite bank, and this fortress – now a tree-grown mound called **Baile Hill (23)** – can be reached by crossing Victorian **Skeldergate Bridge (24)** and mounting the city wall. After skirting round Baile Hill, this section of the wall encloses the now fashionable Victorian terraces of Bishophill: to the right, from near **Victoria Bar (25)**, can be glimpsed the Anglo-Saxon tower of St Mary Bishophill Junior, York's oldest parish church.

Next comes **Micklegate Bar (26)**, the south-western gate of the city and the most impressive of them all – probably because it looks down the main road from London, and it was here that York's civic dignitaries customarily welcomed visiting monarchs coming from the capital. Out-

The Shambles

side it stands the Bar Convent Museum of Roman Catholicism in York, displaying a splendid Classical chapel (with priest's hole) and relics of local Catholics who suffered for their faith. Many of them died on the Knavesmire, a mile or so further down the London road. Now the site of York's famous garden racecourse, this was once the execution place of the city's felons, or 'knaves'.

At this point visitors have the choice of continuing round the wall to Lendal Bridge or making an interesting detour down Micklegate. Railway enthusiasts should stay on the wall: those interested in churches should opt for Micklegate.

From Micklegate Bar a particularly high stretch of wall continues to Lendal Bridge, providing fine distant views of the Minster. To the right it passes the massive modern railway offices, partly built on the site of York's first station of 1840, whose deserted platforms can still be seen. This was the creation of George Hudson 'the Railway King' – entrepreneur, thrice Lord Mayor of York and finally (when the awesome extent of his corruption, bullying and fraud was exposed) disgraced crook.

Opposite, but outside the wall, is the present **Station (27)** of 1877, renowned for its breathtaking 800 feet of curved roof-tunnel in ornate Victorian ironwork. Behind it stretch acres of sidings and carriage works, a reminder of the continuing importance of railways in York's history. It is fitting that Britain's **National Railway Museum (28)**, with its unrivalled collection of historic locomotives and royal carriages, should be sited a short walk from the station. During summer weekends one of its veteran locomotives can often be seen 'in steam', preparing to haul a train full of enthusiasts to Scarborough.

Micklegate (29) itself is not to be missed. It's name, appropriately, means 'the great street', and it is probably the stateliest in the city. Curving down a hill (one of the few

The city wall

in level York) it passes some exceptionally grand Georgian mansions, as well as the much altered priory church of Holy Trinity – near whose east end, on Trinity Lane, is the charming timber-framed house called Jacob's Well. At the foot of Micklegate hill, opposite the street recently renamed after George Hudson (York has always had a sneaking admiration for the old reprobate), is another part-medieval church, St Martin-cum-Gregory, and further on to the left yet another, St John's (now the Arts Centre) with its pretty brick and timber tower.

The most fascinating of all the city's many parish churches is reached by turning left here into North Street, where slender-spired All Saints and its attendant timbered cottages face the red-brick colossus of the Viking Hotel. Lining its atmospheric interior is York's finest display of stained glass windows outside the Minster – notably the second from the east on the north side, wherein a long bearded benefactor distributes charity to crippled beggars and pilloried prisoners. The next window to the east depicts the end of the world as a fifteenth-century strip-cartoon, and across the church a hierarchy of glass angels lead popes, kings and citizens (one wearing medieval spectacles) into heaven. Flanking the roof above – recently and controversially repainted in glowing colours – are more angels playing musical instruments.

Across the Ouse from All Saints is the long, battlemented river front of the Guildhall, with the dark barred archway of its watergate below. This watergate marks the crossing point of the long-vanished Roman bridge, and from it an underground passage – York's oldest thoroughfare – follows the line of the Roman road beneath the Guildhall, to emerge above ground as

Stonegate and head straight for the place that was once the Roman headquarters building, and is now the Minster.

To trace its course, cross Victorian **Lendal Bridge (30)** and turn right down Lendal to the crimson-painted **Mansion House (31)**, begun in 1726 as the official residence of York's Lord Mayors. Every Lord Mayor still moves in during his year of office, to enjoy the services of its butler and cook and the use of its magnificent state room for official functions. There, too, are guarded the city's ancient silver mace and great medieval two-handed sword, always borne before the Lord Mayor in civic processions and represented in the city's heraldic arms, together with the scarlet and ermine 'cap of maintenance'. They proclaim York's proud status as a county in its own right, granted by King Richard II in 1396.

Immediately behind the Mansion House (via an archway) is the **Guildhall (32)**, not only the nerve-centre of York's government for five centuries, but also – as the flame-scorched masonry underlines – a symbol of its indomitable spirit. Built during the 1440s, in 1942 the hall was gutted by German incendiary bombs. It burned uncontrollably for twelve hours but even before the fires died down the decision was taken to reconstruct it in its original form. The only variation is the window depicting the great events of York's long history.

That history is epitomised by **Stonegate (33)**, the street connecting the Guildhall with the Minster, the civic and the spiritual focus of the city. The Via Praetoria or imperial way of Roman Eboracum, the 'steingata' or stone-paved street of Viking Jorvik, it is a patchwork of Norman, Medieval, Stuart, Georgian and Victorian houses, interspersed with the shop-fronts of modern York – the 2000 year-old city whose story is the story of England.

Tour 1
High Cliffs, Esk Dale and Captain Cook

54 miles. This tour explores the most northerly area covered in the guide book. It includes the coast from near Whitby to Loftus, passes the charming village of Staithes – perched in a narrow valley – and skirts the highest cliffs in England. The priory at Guisborough is visited before a look at Great Ayton, where Captain Cook went to school and lived most of his childhood. The tour returns to its starting point down the length of the delightful Esk Dale, following the River Esk from near its source in moorland, through fertile valley floors and steep gorges, on its route to the sea at Whitby, where it forms the harbour. It was here in Whitby that Cook learnt his seamanship, and the ships were built in which he discovered Australia. Apart from a few steep short sections in Esk Dale the route is fairly easy for cyclists.

The tour starts to the north of Whitby ★ in the village of Lythe ★ above Sandsend ★. The strange shape of the cliffs here was caused by old alum workings. In Mulgrave Woods nearby, it is possible to see various castle ruins in a very attractive setting. The entrance to the woods is on the left through a gate below St Oswald's Church. The church, with its Saxon relics, lies on the road from Sandsend and Whitby where it climbs steeply up the hill and enters Lythe.

Coming up the hill, take the first side road to the right, at **(A)** on the map. It is signposted to Goldsborough. Follow the lane along fairly flat ground to where it ends near the cliff edge at Kettleness. From the car park the view north is dominated by the 700 ft high cliffs at Boulby ★. The village of Runswick Bay ★ nearer at hand, nestles at the foot of the cliffs.

Go back past the Fox and Hounds Inn in Goldsborough, but bear right at **(B)**, the junction in the village. Rejoin the A174, turning right to East Barnby and Saltburn. Do not go left up the B1266 towards Guisborough, but keep on the A174 via Hinderwell, to take the third side road on the right to Port Mulgrave ★, ½ mile away. This mining port with its artificially created harbour was used for shipping ore in the last century.

Port Mulgrave makes a dramatic contrast with the much older village and harbour at Staithes ★ just up the coast,

which is reached from the next turning off the main road. Turn right by the sign, proclaiming 'Captain Cook's Village, and park in the municipal car park on the right. This is the starting point for **Walk 1**.

To continue the tour go on northwards up the A174 past the potash works, the only remaining mining industry left in the area. A short detour, at **(C)**, to Boulby ½ mile to the right can be made by those interested in industrial archaeology, as below the cliffs is a marked trail showing how alum was mined and processed for use in tanning. Through Easington and past the Tiger Inn, the road enters the village of Loftus ★. Turn left at the traffic lights down the B1366 to Liverton and Guisborough ★. Go past the Station Hotel, through Liverton Mines and a short section of open country. In Liverton stop to see the unspoilt eighteenth-century church at **(D)**, which lies down a side track on the right as one enters the village.

In the village centre, turn right down a side road to Moorsholm, 1¾ miles away. This takes you through some pretty farmland, passing the Toad Arms in Moorsholm, until the A171 is reached. Turn right towards Guisborough and Teesside. Descending the steep Birk Brow (a dual carriageway) there is a good view of Guisborough Woods ahead. The priory in Guisborough is on the right as you enter the town (see **Walk 8**).

Continuing the tour, follow the signposts to Stokesley and Middlesbrough, turning left to Pinchingthorpe and Great Ayton ★ along the A173. Roseberry Topping ★, the conical hill which miners have taken a bite out of, can be seen on the left. There is a suggested short walk to the top from Newton under Roseberry. Over the railway bridge you enter Great Ayton. If intending to visit Captain Cook's Museum, or just to look around the town, go straight on at **(E)**, where the main road bears right at a garage.

At the other end of town, immediately after going over the river bridge, the A173 bends sharply to the right. Go straight on to Kildale ★. Captain Cook's Monument ★ is a predominant landmark to the left (there is a suggested stroll to the obelisk). Our road approaches a 'Give Way' sign. Go left, following the directions to Easby and Kildale, ¾ mile and 3 miles away respectively.

In Easby go on to Kildale, noting attractive Pill Hall on the right. Under the railway bridge, continue towards Kildale at **(F)**, which marks the point where the road bends left at a junction to go under the railway line again. The Moors become visible on the right, just before the attractive village of Kildale is reached. As the road goes over the railway line look left to see the isolated railway cottages, built to house railway staff when trains were more frequent than today.

Turn right over the bridge, at **(G)**, to Westerdale ★ 3 miles away, and go over the railway yet again. The road then crosses a cattle grid to enter moorland. This sudden switch from pasture to moorland is typical of the region. The road climbs a little and Great Hograh Moor, where early Man eked out an existence, is to the right across the valley. As the road descends into the valley, watch out for a side road on the left, at **(H)**, before the ford. Take this route to Castleton ★.

After crossing a bridge by Dibble Bridge Farm, the road climbs the side of a hill. Go over the cross-roads, to turn left at the junction where a road comes down from a ridge on the right, and enter Castleton. Our road goes straight through the long village which has several side turnings. Ignore all the signs except those to Danby Lodge Information Centre ★, which is reached by crossing the River Esk and the ever-present railway line. The Centre at **(J)**, is a good place to gather further information about the Moors. The Centre is on the right with a large picnic area and there is a suggested short walk in the area. The car park is on the left hand side of the road.

Leaving the Centre, continue in the same direction down towards the river and under the railway bridge. Turn left in the direction of Houlsky along the valley floor, going over the railway bridge into the village. Follow the signpost to Leaholm, going under or over the railway line three more times, before arriving at this attractive centre for walking.

Our route then goes on to Glaisdale ★ (see **Walk 7**) with several twists and junctions in the road, but keep following the signs. There are two ways out of Glaisdale to Egton Bridge ★. Both ways pass the pretty Beggar's Bridge over the Esk. This is also the starting point for an attractive short walk through woods by the river.

Go under the railway bridge and turn right at the next junction, at **(K)**, but do not go on to Egton. Turn right again at point **(L)** to Egton Bridge. The road goes down a steep slope, under the railway once more, and follows a pretty section of the River Esk into the village of Egton Bridge. Turn left by the bridge over the river, past the inn on the left, under the railway – for the last time – and climb the steep hill into Egton. Go on to rejoin the main A171, and turn left, – if returning to Whitby go right here at **(M)**. Take the next right, almost at once, to Lythe. Follow this lane through farmland, past a road coming from the right, to a cross-roads at **(N)**. Turn right here to go along a ridge above Mulgrave Woods. Here the castle ruins are visible amongst the trees. This lane leads us back to our starting point.

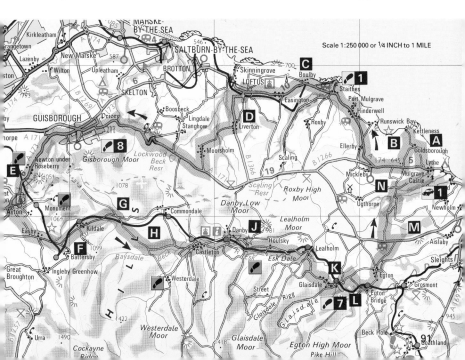

91

Tour 2
Hole of Horcum and the coast

60 miles. This tour explores the magnificent coast between Whitby and Scarborough, and gives an opportunity to see the moorland between Pickering and Sleights which includes the dramatic Hole of Horcum. There are three convenient starting points near Pickering, Whitby or Scarborough. The tour is described as starting from Scarborough at (A). Apart from a short section along the main Scarborough to Pickering road, the route follows roads and lanes that do not carry a great deal of heavy traffic, and in that respect is ideal for cycling, although there are some very steep sections.

Take the A170 from Scarborough ★ to Pickering ★ , and just beyond the second roundabout (the one after the railway station) turn right up the A171 into Scalby, now a suburb of Scarborough. Go past the hospital on the left and after the road crosses the channel built to relieve flooding in Ryedale, turn left at (B), towards Hackness ★ .

The road soon leaves the houses and climbs the hill. Behind, there are views of Scarborough Castle. In the hamlet of Suffield bear left and go down the avenue of trees – part of the Hackness Hall estate – under the footbridge, and past the large Hall set in parkland to the left of the road. The road then bends sharp left and right again. Do not go to Forge Valley on the left, (to enjoy this see **Tour 8**) but keep straight on, with the houses of the village set above the road on the right. The Grange Hall Hotel is on the left, and shortly afterwards, at point (C), a side road enters from the left. Go down this road to Troutsdale, crossing a tributary of the River Derwent, and carry on along the attractive valley floor. This is mainly pasture land, but the slopes are wooded: the whole area is peaceful and quiet.

At the end of the valley the road twists and climbs up to Cockamoor Hall. The view from the picnic site here back along the vale is very pleasant, and there are some earthworks whose original purpose has puzzled many archaeologists. The route progresses through open farmland, with good views across the Ryedale Plain ahead, until it drops down into Snainton where it meets the A170. Although our route takes us right, towards Pickering, motorists might like to make the mile or

so detour to the left to the village of Brompton ★ , and look at the church where the Lakeland poet William Wordsworth was married.

Turning right in Snainton, go along the A170 until the very attractive village of Thornton Dale ★ is reached. A pause here to walk down by the beck to the left is worthwhile. Our route goes right at the green, at (D), along a quiet road to Whitby ★ . This way leaves the traffic behind, climbing a wooded slope. On the right the entrance to the Dalby Forest Drive is passed and the road joins the A169 Pickering to Whitby main road by the Fox Inn.

Go right, and continue along a fairly level section of road until you reach a large car park on the right. Stop here to cross the road to look at the Hole of Horcum ★ (see **Walk 6**) a dramatic declivity in the moorland, and a favourite place for hang gliders. The route continues down a steep hill, with a notice on the left warning United Buses to stop and change gear. The whole vista of the Moors is ahead. Below on the left is Saltergate Inn ★ on the old way that saltermen used to take from Whitby to Pickering. Past here, on the right, is the Fylingdales Early Warning Radar System. Look, however, to the left: the single track of The North Yorkshire Moors Railway ★ can be seen as it turns across Fen Moor. This is a swampy section of the Moors, where the engineer George Stephenson had bracken, wood and sheep skins sunk into the bog to form a base for the railway line. At the dip by Eller Beck keep on the A169 as it climbs up and out of the valley towards Whitby.

Cross high open moorland until the road starts another steep descent down Blue Bank. At point (E) turn right to Littlebeck ★ and turn down this narrow steep lane (coaches are warned not to try) with its 1-in-3 and 1-in-5 slopes. At the bottom by the old mill there is a suggested short walk to Falling Foss. Turn right up the 1-in-4 hill at the junction over the stream to join the B1416. At this point is the entrance to the attractive May Beck ★ , with its farmland and nature trails. If you have time this is a pleasant place to picnic, rest or take a stroll.

Go right a short way along the B1416 to point (F), and turn left here to Sneatonthorpe. Go past the mournful Soulsgrave Farm and descend the valley side. In Sneatonthorpe turn right, to Hawsker ★ , past the entrance to the camping site and over the stream. The road bends sharp left. After this bend go straight on into

Stainsacre, to climb up the hill to the A171 where you turn left to Whitby.

In Whitby outskirts look out for a crossroads before the modern bridge over the River Esk. Go right, at **(G)**, and then take the third right up the hill towards St Hilda's Abbey. After the houses the road goes onto flat farm fields up to a T-junction. Turn left and go into the car park by the abbey, above Whitby. To explore the old town, walk down the steps — motor traffic cannot come up this way. Alternatively you can explore the abbey or go along Dracula's trail which is clearly signposted.

To continue this tour, go back down the road from the abbey, keeping straight on past the junction and the caravan site to rejoin the A171 just outside Hawsker. Turn left, towards Scarborough. Just

after the road goes over a bridge spanning the old disused railway line, turn left at **(H)** to Robin Hood's Bay ★ . This is an attractive fishing village with a public car park at the top — motor vehicles are not permitted into the harbour area.

Leaving the car park, turn left to Fylingthorpe ★ , and follow this road up onto moorland. Look out for the delightful church on the left beyond the village. Go left at the A171 and continue along the main road for 4 miles to the second road on the left, at **(J)**, turning down this road to Staintondale and Ravenscar ★ . Follow the signs to Ravenscar for a superb view of Robin Hood's Bay. In Ravenscar there is a National Trust Office by the car park and an interesting geological trail.

Go back the way the route came, but continue into the village of Staintondale to meet the A171 in Cloughton. To enjoy this beautiful coast on foot, see **Walk 3**. After 2 miles turn down the A165 into Scarborough.

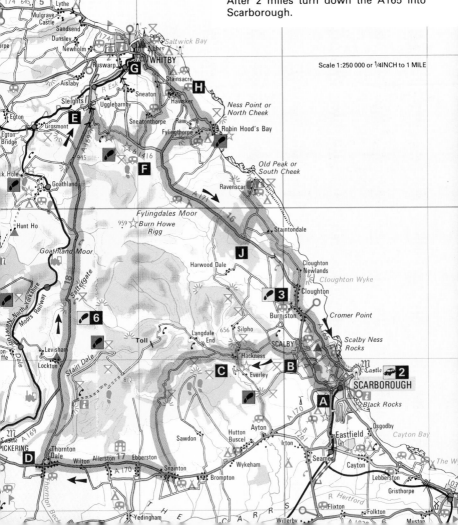

Tour 3
The Five Moors: Wheeldale, Spaunton, Glaisdale, Rosedale & Egton High

50 miles. This tour follows part of the route of the North Yorkshire Moors Railway and explores the eastern half of the Moors with its attractive villages in the beautiful Esk Dale. It includes a visit to a steep incline on a disused section of the line where George Stephenson installed a novel cable system. It also passes a Roman camp and the remains of Rosedale Abbey. A highlight of this outing is the fascinating museum at Hutton-le-Hole. The tour starts from Whitby near (A) but it can be equally well started at (D) if coming from Scarborough or (G) if driving from York or Helmsley. There are sections that cyclists will find steep.

Out of Whitby ★ take the A171 (sign-posted to Guisborough ★) up the hill out of the town towards the north. Beyond the roundabout turn left down the A169 towards Pickering ★ at point (A). After a short drive through farmland the road dips into the village of Sleights ★ at the bottom of Blue Bank and then climbs steeply onto the bleak moor above the town. There is a parking spot at the top with views to the cliffs of Robin Hood's Bay ★ .

Take the second side road on the right at (B), which is sign-posted to Goathland ★ , and immediately turn right again. The road goes down into the hamlet of Beck Hole ★ . It is possible to take some pleasant strolls here, including one to Beck Cottage at the bottom of the disused railway incline, and another to see a waterfall. The pretty public house serves tea in season and it is pleasant to sit by the bridge over the stream or on the village green.

Leaving the valley go up the hill into Goathland. Watch out for sheep 'mowing' the grass on the broad green. Railway enthusiasts will want to look over the collection of rolling stock in the railway

Scale 1:250 000 or ¼INCH to 1 MILE

station or ramblers may want to go on **Walk 5** which starts from here. The village is well served with hotels, public houses and a good selection of shops.

To continue the tour go right at the car park and through the village turning left after the church to rejoin the A169 at **(C)**. Turn right and drive over the moors with the famous Fylingdales early warning radar domes on the left and pass the old Saltergate Inn ★ at the bottom of the Hole of Horcum ★. This is also the start of **Walk 6**. There is a parking place at the summit. Drive on until **(D)**. Turn right to Lockton and go on through the pretty village of Levisham ★ and down the slope to the railway crossing at **(E)**.

The road then enters forest and becomes a dirt surface. This section is attractive with several places to picnic or take a stroll in the forest. The road surface becomes tarmac near the hamlet of Stape. Follow the signs to Cropton ★ but pause at the parking place on the right for a splendid view of Elleron Lake, the hills and moors. It is a short walk from here to see the site of the Roman camp at Cawthorne ★.

Keep along the road to Cropton and at **(F)** beyond the village turn sharp right then left to Lastingham ★ and look at St Cedd's Well on the right. Go right in the village by the church and right again at the T-junction to Hutton-le-Hole ★ at **(G)**. Hutton-le-Hole is a typical example of a Moors village, scrupulously neat and well kept. Stop in the large car park as a visit to the local history museum is recommended. (Also see the map to plan a short walk). Leaving the car park retrace the route by turning right onto the road then turn left up the steep hill at **(G)** to Rosedale ★ with the warning sign about Rosedale Chimney Bank. Go over the

moorland but as the road starts to descend into Rosedale stop to look at the old iron workings on the left. Rosedale has an abbey the ruins of which are part of the village church. There is a large camping site and some good eating places. **Walk 4** starts here.

From Rosedale follow the signs for Castleton ★, turning right where the road climbs up onto Rosedale and Glaisdale Moors. There is a splendid view over a steep valley on the left. Follow the signpost to Leaholm and Egton Bridge ★. The road is high on the Moors with views to the right towards the Roman road on Wheeldale Moor and Fylingdales radar domes. There are shooting butts by the roadside (watch out for grouse) and several ancient waymarks.

Do not turn right at the first junction to Egton Bridge but go on to **(H)** and down the hill into Glaisdale ★. **Walk 7** begins here. In the village go left: just before the railway bridge is the picturesque Beggar's Bridge to the right of the modern road bridge (there is a short walk along an attractive path through woods by the river). Under the railway turn right to Egton Bridge and then right again. The road goes back under the railway following a most attractive valley bottom by the River Esk.

In Egton Bridge turn right over the river, then left and left again to Grosmont ★ down a gated road, through farmland, down a steep hill and over a ford. Cyclists have a footbridge. Park in the car park: you can picnic in the old ironworks or look at the steam locomotives in the station. Go over the level crossing and left and follow the river to Sleights ★ to return to Whitby.

Lastingham Church

Tour 4
Castle Howard, and Hovingham

48 miles. This is a gentle round tour starting from York, and taking in the western end of the plain that stretches from York up to Scarborough. This separates the Moors on the north from the southern Wolds. Two houses of note, Castle Howard and Sutton Park are included, as well as peaceful Kirkham Priory on the banks of the River Derwent. There are no hills to concern the cyclist and the majority of the route is over quiet country lanes. The tour is taken in an anti-clockwise direction, as Sutton Park is not open until 1.30 pm and motorists leaving York who wished to see the house and gardens would arrive too early with a morning start.

Leave York ★ on the A1079 (directions to Hull) and at the roundabout over the by-pass take the A166 to Stamford Bridge ★ and Great Driffield. On the left hand side of the road is the Yorkshire Museum of Farming which has an interesting collection of rural ironmongery and equipment. Follow the A166 through mainly flat arable land into Stamford Bridge. Turn left at (A), just before the bridge across the River Derwent, which was the scene of the battle in 1066 that Harold won. The inn by the bridge was

Castle Howard

once a manor house and there is a camping site near here.

The road is sign-posted to Sand Hutton. Almost at once the land takes on a more gentle and more interesting appearance. Go right at the T-junction (Sand Hutton 2 miles, Malton 13 miles) into the wood and almost at once turn left to Sand Hutton. Out of the trees in Sand Hutton take the turning to the right to Malton ★ and Bossall ★ , by the war memorial. At the next T-junction, at (B), turn right by the farm house and go straight through Bossall, which has a pretty church with a weather vane in the shape of a dragon.

Follow the signs to Howsham ★ turning right at the next cross-roads. The Hall can be seen across the River Derwent (there is a suggested short walk along the footpath by the river). Go over the bridge and climb the hill to (C). Turn left here towards Malton, and immediately go left again to Westow ★ , passing under the electricity pylons. Just over the ridge, attractive Westow Hall is on the right hand side of the road. Beyond the Blacksmith's Arms public house turn left and go down the hill to Kirkham Priory ★ . On the way the lane passes the start of **Walk 10** (also see the map for a suggested woodland stroll). Kirkham Priory is at the bottom of the valley in a most attractive setting.

Past the priory, go over the river and over the level crossing. This road twists up the hill to join the dual carriageway of the A64, York to Malton, road. There is a cycle track, but take care turning right towards Malton as this can be a busy

road, especially in the holiday season. Where the road descends the hill, about 1½ miles further on, the dual carriageway ceases. Turn left here at **(D)** and pass through Welburn ★, with its Crown and Cushion Inn. There is a short walk here with views over the Castle Howard ★ estate.

Go right at the cross-roads at **(E)**, and down the avenue of trees through the gate house of Castle Howard. The entrance to Castle Howard is on the right. At least half a day should be allowed for visiting here.

The route goes straight along the avenue with its gentle switchback road. There is a short walk here before our route reaches the edge of Slingsby ★ at **(F)** on the B1257. Our route turns left to go down to the attractive village of Hov-

ingham ★. There are several good public houses here, the Hall, a village green and stream, and many pretty houses. There was an attempt to turn Hovingham into a spa to rival Harrogate. Luckily the plan failed. **Walk 11** starts here.

In Hovingham take the road off to the left by the Worsley Arms, sign-posted to Yearsley and Brandsby. This goes up by the side of the Hall, parts of which are open to the public, and where music festivals have been held in the riding school. This part of the tour goes through pleasant parkland, and over a cross-roads to meet the B1363 at **(G)**. Turn left.

The road is fairly flat and twists and turns through farmland until it enters the village of Sutton-on-the-Forest ★, on a dog leg in the road. Here is Sutton Park with its beautiful gardens, which are open to the public. A straight run down the B1363 takes us back to York.

Scale 1:250 000 or ¼ INCH to 1 MILE

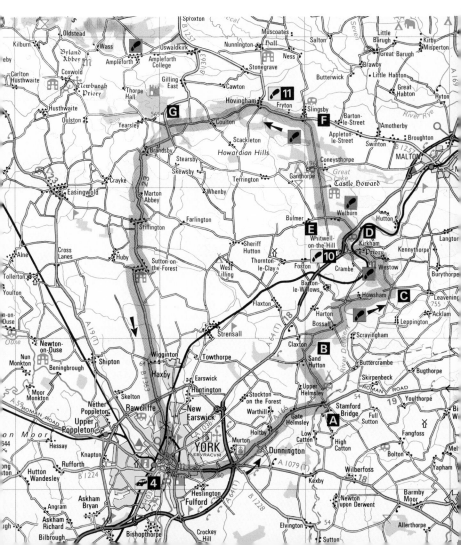

Tour 5
Marston Moor; peaceful Abbeys and Priories

72 miles. This tour follows the course of the river Ouse and the Ure up to the ancient Norman town of Boroughbridge to the north-west of York. It then visits the Roman settlement at Aldborough and some delightful villages bordering the Ure until it reaches 'claret coloured' Beningbrough Hall. This is followed by a pleasant drive via the attractive town of Easingwold to Newburgh Priory, for which the village of Coxwold provides a perfect setting. A short section covers the ruins of Byland Abbey and goes along the foothills of the Hambleton Hills to Ampleforth, home of the Catholic public school. We return through the village of Sutton-on-the-Forest with its impressive Hall and extensive gardens. The tour presents no problems for cyclists.

Leave York ★ on the Tadcaster road going south and turn right at the traffic lights up the B1224 towards Wetherby ★. This road soon goes into open farmland passing through Rufforth before reaching Long Marston. At **(A)**, in Long Marston, turn right by the Sun Inn at the crossroads towards Tockwith. Leaving the village the road curves left, with open fields to the right. This is the site of the famous Battle of Marston Moor ★. A monument on the right hand side of the road records the battle site. Tockwith village has some attractive houses and an inn, 'The Boot and Shoe', with an unusual sign.

After Tockwith, where the sign ahead warns 'No access to A1 north', turn right to Cattal ¾ mile away. The road crosses the River Nidd by means of an interesting packhorse bridge. Immediately turn right and follow the directions to Kirk Hammerton ★, 2 miles away. Just before Cattal railway station turn right and then right again, still following signposts to Kirk Hammerton. The village is entered shortly. Pause to visit the Saxon church on the bend in the road opposite the small village green.

Go on over the level crossing and turn right down the A59 towards York. Take the first left at **(B)** towards Nun Monkton★ just before the garage on the right hand side of the road. Pool Bridge Farm, selling fishing permits, is passed on the left. After going through lush farmland the

road ends in the peaceful village of Nun Monkton with its Georgian houses clustered around the large village green with a duckpond and maypole. (There is a suggested stroll by the river here).

Go back to the A59 to **(B)** and turn right towards Harrogate. In Green Hammerton about 1 mile up the road do not follow the traffic up the A59 where it bends left but go straight up the little-used B6265 to Boroughbridge ★. The road goes up and down like a gentle switchback through open country passing a modern wind vane on the left before arriving at Boroughbridge.

Leave the town in the direction you came but bear left at **(C)** as directed to Aldborough ★ – the old Roman town of Isurium. Part of the city walls and a tiled floor are visible in the grounds of the excellent museum. To visit the museum, bear right in the village and go past the green with its maypole.

To continue the tour go back down the hill following the sign-posts for Lower Dunsforth and Ouseburn. Both these villages are unspoilt and set in pleasant farmland. In Ouseburn turn left by the Crown Inn and then left again at **(D)** sign-posted to Aldwark. Immediately after the toll bridge, which is moderately priced and single file, turn right which is sign-posted to Beningbrough Hall ★. The road runs past the runway at the busy RAF base at Linton-on-Ouse. There is a camping site on the banks of the river here. The village of Newton-on-Ouse is laid out in the grand manner with tree-lined streets. While in the vicinity be certain to see Beningbrough Hall.

Just before the end of Newton-on-Ouse village turn left to Tollerton. On a clear day the White Horse of Kilburn ★ can be seen directly ahead on the steep slope of the Moors. At the next junction go left. Tollerton is sign-posted as 1¼ miles away. An old windmill, now a private house, makes a contrast with the hi-tech wind power vane we passed outside Boroughbridge. There are several good public houses in Tollerton. Go through the village and left at **(E)**.

At the cross-roads past the village go right, at **(F)**, to Alne and Easingwold ★. Beyond Alne take the left fork. After passing over the railway bridge the road bends sharply to the right. Immediately turn left and go into Easingwold. There is a camping site here and a good selection of shops. Cross straight over the busy A19 and go up an attractive street with well-proportioned houses set back from the road. Turn left at **(G)** – the cross-roads

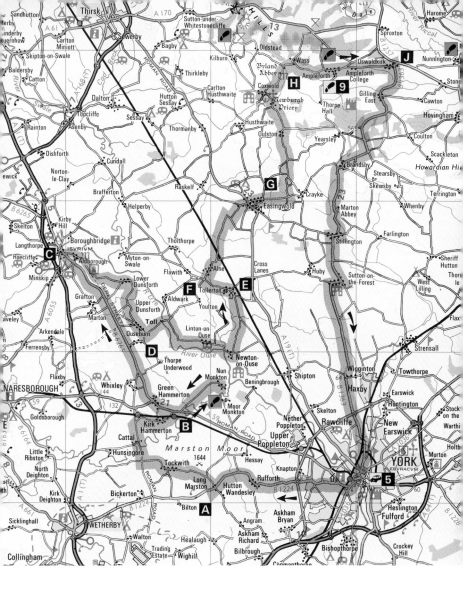

– where it is signposted to Coxwold ★ . Go straight ahead over two cross-roads and through pleasant rolling pastureland. The road then runs alongside a wall on the right that eventually joins the entrance gates of Newburgh Priory. If it is afternoon the Priory may be open and a visit is well worthwhile.

In the very charming village of Coxwold once home of the author William Sterne, turn right at the cross-roads to Byland Abbey ★ and Wass ★ . Almost at once the beautiful ruins of the Abbey are visible. Further on you come to Wass which was built with stones taken from the Abbey.

In Wass turn right at **(H)** at the Wombwell Arms and look out for the natural spring tap on the right for free refresh-ment. Our route takes us along the lower slopes of the Hambleton Hills into Ampleforth ★ . In the woods above the road are some ancient earthworks and pleasant short walks. Ampleforth is a long village with the famous Catholic public school at the far end. (**Walk 9** takes you through part of the school grounds). The school church was designed by Sir Giles Gilbert Scott, architect of Liverpool's Anglican Cathedral. Beyond Ampleforth do not take the road to Helmsley ★ but go on to Oswaldkirk ★ and look out for the church on the right. At the junction with the B1363, at **(J)**, turn right towards York.

The village of Sutton-on-the-Forest, on a dog leg in the road, has an attractive Hall and gardens. It is a restful place to stop before returning to York.

Tour 6
Malton and Kirkham Priory

56 miles. The tour starts in York, but could be begun in Malton, at (H) on the map. The route visits castles, manor houses and an abbey, all on the plain of Ryedale. There are few hilly sections to deter cyclists, and the roads out of, and into, York are chosen to be relatively free of motor traffic.

Leave York ★ in a north-easterly direction on the Huntingdon Road to New Earswick ★ , the model village created by Rowntree at the turn of the century. The River Foss is now on your left. Go through Huntington ★ to Towthorpe and Strensall. Bear left in Strensall, at (A), to go under the railway and follow the signs to West Lilling. The countryside between the villages is flat common land, and between Strensall and West Lilling the road crosses several small streams, which drain what was, until recently, very marshy ground.

As the road goes under the second set of pylons, near Westerfield Farm on the left, keep straight on avoiding West Lilling. Soon you will enter Sheriff Hutton ★, with its historic ruined castle. The castle is in a farm, but can be entered for a small donation to a charity.

Leaving the village, continue in the same direction, past some pleasant farmland, including 'The Cape of Good Hope Farm', to climb a small hill and meet a T-junction. To the right is Terrington ★ . Go left and immediately turn right, towards Hovingham ★ . The lane then goes

through some attractive parkland before dropping down off the ridge into Hovingham at a bend in the B1257. Hovingham claims to be prettiest village in Yorkshire, with its Hall, stream, stone cottages and village green. **Walk 11** starts here.

Go north out of Hovingham to (B) on the map, leaving the B1257 as it bends left, and going straight ahead to Nunnington Hall ★ . As the road goes down into the valley of the River Rye, go straight over the pretty bridge to visit the Hall, or left at the cross-roads to look over the church and the village of Nunnington. (There is a short walk by the river here).

Our route goes right at (C) on the map, to Ness, and then loops back to rejoin the B1257 in Slingsby ★ , which has an interesting manor house that is still uncompleted, although it was started in 1640! Turn left at (D), and then left again at (E), in Barton-le-Street to join a country lane that goes to the attractive hamlet of Butterwick by the banks of the River Rye.

At point (F) on the map, turn right, to pass through Brawby, which lies on a sharp bend in the road. The lane crosses a narrow bridge over the River Seven. Note the high flood banks in the fields. Entering the outskirts of Great Barugh, go right, down the main street, then left and right again, following the sign-posts to Little Barugh and Kirby Misperton. The road passes the entrance to the pleasure park of Flamingo Land.

At the roundabout (G), go right towards Great Habton, and turn left at the lane to Ryton. This section of the tour passes some attractive houses before going through Ryton and over the River Rye again. As the road bends left to join the

Malton

A169, Eden Camp, a prisoner of war camp museum, is on the right. Go right and cross over the by-pass through the village of Old Malton, before entering Malton ★ itself. There is a Roman museum in the market square, as well as a good selection of shops and hotels. Go over the level crossing, having turned left at the traffic lights, and at **(H)**, immediately after the crossing barrier, turn right to go up a straight road out of Norton. The road rises up a slight hill in open country. Continue along the road until the crossroads at **(J)**, turning right to Kirkham Priory ★. The road meets a T-junction, where we turn right, descending into the valley with fine views of the ruins. On the way the lane passes the starting point of **Walk 10** and a suggested stroll in Howsham Woods. Turn right in Westow ★, leaving the Blacksmith's Arms and the Hall, to go over the ridge and under the pylons to the T-junction at **(K)** on the map.

Turning right, there is then a fairly straight section of road until a sharp bend to the left, signposted to Stamford Bridge ★. Go straight on, at **(L)**, over the narrow packhorse bridge, past the mill, into the delightful village of Buttercrambe ★ – a place where nothing has changed since the eighteenth century.

Out of the village, the lane goes into a small wood. Take the side road on the left to the outlying houses of Stamford Bridge. At **(M)**, go right along the A166. At the roundabout over the York by-pass, the A64, is the Farming Museum, which makes an interesting end to the tour.

Scale 1:250 000 or ¼INCH to 1 MILE

Tour 7
The 'two prettiest villages in Yorkshire'.

60 miles. This tour from Malton gives the opportunity to visit Castle Howard or pass some time at the adventure world of Flamingo Park at Kirby Misperton. There is a section up lonely Bransdale, and the route also passes attractive Nunnington Hall and the interesting local museum in Hutton-le-Hole. There is, therefore, at least one place to suit everyone's taste, with the added bonus of a pleasant country drive. Although the directions are given in a clockwise direction, if a visit to the Flamingo Park is intended it is suggested that you go anti-clockwise from Malton as the Park becomes very crowded from midday in the holiday season. Apart from the section in Bransdale there should be no problems for cyclists.

Leave Malton ★ from the traffic lights in the centre on the B1248 towards York ★ . As the road goes up a slope turn right at the sign to Castle Howard ★ . Shortly the road leaves Malton, passes over the busy by-pass and runs along a ridge with views of farmland on either side. Just beyond Coneysthorpe the Great Lake of Castle Howard can be seen on the left. Turn left at **(A)** (there is a place to park on the right) and go up the impressive drive towards the obelisk. There is also a camping site by this junction. Going through a narrow gate: the main car park and entrance to Castle Howard are on the left.

Continuing, go over the small canal and through the imposing gatehouse before turning right at the cross-roads at **(B)** towards Bulmer, 1 mile away. This is an attractive village built in stone with wide grass verges and a Norman church. There are views of open country to the right before the road twists down a 1-in-6 slope. The ruined castle of Sheriff Hutton ★ is visible now: 1¼ miles ahead you will enter the village of Sheriff Hutton. The grounds of the castle can be viewed by asking at the farm house. A small donation to charity is expected.

At the cross-roads, at **(C)**, go in the direction of Hovingham ★ . This part of the tour wends its way across the plain before rising over a small ridge to give a distant view of the Moors ahead. In Hovingham stop to walk around the village that claims to be the prettiest in

Yorkshire (so does Hutton-le-Hole!). The Hall, home of the Worsley family, is most impressive and the family name is reflected in the Worsley Arms hotel. Hovingham is also the start of **Walk 11**.

Go north up the B1257, but as this road bends left, take the side road straight ahead to Nunnington Hall ★ . To see the Hall, go over the pretty packhorse bridge to the car park on the left. (There is a suggested short walk in the area.) The tour goes left at the cross-roads at **(D)** to pass the thirteenth-century church and the Royal Oak Inn on the right. Go along the ridge and down the 1-in-6 hill, to rejoin the B1257. Turn right and go up to Helmsley ★ . This is an attractive market town with several fine inns, a castle and a well-equipped information centre.

Take the A170 out of the town towards Pickering ★ and Scarborough ★ and before leaving the houses of the town turn left up to Carlton, 1½ miles away. The road climbs up a gentle slope through some trees and the unspoiled village of Carlton. Beyond the village Carlton Grange has a camping site for Caravan and Camping Club members. The woods in this area have plenty of places to park a car and to take a stroll. Bransdale is also the place where **Walk 12** begins.

Just beyond where the road dips to the bottom of a valley to cross a stream, stop to look at the isolated and delightful little church of St Mary Magdalene in the trees on the right. A telephone box by the roadside indicates this spot. The way ahead passes through woods, moors and the side of a valley with pleasant views to the right before reaching the head of the dale. The end of the valley is in the care of the National Trust. Go through two farm gates to reach St Nicholas's Church set above a stream and the beech trees below. The route back from Cockayne ★ is sign-posted all the way to Kirkbymoorside ★ and has good views of the plain and wolds ahead. In spring look out for the primroses and bluebells in the trees. At the signpost giving directions to Fadmoor and Gillamoor ★ go left to Gillamoor.

Turn left, at **(E)**, in Gillamoor and pause by the seat next to the church to look at the splendid view up Farndale. The road drops down to the valley floor and at the next junction go right to Hutton-le-Hole ★ . If this tour is being done in early spring go up Farndale (see **Tour 10**) to see the masses of daffodils. On this tour the road crosses a couple of streams before climbing a slope to join the road coming down off Blakey Ridge. Turn right to the charming village of Hutton-le-Hole ★ . Decide for yourself whether it, or Hovingham ★ , is the prettier. It is a difficult choice. If there is time, visit the museum of local life (or use the map to plan a short walk). Follow the road down the slope to Kedholm and towards Kirkbymoorside.

At the junction with the A170 go straight over the main road towards Marton and Normanby. This way takes us through farmland and beside the River Seven. There is a camp site in Normanby. Great Barugh is 2½ miles further on and in this hamlet turn left, at **(F)**, to go up the main street and then left again at the T-junction to go to Little Barugh. Take care to turn right almost at once to follow the route to Kirby Misperton. The en-

trance to the Flamingo Park is on the left as one enters Kirby Misperton.

At the roundabout turn right towards Great Habton but do not go all the way. Turn left, at **(G)**, 2½ miles down the road, shortly after the British Gas drilling site on the right. The signpost says to Ryton. There is a pleasant drive past some attractive houses and fields through Ryton and past Eden Camp, now open as a Prisoner of War museum, to meet the A169. Turn right and enter Malton via the old town which has not been redeveloped and retains the feel of a separate village. There is a large public car park on the right just before the centre where one should stop and explore Malton on foot.

Scale 1:250 000 or ¼ INCH to 1 MILE

Tour 8
Pickering, Goathland and a forest drive

48 miles. This tour takes us through delightful Troutsdale and Wykeham forest. The tour starts in the bustling market town of Pickering where a castle, a museum, a preserved railway and an attractive town centre should provide something to interest everyone. A drive over the Moors is followed by a detour to a section of Roman road high on Wheeldale Moor. After the moorside village of Goathland the opportunity is given to explore the nature trails of Littlebeck before a trip through Silpho forest. There is a detour round Scarborough for those whose wish to start there and to take in the beautiful Forge Valley. There is a section along a forest drive before returning to Pickering. A few short steep sections out of Rosedale and up into Silpho forest should not daunt the more active cyclist.

Pickering ★ is an attractive market town and is the terminus of the North Yorkshire Moors Railway ★ . Go out of Pickering towards Helmsley ★ and Kirkbymoorside ★ . In the village of Wrelton, at **(A)**, turn right to Cropton ★ . After passing through farmland fork left then just over the stream go straight on, sign-posted to Rosedale Abbey ★ . Look out for the right turn at **(B)**, to Egton Bridge ★ .

This takes us up and over the Moors. There are extensive views to the right over Wheeldale Moor and the Roman road which is a feature later in this tour. Take the road to the right, at **(C)**, high on the Moors to Egton Bridge. The road goes along a ridge with the fertile Glaisdale valley on the left.

In Egton Bridge, an attractive village on both banks of the River Esk, turn right, before the bridge, to Goathland ★ . The road climbs out of the valley. Go left at Key Green farm (weary cyclists might like to rest at a convenient bench on the left overlooking the dale below) then follow the sign to Goathland. At **(D)**, look out for the sign on the right to 'Roman Road Ancient Monument'. This is a ten minute sedate drive and well worth the detour. Past the gate, moorland is reached with several old waymarks by the roadside indicating that this was once a major route across the Moors. This descends

into a valley where there is a ford across a stream which is an attractive place to stop. On the Moors, on the next high ground, you can see the old Roman road which went from Malton to Goldsborough, a signal station on the coast near Whitby ★ . Where the tarmac road finishes at the edge of the woods is also a quiet place to stop. The Roman road is well-preserved since the stones were not used for building materials because of its isolated position and it was soon buried under the soft peat until its recent excavation.

Go back down the road through the gate and, at **(D)**, turn right to Goathland. Goathland is a well-kept village with several places to stay or eat. There is also a camping site. **Walk 5** begins here. Go through the village and over the railway line to join the main A169 road. Turn left to Whitby and just past the car park at the top of Blue Bank look out for a turning on the right to Littlebeck, at **(E)**. Coaches are warned not to take this narrow road with its steep 1-in-5 and 1-in-3 slopes. At the bottom by the old mill follow the route to Littlebeck and Falling Foss (there is a suggested stroll here). Shortly after the pretty ford there is a junction with Sneaton and Whitby to the left. Go right here, up the 1-in-4 hill. The land becomes moor on either side.

Where this road joins the B1416 on the right is a no-through road leading to Falling Foss and another to the forest walks of May Beck ★ . If you have time these make a pleasant diversion.

Go right along the B1416 to Scarborough and right again at the junction with the A171. The road goes over rolling country. Look for a road on the right to Harwood Dale after about 3 miles. At **(F)**, go up into trees and past Rosalie's coffee house and the Mill Inn. The road climbs up out of the valley to reach a picnic site at Broxa forest at the top of Reasty Bank. Follow the road to Scarborough straight ahead. As you leave the forest you may catch a glimpse of the sea and the castle at Scarborough ahead. Follow the signs for Scalby. Go right in Scalby along the A171, past the hospital, and turn right at the roundabout where the A170 is sign-posted to Pickering ★ at **(G)**.

Leave the town on the A170 towards Pickering and turn right in the village of Ayton ★ , at **(H)**, to Hackness ★ and Forge Valley. This deep fissure was made by the Derwent River flowing away from the sea when its natural outlet at Scalby was blocked at the end of the Ice Age: it is now laid out with several places to picnic and to take short walks in the woodlands. Notices in the car park indicate the wild-life and flowers that can be found in the nature reserve. In Hackness go left to Langdale End. Hackness Grange is on your left with its large lake and extensive grounds. At the next junction do not go to Snainton and Troutsdale but go to Langdale End ½ mile away. Over the stream in Langdale End look out for St Peter's Church on the left before continuing up the valley towards the forest drive. There is an imposing hall on the left with a village post office entered via the vegetable garden at the rear.

Crossing a stream, you will see ahead, at **(J)**, the sign warning that there is a toll ahead and no route for caravans. The fee is paid by inserting coins in a machine to obtain a display ticket. On the left there are some marked walks. The route through the forest is well sign-posted with several points to stop. At High Staindale with its lake there is a special trail for the disabled. (See the entry on Bridestones and the map to plan a stroll). At Sneverdale picnic site there is an assault course for the energetic while the more sedentary will enjoy relaxing by the streams or looking round Dalby Forest Centre with its maps and exhibition.

Leaving the forest drive, turn left at the junction to Thornton Dale ★ , at **(K)**, and then right up the A170 to Pickering to complete the tour.

Scale 1:250 000 or ¼ INCH to 1 MILE

105

Tour 9
Helmsley, Osmotherley and the high Moors

55 miles. This route goes to beautiful Rievaulx Abbey and the lonely village of Old Byland. Past the pretty village of Hawnby it climbs to the heights of Arden Great Moor before descending to Osmotherley. A short section follows the edge of the Moors to Carlton in Cleveland and then turns right to the quaintly named Chop Gate. Up and over the end of Bilsdale, then into the start of Eskdale, the way climbs to the high ridge of Blakey before entering lush Farndale. The tour finishes and begins in the pleasant market town of Helmsley. There are some steep sections for cyclists.

Leave Helmsley ★ to the West going up the B1257 towards Rievaulx ★ . The second side road on the left, at (A), goes down a slope to the village of Rievaulx with its splendid Abbey. If a visit to the terraced gardens is intended do not go down the hill but turn sharp left through the gate along the drive. The Cistercian abbey is best seen at dusk or early morning when the mists rise from the Rye to swirl around the ruins. Past the Abbey turn right over the river signposted to Scawton ★ and Old Byland ★ . Then turn right again over another bridge, at (B), to Old Byland and past the white farmhouse. This single track road runs alongside the stream then climbs up with views over the valley. Watch out for pheasants darting from the hedges. In isolated Old Byland turn right to Hawnby 5 ¾ miles on, but if you have time turn left and visit the twelfth-century church behind the houses on the left.

The road to Hawnby passes over some flat ground and descends into a valley with woods on the right. The lane climbs up to a T-junction with clear directions to the right to Hawnby. As a landmark, a large TV mast can be seen ahead. Descending a steep hill, the old bridge across the stream in Hawnby soon becomes visible. Over the bridge keep to the right towards Osmotherley ★ 9 ¼ miles on. The narrow road leaves the attractive valley and goes over a cattle grid to enter pleasant moorland with pretty dales and woodland. There are several places to park and picnic together with streams and a ford. Soon you will catch a first

glimpse of the Cleveland Plain. The way ahead descends into pasture and the attractive town of Osmotherley, which is entered by going right at the junction. There is a youth hostel here and a camping site as this is on the long distance Cleveland Way. It is also a good place to stretch your legs (see map).

Go straight on through the village past Colbeck reservoir on the right. Passing over a cattle grid, descend the hill and turn right into Swainby ★ with the ruins of Whorlton Castle further on. After the village join the A172, turning right towards Middlesbrough. Take the first right turn, at (C), to Faceby. Go through Faceby into Carlton in Cleveland ★ . This is a most attractive village with an unusual inn sign. Take the road to the right at (D) to Chop Gate ★ . Over a cattle grid this way climbs onto moorland with marvellous views of the Moors. When the descent into Seave Green ★ is completed, and the B1257 reached, turn left and then almost immediately right at (E) to visit St Hilda's Church. Past the hamlet of Urra rejoin the B1257 briefly, turning right by the Forestry Commission car park on Hasty Bank to Ingleby Greenhow ★ . Follow the steep drop into Ingleby Greenhow – turning right at the T-junction, at (F), to enter the village. In the last century this was a mining centre. **Walk 2** begins here.

After the village of Battersby ★ , turn right at (G) towards Kildale ★ . Go over the railway crossing and turn right to Kildale and Castleton ★ , passing under the railway to enter Kildale. Beyond the village the road crosses the railway by a bridge and meets a cross-roads. Go right at (H) to Westerdale ★ . Pass over the railway line yet again and climb up Kildale Moor before descending to a ford and a stream.

In Westerdale there is a youth hostel with an attractive packhorse bridge which the road now by-passes. The village is an isolated arm of pasture land reaching into the Moors (there is a suggested stroll onto the moor here). Beyond the village go straight on to Farndale. The road climbs up a ridge with the ground falling away on either side to reach a point high on the roof of the Moors where four ways meet. This is Ralph's Cross ★ and the whole of the Moors can be seen from this summit. Hopefully the day will be fine and the land will not be covered with a 'roak', one of the sea mists that can sweep so suddenly up the dales to blot out the landscape.

Go right to Farndale and Hutton-le-

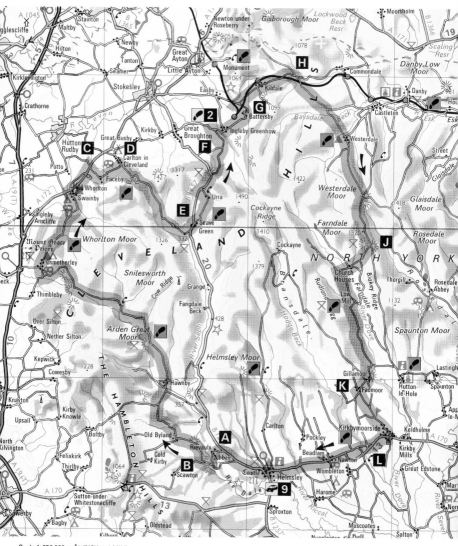

Scale 1:250 000 or 1/4 INCH to 1 MILE

Hole ★ along Blakey Ridge and past the lonely Lion Inn until a road joins from the right at (J) with directions to Farndale. Turn here leaving the parking area on the left and go down the steep slope to cross a cattle grid and enter pasture land again. Keep straight on, ignoring a road to the left. Go straight over the cross-roads taking the road past the Feversham Arms. Climb up the steep side of the valley and go left at the T-junction. The road then runs along the valley side, past the quaintly named Toad Hole farm, and enters the attractive hamlet of Low Mill with its picnic area and weir (see the map to

plan a short walk by the stream here). Continue along the valley and go right into Gillamoor ★ . There is a splendid view back up the dale from near the church. Go through Fadmoor and at (K) turn left to go into Kirkbymoorside.

Turn right up the A170 towards Helmsley ★ but keep an eye out for the sign on the right, at (L), to St Gregory's Minster. This short detour to the attractive church with its Saxon sundial will not be regretted. If there is time and the weather is good the short walk up Hodge Beck (see map) is a relaxing way to finish the tour before returning to Helmsley.

Tour 10
Farndale and the haunting ruins at Rievaulx

84 miles with optional excursions. This tour has been designed so that two sections – one of 20 miles up Farndale, which should not be missed if it is spring; and a 12 mile meander in the foothills of the Hambleton Hills – can easily be omitted if time is pressing. The route has been designed so that the steep hills up and onto the Hambleton Hills are avoided for cyclists.

The route starts in Thirsk ★ , now a quiet market town since the construction of the by-pass to the east. Go out on the A170, with its warning signs telling caravans not to go up the steep Sutton Bank ★ to Helmsley ★ . Over the busy by-pass, take the second turning on the right at **(A)**, towards Kilburn ★ . Down this side road Osgodby Hall, a fine Jacobean building, can be seen on the left before the T-junction. Turn left here to Kilburn. On the left is The White Horse of Kilburn on the escarpment face, cut by schoolchildren in the last century. The road goes down a slope into the delightful village of Kilburn, the home of a well-known master carpenter, whose work with its distinctive signature of a mouse can be seen in many churches and cathedrals. Go on through the village. After a couple of miles the lane bends sharply right and there is a T-junction. Turn left here. At once the attractive village of Coxwold ★ is entered, with Shandy Hall the home of the author William Sterne on the left, opposite the church where his father was vicar. Both places are worth a visit.

At the cross-roads in the centre, point **(B)**, turn left to Byland Abbey ★ and Wass ★ . The ruins of the Abbey are to the right of the road and should not be missed. Wass is a typical village, built in a local stone, most of it taken from the Abbey after the Dissolution. Do not go up the hill to Helmsley, but turn right at the Wombwell Arms, and along a level road through pleasant country into Ampleforth ★ . On the left is Studford Ring (see the map to plan a walk to this interesting

Scale 1:250 000 or ¼ INCH to 1 MILE

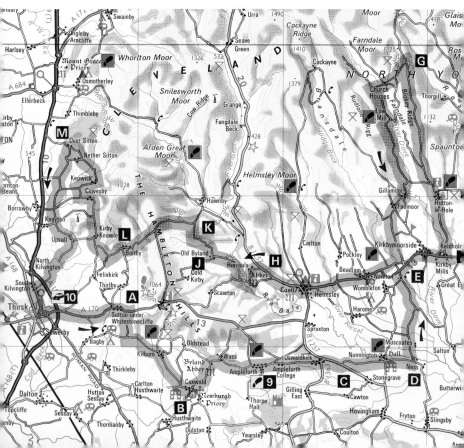

earthwork). Beyond the village is the Catholic public school, with its church, designed by Sir Giles Gilbert Scott. **Walk 9** starts here.

Continue on to Oswaldkirk ★ , with its historic church on the right below the level of the road just before the B1363. Go left up the hill, and at once turn right down the B1257. Take the first left, at **(C)**, to Nunnington Hall ★ . This road traverses the edge of a ridge, with fine views on the left to Nunnington. Both the church and the Hall are worth seeing. At the cross-roads go straight ahead to continue the tour, but cross the bridge on the left to see the Hall (there is a suggested short walk here).

The next place reached is the small hamlet of Ness where we turn left, at **(D)**, to cross the River Rye. Go straight across the plain, with the Moors visible ahead, following the signs to Kirkbymoorside ★ .

At **(E)** on the map, the A170 is reached, with Helmsley to the left, Kirkbymoorside to the right. To look at Farndale go right, or if missing out this part of the tour, go straight ahead to St Gregory's Minster, and miss out the next paragraph.

Having turned right onto the A170, go straight ahead at the roundabout and take the turning on the left to Hutton-le-Hole ★ , at **(F)**. This is an attractive moorland village with an excellent museum of rural life. Go straight up the ridge towards Castleton ★ and continue along this road, with views both east and west high on the moor, until the Lion Inn can be seen ahead. Turn sharp left, before the inn, at the car park at **(G)**, down the steep lane to Farndale. Go straight past the houses and over the valley floor, crossing a stream. Turn left again to drive down the side of the valley until Low Mill. There is a car park here and a suggested stroll. Continue along the side of the valley to Gillamoor ★ . The church on the left has a magnificent view back up the dale from a convenient seat beside it. Follow the signs to Fadmoor. In Fadmoor, go left, then right at once, to pass through farmland. By Starfits Farm there is a cross-roads where we turn right to cross Hodge Beck to St Gregory's Minster which is full of Saxon relics. Pause here to look at the church, or stroll up to Hodge Beck.

Continuing the tour, go straight on to join the A170, and go right into Helmsley ★ . This is a thriving market town with several good inns, a castle and a range of shops. Take the B1257 out of the town and turn down the second road on the left, at **(H)**, to Rievaulx ★ , the highlight of the tour. Both the Abbey and the terraced gardens equal the best of their kind, and should not be missed.

Past the Abbey, turn right to cross the bridge over the River Rye, and then right again over the stream, at **(J)**, to pass the large white farmhouse on the right as the road bends left. Stop in Old Byland ★ to visit the minute church hidden behind the houses on the left of the Green.

Go right and down into the valley, and up again to a T-junction at **(K)**. Turn left, but admire the view over to the right towards Hawnby, before going straight over the old drover's way. This was once used to drive cattle from the north of Scotland to the hungry towns in the south of England. This route takes us down Sneck Yate Bank into Boltby.

At point **(L)** on the map either follow the signs to Thirsk ★ , or for a quiet detour, turn right beyond the village to Kirby Knowle. This little area has an air of absolute calm, as it is not on any main or minor through route. Follow the signs to Cowesby and after that turn right to Kepwick and Nether and Over Silton ★ . Our route goes left to Knayton and Upsall, where we turn right following the signposts back into Thirsk.

Helmsley Castle

Walk 1
Staithes and the coastal path to Runswick Bay

This walk starts in the small fishing port of Staithes, once famous for its herring fleet. Huddled at the base of the cliffs, Staithes remains a close community and it is still possible to see old women wearing traditional bonnets. From the village, the route runs along the cliff tops to the sheltered, sandy beach at Runswick and returns inland through pleasant countryside. The walk can be shortened by turning inland at the Victorian artificial port of Port Mulgrave. Allow 3 hours for the full walk and about 1 hour for the shorter alternative.

Staithes★ (NY-100) (78-18) is on **Tour 1**. It lies between the A174 and the sea, just south of Loftus. United Buses run a service along the A174 that stops at Staithes.

From the car park, go down the steep lane into the village. Staithes is built on the south side of the narrow cleft in the cliffs where Staithes Beck flows out to the sea, with the crumbling rock face of Cowbar Nab to the north. The houses seem to cling precariously between the cliff and the sea and indeed many have disappeared into the sea over the centuries.

The Cod and Lobster public house, on the sea front, was last rebuilt in 1953. Lobster is now the main catch.

Turn right on the seafront and walk up Church Street. The Cleveland Way bears left up a gulley and past a farm. Leave the farm on your right and follow the footpath across the fields. This is a much used path and clearly marked. The path bears to the right and then climbs to follow the cliff edge.

Go past Beacon Hill, on your right, and follow the path as it curves round to the right into Port Mulgrave ★ . The harbour is at the base of the cliffs, only approached by a steep path. It was blasted out of the rocks in the last century to form a loading place for iron ore carriers, the ore being transported from the inland mine through a tunnel under the village. To take the short walk, turn right here at **(K)** and read the last paragraph now.

To continue the longer walk, leave the village on your right and carry on along the Cleveland Way. As you walk along the edge of the cliffs, Runswick Bay ★ comes into sight. Just past two small ponds, turn sharp right **(A)** and follow the path into the village. Runswick, like Staithes, grew up as a fishing community but its whitewashed cottages with their neat gardens form a complete contrast. Many are now holiday homes.

If you have the time, turn left at **(B)** to explore Runswick Bay. There is a sailing

Staithes

Scale 1:25 000 or 2 ½INCHES to 1 MILE

club here and a long, curving, sandy beach. Farther along is Hob Hole, partly natural caves and partly old jet workings.

If not, turn right at **(B)** and walk up Runswick Lane, past the post office, until you reach the outskirts of Hinderwell. The name is a corruption of St Hilda's Well and the village lies on a route linking various holy places which ran as far North as Lindisfarne, just south of the Scottish border. At **(C)** turn left up the narrow track to join the main road at **(D)**.

Turn right at **(D)** and take the first road on the left. Keep straight on past the houses into open fields and turn right at **(E)** down Back Lane. At **(F)**, turn left down a path leading towards the wood. Cross the footbridge over the stream, go through the trees and take the path going off to the right at **(G)**. Follow this path into the wood, past a clearing on the left, to join another path from the left just before the wood ends **(H)**.

Cross the stream by the footbridge and turn right up the slope towards Seaton Hall. Leave the hall on your left and continue on to the right hand edge of the housing estate, where there is a passage between the houses. Go down here and follow the road in the estate to rejoin the main road. Turn left and then right down the road back to the car park.

For the shorter walk, turn right at **(K)** and go up the road to the telephone box at **(L)**. Go right here up the lane and turn sharp left by the last house, at **(M)**, to follow the footpath downhill to the main road visible ahead. Cross this busy road with care to the lay-by on the other side at **(N)** and climb over the stile. There is a path going down to some trees in the valley. Turn left and cross the stream by the footbridge. At **(P)**, turn right to rejoin the longer walk.

111

Walk 2
Greenhow Bank and Ingleby incline

This walk starts in the village of Ingleby Greenhow and climbs up the old railway incline which formed the northern end of the line that carried iron ore across the Moors from Rosedale. The route then follows the Cleveland Way along the edge of the escarpment, giving glorious views across the Moors. The walk passes an old Bronze Age burial site, and returns through pleasant farmland to the village. For the less energetic there is a shorter walk of 4 miles which avoids the climb to Greenhow Bank. This takes under 2 hours, while the full walk of 7 miles takes nearly 4 hours.

Ingleby Greenhow ★ (93) (NZ 58-06) lies on **Tour 9** and is reached by turning right off the B1257 by the Forestry Commission car park on Hasty Bank and descending the slope of the escarpment.

Park by St Andrew's church and walk down the lane to Ingleby Beck. Cross over the stepping stones and at **(A)** turn left up the stone steps and walk through the green gate at the top, with the field on your right hand side and the wood on your left. The path down by the side of the wood is a bit overgrown. Where the path ends, cross over the stile and keep to the left hand side of the field. Over the rise a farmhouse becomes visible and two stiles, one in the near field and one in the farther one. Go between the two.

Over the second stile, follow the direction of the waymark sign towards the gate on the other side of the field. Go over the stile by the gate, leaving the farm on your left, and cross over the little ditch. Go straight across the next field, aiming for Low Farm which is now visible ahead. From here you can see the scar left by the old railway incline going up to the top of Greenhow Bank, which is where we are heading. At the far side of the field follow the yellow waymark sign to Low Farm, keeping to the left hand side of the field. Bear right, skirting the garden, and at the entrance to the farm turn right and walk up the track to the road. Turn left by the public footpath sign into the metalled road. At **(B)** a Public Footpath sign goes off towards Wood's Farm. For the shorter walk turn left and read the last paragraph.

To reach the incline, continue along the road until you reach a junction, with a Public Footpath sign on the left hand side. Go left here through the stone entrance to High Farm and over a cattle grid. Cross the stream by a little bridge and go down the metalled track through a field. You can see the farmhouse amongst the trees ahead. Go over another cattle grid and down the drive. As this bears left towards the farm, go straight ahead over the stile marked with a yellow arrow and along the right hand edge of the field.

At the end of this track go over a stile and keep on the right hand side of the field, aiming for a gate about 50 yards away. Go through the gate and bear left towards the houses on the far side of the field at **(C)**. These are old railway cottages that were built to house the workers who worked at the foot of the incline. Cross a stile in front of the cottages and turn right along an asphalt track to a turning circle. You are now at the bottom of the incline.

The incline is just under 1 mile long but the gradient is mostly 1 in 8 or less and not difficult to climb. Where the track forks, do not bear right but go straight on up towards the top of the incline which is visible ahead. Near the top, climb over a stile by a gate and walk through a cutting. There are some old railway sleepers here and the remains of the winding house that used to haul the wagons up the incline. At the top of the incline, at **(D)**, path bears round to the right along the bed of the dismantled railway. Although there is a path to the left at this point which joins up with the Cleveland Way and cuts off 1½ miles, this is not a right of way. You should therefore continue along the route of the disused railway. After about ½ mile this joins the Cleveland Way, which comes in from the right, and 200 yards after this the Cleveland Way turns sharp left and heads due north along a wide stony track. This section is not shown on the map opposite because of space but is easy to follow.

Continue along the Cleveland Way to **(E)**. Here there is a green gate across the Cleveland Way with a wooden wicket gate next to it. Turn left just before the gate down the path leading to Ingleby Bank. At **(F)** go through a gate and continue down the stony path into the plantation. When you reach Bank Foot Farm, go through the farmyard and down the road past the cottages. Just past the last house you will see three prominent trees, two on your left and one on your right. Turn sharp left through a gate past the trees **(G)** and go down between two fields.

At the end of the field, don't cross the stile but follow the yellow arrows into the field to the right of the stile. Ingleby

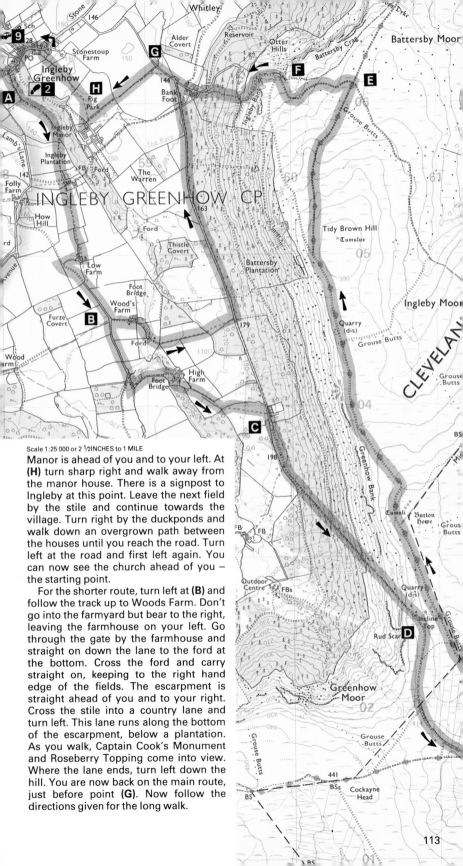

Scale 1:25 000 or 2 ½INCHES to 1 MILE

Manor is ahead of you and to your left. At
(H) turn sharp right and walk away from
the manor house. There is a signpost to
Ingleby at this point. Leave the next field
by the stile and continue towards the
village. Turn right by the duckponds and
walk down an overgrown path between
the houses until you reach the road. Turn
left at the road and first left again. You
can now see the church ahead of you –
the starting point.

For the shorter route, turn left at **(B)** and
follow the track up to Woods Farm. Don't
go into the farmyard but bear to the right,
leaving the farmhouse on your left. Go
through the gate by the farmhouse and
straight on down the lane to the ford at
the bottom. Cross the ford and carry
straight on, keeping to the right hand
edge of the fields. The escarpment is
straight ahead of you and to your right.
Cross the stile into a country lane and
turn left. This lane runs along the bottom
of the escarpment, below a plantation.
As you walk, Captain Cook's Monument
and Roseberry Topping come into view.
Where the lane ends, turn left down the
hill. You are now back on the main route,
just before point **(G)**. Now follow the
directions given for the long walk.

Walk 3
Hayburn Wyke and Cloughton Wyke

This walk explores the coast above Scarborough, visiting the sheltered inlets of Hayburn Wyke and Cloughton Wyke. The route follows first the track of a disused railway line, now reclaimed by wild flowers, and then the coastal path of the Cleveland Way. This runs along the cliff-tops, offering magnificent views of the rocky coast. There is also the option of following the Cleveland Way down the coast below Cloughton Wyke for a view south to the Scarborough promontory. Allow about 2 hours for the shorter walk and 3 hours for the longer.

Cloughton (101) (TA 01-94) is on **Tour 2**, north of Scarborough ★. Where the A171 turns sharp left, turn right down a narrow lane with the Cober Hall Guest House on the corner. Park in the lane. The 115 bus stops in the village: phone (0723) 375463 for times of buses.

Walk down the lane towards the sea, passing Court Green Farm on your left. Where the track crosses the disused railway line **(A)**, go down the steps to the left and walk north along the old railway track. This is now a pleasant, silent path, with shrubs and many varieties of wild flowers recolonizing the permanent way.

Where the road to the Hayburn Wyke

Hayburn Wyke

Hotel crosses the track, there is a gate. Just before here, at **(B)**, turn right and go up the embankment and into a field. At **(C)** turn right to join a track from the hotel which takes you over a stile and into the woods. Shortly after this, the Cleveland Way comes in from the right.

Continue along the path, turning left to follow the Cleveland Way down through the woods to Hayburn Wyke **(D)**. Wyke is the Yorkshire dialect for 'a small sheltered bay', which accurately describes this sandy inlet. The beach and woods are a Nature Reserve, in the care of the Yorkshire Naturalists' Trust. Hayburn Beck runs into the cove through a deep channel in the clay, which has exposed the underlying rock. Numerous fossils have been found on the beach: undoubtedly the most dramatic was a footprint of a three-toed dinosaur.

To return, retrace your steps as far as the point where the Cleveland Way leaves the path on your left, midway between **(D)** and **(C)**. Turn left here across a stile and follow the Cleveland Way back along the coast. The path first runs along the top of the woods and then follows the edge of the cliffs, between the fields and the sea. Like all this coastline, the cliff face is soft and crumbling and it is not safe to climb down to the beaches below.

Follow the cliff path south to Cloughton Wyke, a shingle inlet enclosed by 100 ft cliffs. There is a fine view from here across to Hundale Point: in spring its cliffs are covered with nesting sea-birds. A grassy track leads down to the beach from a small car park.

For the shorter walk, turn right at **(E)** to follow a footpath across a field. Bear right to cross the next field diagonally, making towards the farmhouse, and rejoin the lane at **(A)**.

For a longer walk, continue along the Cleveland Way as far as Crook Ness **(F)**, passing Hundale Point and the Coastguard lookout at Long Nab. You cross the southern boundary of the North York Moors National Park just before Long Nab. At Crook Ness, the Cleveland Way turns sharply inland but there is a narrow concrete path leading down to the shore through the gap in the cliffs. From here, there is a good view of Scarborough's Castle Cliff.

For drivers, Crook Ness is a good point to turn and retrace your steps. If you have come from Scarborough by bus, you may prefer to continue south. The distance into Scarborough is about the same as the distance from Haven Wyke to Crook Ness and is well sign-posted.

Walk 4
Rosedale – a peaceful valley once the centre of a mining boom

This walk, starting in Rosedale Abbey, covers two contrasting but typical aspects of the North Yorkshire Moors. The first half of the walk goes down either side of a quiet dale and can be done as a complete tour. The second half climbs up onto the edge of the moors, visiting one of the old ironstone mines that made Rosedale Abbey a boom town in the last century, and returns through pleasant farmland. Allow about 3 ½ hours for the full walk. There is no public transport to the village so the only means of access is by car or bicycle.

Rosedale Abbey ★ (94,100) (SE 72-95) is on **Tour 3** and is reached by a minor country road which turns right out of Hutton-le-Hole ★ by the folk museum and then left to run north across Spaunton Moor. In the nineteenth century this unspoiled village was the centre of a mining boom and a railway was built to carry iron ore across the moors to Ingleby Greenhow ★ .

Park at the public car park by the Milburn Arms Hotel. Turn left out of the car park and right to the village green. Walk down the right hand side of the green and bear right down the road past the school. At the west end of the church is a small turret with a winding staircase which is the only remains of Rosedale Priory, a Cistercian nunnery founded in 1158.

Just past the church you will see two footpath signs on the left hand side of the road, within a few yards of each other. Turn left down the second footpath at **(A)**, crossing a stile over a wall. After about 15 yards you will come to a T-junction. Turn right and go past the recreation ground into a caravan site. Bear right where the path forks and continue until you come to a curious stone hut on the left containing a spring which spouts from a pipe set in the wall. This is Waterhouse Well which is marked on the map and was probably once a source of water for the priory.

Opposite the well there is a footpath sign. Follow this through a cow gate and into a field. Keep to the left-hand side of the field, continuing in the same direction

as before. Cross a stile into the next field and follow the path, which gradually descends towards the stream on your left. Cross another stile into a little wood by the stream. You will see a footbridge across the stream on your left. Do not cross the stream here but carry straight on, keeping the fence and stream on your left. Go over a stile into the next field and make for the gate on the opposite side of the field. Go through the gate and bear diagonally left towards a stile near the stream. Follow the stream through two fields and at the far corner of the second field turn right up the hill and go left through a gate at **(B)** into a farm road.

Turn left down the road and go over two branches of the stream. Past the second branch turn left into a field and make for the white fence which marks a footbridge across the stream. Go over the stile and across the footbridge. Low Thorgill Farm is now ahead of you. When you reach the farm, go through a gate between two barns into the farmyard and leave by a lane on the opposite side.

Turn left at **(C)** where the lane meets a tarmac road and walk along the road until you reach the Red House on your right. To return to Rosedale, turn left just beyond the house at **(D)** down a footpath which leads back to Rosedale. (For a longer walk, see the next paragraph.) Cross a stile by the stream and go down the right hand edge of the field. There are lovely views ahead and to the left looking down into Rosedale and across to Northdale Rigg. Go over a stile and down some steps by the side of a house to reach the road. Continue down the road, crossing the stream, and turn left at the bottom. This brings you back into the village.

For the moorland walk, turn right at **(D)**, crossing the stile. Leave the Golf Club headquarters on your right and just beyond a shed turn right at the footpath sign to follow the roped-off path across the golf course. Where the golf course ends, go over a drystone wall by some steps and turn left towards a second set of steps over another drystone wall coming down at rightangles. This section is quite steep and there are lovely views behind you across the valley. Continue along above the drystone wall until you reach a stile leading onto the moors.

The path follows a wire fence with wooden posts and then turns away to the right to go up through a cutting. As you come out of the cutting the ruins of the ironworks are visible ahead of you. Turn right and walk up a track towards a prom-

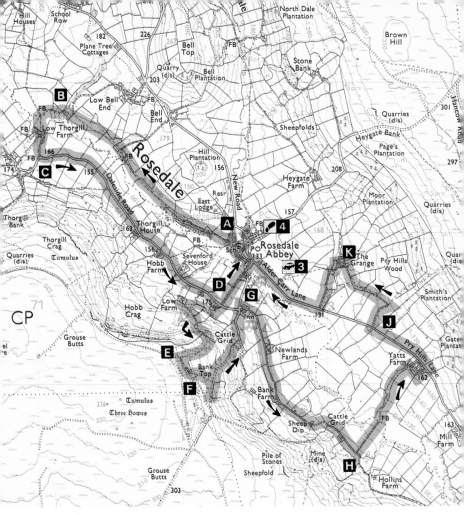

Scale 1:25 000 or 2 ½ INCHES to 1 MILE

inent tree. The track takes you to the right of the three houses ahead of you. At **(E)** turn left down a level track which goes behind the houses. The ruins are now directly ahead and there are glorious views of the valley below and across the moors towards the coast. One can see the Wolds on the other side of the Vale of Pickering.

Just beyond the houses turn left at **(F)** and follow a fairly clear track down to the road. Turn right up the road to look at the ironworks. The surviving wall with its eight arches gives some idea of their scale. Walk back down the hill, going through a gate at the side of the cattle grid, until you reach the White Horse Farm Hotel. Turn right here at **(G)** by the public footpath sign and walk through the car park and along a track which goes past several houses. Up the hill on your right is the site of Hollins Mine which opened in 1856 to mine an 18 ft vein of ironstone.

Cross the cattle grid and carry on down the path. 400 yards or so before Hollins Farm turn left and cross the stile at **(H)**. Walk straight down through the field towards the stream and cross by the concrete bridge. Continue up through the field towards Yatts Farm, keeping close to the trees on the left. Keep the farm on your right and the stream on the left, as indicated by the signs painted on the gates. At the road turn left towards Rosedale Abbey.

Turn right by the footpath sign at **(J)** and walk up the hill towards a plantation, keeping close to the drystone wall on your left. At the corner of the wall turn left and walk towards The Grange, keeping the wall on your left. Turn left just before the farm at **(K)**, and go through a gate. Walk through the farm and downhill along the farm road. Go across a small ford and follow the sign-post back down to the road. Turn right and walk back along the road to the village.

Walk 5
Goathland – a moor, a Roman road and a unique waterfall

The two walks described here both start in the village of Goathland, which lies round the edge of a large common, and take you through moorland to the Mallyan Spout. This is a dramatic waterfall which plummets over 70 ft down the side of a narrow gorge. The wild open moorland which surrounds Goathland forms a striking contrast to the smooth well-kept grass of the common, kept short by grazing sheep. The longer walk also goes up onto the moors, where there is a well-preserved stretch of a Roman road which originally ran from Malton to near Whitby. Allow 3-4 hours for the longer walk and about 1 ½ hours for the shorter.

Goathland ★ (94) (NZ 83-01) is on **Tours 3 and 8**. It lies on a tributary of the river

The Mallyan Spout

Esk and can be reached by turning west off the A169, south of Sleights. Steam locomotives operated by the North Yorkshire Moors Railway ★ run from Grosmont to Goathland and there is also a local bus service from Whitby ★.

From the car park in the centre of the village, turn right and walk up the main street which runs through the centre of the common. Bear right beyond the Church at **(A)**. Just after this, the two walks diverge. (For the shorter walk, read the last paragraph now.)

For the longer walk, turn left onto the moor and follow a track that leads gradually uphill. There are several sheep tracks here and you need to choose one that aims for the ridge ahead of you. Keep the small lake on your left and avoid paths going downhill. When a cairn becomes visible, aim for that.

This is typical moorland, carpeted with bracken and heather, and you will probably put up some red grouse. As you crest the rise, the ground ahead falls away steeply and the tarmac road to Hunt House become visible. Go down the hill to the house **(B)** and walk down the path to the Youth Hostel. Leave the hostel on your right and at **(C)** turn right and cross Wheeldale Beck by the stepping stones.

Go up a fairly steep section to the top of the ridge and continue until you come to the Roman road at **(D)**. The construction of the road, with culverts, curbs and infill, is almost intact – no doubt because its isolation meant that the stone was not looted for other buildings. Nineteen centuries ago, Roman legionaries marched ten abreast along this road to get from their camp at Malton to the coastal station at Goldsborough ★, north of Whitby.

Turn right and walk beside the road until it comes to an end. Go through the gate and follow the drystone wall on your right to reach a stile at **(E)**. Go over the stile and walk down the hill to a small stream. Turn right and cross the stream at the second footbridge, where it meets a second stream just above a ford. Then turn right up the track to join the road at **(F)**.

Turn left and walk along the side of the road. At **(G)**, turn left and follow the track across the bracken to meet the road at **(H)**. (The shorter walk comes in from the right here.) Turn left and follow the road as it bends sharp right. Just before the bridge, turn right down the signed footpath to the Mallyan Spout and follow the banks of the stream. The fact that this waterfall is called a spout rather than a force gives you some idea what to expect

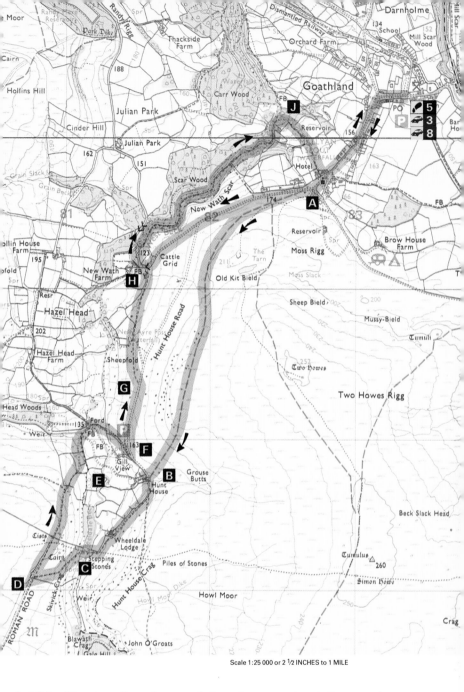

Scale 1:25 000 or 2 ½ INCHES to 1 MILE

but it is still a dramatic and unexpected sight, located on a bend in the stream so that you come on it suddenly. Its sheer drop is the result of exceptionally hard rock, which has prevented the normal process of erosion.

Continue along the bank of the stream until the path forks (J). Turn right here and go up the steps to rejoin the road by the Mallyan Spout Hotel. Turn left to retrace your steps to the car park.

For the shorter walk, carry on down the road at (A), passing some houses on your right, and bear right at the road junction. The road runs along the edge of the moors, with high ground on your left and West Beck, set among trees, on your right. The road dips down into the valley and rejoins the longer route just before the bridge (H).

119

Walk 6
The Hole of Horcum and Newton Dale

The two walks described here take you to a dramatic landscape now known to be the result of a sudden torrent of water escaping from the enormous ice-dammed lake which once filled Esk Dale. It was this water which gouged out the Hole of Horcum and cut a gigantic groove through the moors to form Newton Dale. Both walks go south across Levisham Moor and along an ancient dyke to West Side Brow, above Newton Dale, returning through the Hole of Horcum. The longer walk (allow 3 ½ hours) also visits the village of Levisham, which still has a maypole, while the shorter (allow 2 hours) returns through Dundale Griff, a tree-lined ravine.

The **Hole of Horcum** ★ (94,100) (84-93) is on **Tours 2 and 3**, north of Pickering ★ . Just before the A169 drops steeply down to the Saltergate ★ Inn, there is a large car park. Alternatively the 92 bus goes along the road: phone (0723) 375463 for details.

From the car park, walk north down the main road. There are good views of the Hole of Horcum below you, once full to the brim with water. Its steep sides and warm upcurrents of air now make it ideal for hang-gliding.

As the road descends, Lockton High

Hole of Horcum

Moor can be seen to the north, with Saltergate Inn in the foreground. At the hairpin bend, turn left onto the stony track that runs along the northern edge of the Hole of Horcum at **(A)**.

Follow the level track as it bears round to the left onto Levisham Moor. All this land was purchased by National Park Authority in 1976, to preserve what was felt to be a critical area of heather moorland.

The moor is also of archaeological interest, with numerous earthworks and tumuli. Finds excavated by the local archaeological society can be seen in the Rotunda Archaeological Museum in Scarborough ★ .

Past Seavy Pond, the path crosses a boundary dyke which was probably built as a defence by local tribes. It is worth turning right here to follow the dyke to West Side Brow. From here you can look down into Newton Dale. At the north end, the water which was released when the ice dam melted has carved out a channel several hundreds of feet deep and exposed strata 150 million years old. The vale is now thickly planted with conifers and the North York Moors Railway ★ line runs along its floor.

Green hairstreak butterflies are found on the scrubby grasslands of the moors, cliff tops and limestone hills. Normally seen flying in May or June

Retrace your steps along the dyke, turning right to follow the path to Dundale Pond **(B)**. Here the two walks diverge. (For the shorter, read the last paragraph now.)

The longer walk continues south along the path which leads diagonally to the left. At the moorland boundary, go through a gate and follow the walled lane into the village of Levisham ★ . The main street runs through a green and outside the Horseshoe Inn there is a maypole. This is one of the few villages where the custom of dancing round the maypole is still kept up.

Go through the village and follow the road as it turns sharp left and descends steeply. At **(C)**, turn left along a footpath which climbs back up towards the plateau, bearing left at the fork to keep on higher ground. The path follows the shoulder of the plateau round to the left and then descends through woodland, following the line of Levisham Beck.

At **(D)**, go over a footbridge and turn left along a path that runs between the beck and the wall. Then walk over the fields towards Low Horcum Farm, keeping roughly halfway between the beck on your left and the wood on your right. Leave the farm on your right and follow a wide grassy track to a stile and gate. Cross a narrow stream and continue along the track which climbs steeply to join the main road at **(A)**. Turn right and climb the hill back to the car park.

For the shorter walk, turn sharply left at **(B)** onto a wide grassy track. This leads into the steepsided valley of Dundale Griff (griff is dialect for a side valley.) Keep to the right of the narrow stream at the bottom and at **(D)** turn left to cross first the stream and then Levisham Beck. You are now back on the main route.

Scale 1:25 000 or 2½INCHES to 1 MILE

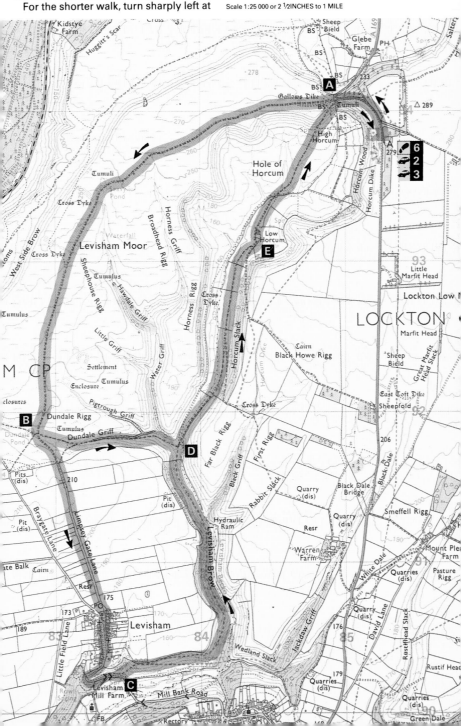

Walk 7
Glaisdale, Egton Bridge and the River Esk

This walk starts near the Esk Dale village of Glaisdale in the northern section of the Moors and goes along an old packhorse way which runs through woods by the River Esk. The walk then takes you

Scale 1:25 000 or 2 ½ INCHES to 1 MILE

through pleasant pasture land in typical dale country and returns via country roads through the charming village of Egton Bridge and across a high arched packhorse bridge. It is possible to miss out the middle section of the walk by climbing a steep section of country road. Allow 2 ½ hours for the full walk.

Glaisdale ★ (94) (NZ 77-05) is on **Tours 1 and 3** and lies inland from **Whitby** ★ on one of the minor country roads that criss-cross Esk Dale.

Park by the station and turn left down

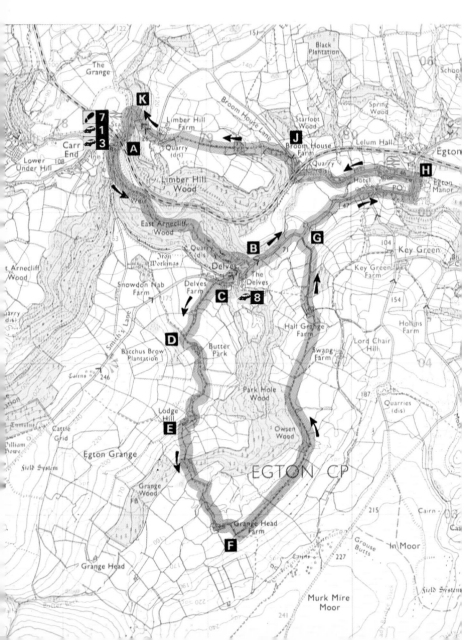

Egton Bridge

the road towards Egton Bridge ★ . Just before the railway bridge, turn right down a footpath at **(A)**. Cross the footbridge and follow the track into the woods. The path bears away from the river and then back again to follow the line of the river past the weir. It then bears right again and passes to the left of a pond before emerging out of the woods to meet the road at **(B)**. For part of the way the path follows the old packhorse way and you can see the original paving stones, worn down by horseshoes.

For the shorter walk, turn left at **(B)** and go up the road to rejoin the longer walk at **(G)**. For the full walk, turn right and go down a steep section of road. Just before Delves Farm, turn left at **(C)** down a farm track. This turns sharp left at **(D)**, where a path comes in from your right, and goes towards Butter Park Farm. Walk past the farm and down the track to Lodge Hill Farm. Go past this farm and through the gate on the left at **(E)**. Cross the field diagonally and go over the footbridge at the bottom of the valley. Then go uphill, aiming for the gate to the left of the field ahead. Go through the gate and keep to the left hand edge of the next field until you reach another gate. This brings you onto the right hand side of the next field.

Go across this field, heading towards Grange Head Farm.

Leave the farm to your right. At **(F)** the track turns sharp left and continues for about 1½ miles before it reaches the road at **(G)**. Turn right and go down the hill into the village of Egton Bridge which lies on either side of the River Esk in a steep-sided valley. There are some craft shops, cafes and a village pub which make it a pleasant halfway house.

Go over the bridge and turn left at **(H)** to walk down the road with the river now on your left. This is a quiet country lane. Go past the last houses in the village and up the steep hill under the railway bridge. As the road levels out, turn left down a footpath at **(J)** which leads into a field. Go up the track by the wood and over two fields, aiming towards a spur in the wood ahead. Follow the track through the wood, still keeping in a straight line. In the next field go on up the slight slope, walking by the left-hand edge of two fields. As the path crests the ridge, Limber Hill Farm is visible ahead. Bear left before the farm towards the disused quarry to join the tarmac road at a sharp bend.

Go left down the hill and turn left at the road junction at **(K)**. Cross Beggars' Bridge and go under the railway bridge to return to the station.

Walk 8
Guisborough and the northern edge of the escarpment

This is a circular walk starting in the ancient market town of Guisborough, now a dormitory town for Middlesbrough but still retaining much of its character. The walk passes the ruins of Guisborough Priory and goes through farmland before joining the Cleveland Way to climb up onto the escarpment which lies just south of the town. The second half of the walk doubles back through Guisborough Woods along the edge of the moors and returns through fields. A shorter walk which misses out the woods is also shown. Allow 3 ½ hours for the full walk of 7 miles and 2 hours for the shorter walk.

Guisborough ★ (94) (NZ 61-15) is on **Tour 1** and lies on the A171 east of Middlesbrough. It can be reached by bus from Whitby ★ or Middlesbrough.

From the car park, turn left down the A171 and right at the traffic lights. Turn right by the church and walk up the path on the left-hand side of the church. It is worth making a detour here to visit the remains of the Priory which was founded in 1129 by Robert de Brus, an ancestor of the Robert Bruce who defeated the English at Bannockburn to become king of Scotland. The magnificent east wall is still standing.

Pass the old grammar school on the left. At point **(A)** don't turn left but go through the gate and take the tarmac path that crosses the field at an angle. There is a good view of the edge of the moors and the woods ahead: the trees completely hide the town and the main roads on either side. Keep straight on through a swing gate into a small copse at the side of the A171. Turn left up the road and go past the old milepost (21 miles to Whitby). Just before the entrance to Guisborough Hall on the left, turn right and go up a public footpath on the opposite side of the road at **(B)**, sign-posted to 'Foxdale Farm Only'.

Immediately you get away from the main road it becomes quiet again. As the road to the farm bears right, turn left at the Public Footpath sign and cross a stile over a wooden fence. Follow the line of the fence up the right hand side of the field and go through a small metal swing

gate. Keep to the left hand edge of the next field and leave it by a stile in the corner. Go up a rather overgrown track between two high hawthorn hedges. Where the path opens out and becomes pasture, Little Waterfall Farm can be seen ahead through another field. Go towards the stile ahead in the corner of the field. Just after the stile there is a small stream on the left and looking to the right you can see an old railway bridge on the disused railway line. Keep to the left hand edge of this field and walk towards another stile in the corner.

At **(C)** go past the Public Footpath sign onto the main Whitby Road. Turn right immediately for the shorter walk (and read the last paragraph now). To continue on the longer walk turn left down the road and after about 400 yards turn right at the footpath sign just before Waterfall Farm at **(D)**. Turn right almost immediately down the path marked Skelton, 2¼ miles. Cross Waterfall Beck by a green bridge and turn right up a dirt track, following the direction of the blue arrow. Walk up through the fields, keeping to the edge of the trees, until you come to a plantation.

Turn sharp left at **(E)**. After about 600 yards you come to a gate on your right with a waymark sign. Go through the gate and walk up the steep track through the trees. Do not cross the stile but turn right at **(F)** onto the Cleveland Way. The trees are now on your right. Continue along the Cleveland Way, crossing the stile above the quarry. Bear left round the top of the quarry and follow the Cleveland Way down the slope. This is well sign-posted. Cross the stile at the bottom and head for the A171. The Fox and Hounds at **(G)** might be a good place to break your walk.

On the opposite side of the road behind some trees are some rather unsightly alum spoil heaps. The Cleveland Way is shown on the map as starting below these and running south-west parallel to the road before swinging back on itself to pass behind them. The spoil heaps have now been turned into a motocross course for motor bikes and the scrubby hillside to the east of the course is criss-crossed with paths. This makes it almost impossible to keep to the marked route. Instead just make your way up the slope, keeping to the left of the motocross course, and turn right at the top. A clear track now bears left away from the spoil heaps into the trees. This is the Cleveland Way. Keep to the track as it bears round to the left, ignoring a stile on your right. At **(H)** climb over the stile and turn left up

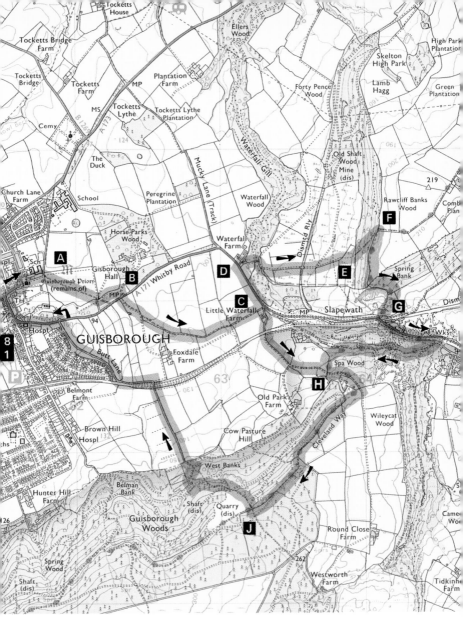

the concrete farm road. Go past the old water works building on the right and continue up the hill, with the trees on your left. Where the path ends, go through the gate and turn right into the field. The Cleveland Way is sign-posted here.

Leave the field by the gate opposite and continue along the Cleveland Way by the edge of the forestry plantation. Where the plantation goes uphill, the Cleveland Way bears left into the trees. Continue along the path through the woods until you reach the disused quarry at (J). Here turn right down a forestry path which brings you into a lane leading back through

Scale 1:25 000 or 2 ½ INCHES to 1 MILE

fields to the A171. Turn left to return to the car park.

For the shorter walk, turn right at (C), at a sign for the Old Park Farm Boarding Kennels. Follow the direction of the arrow up the slope and keep along the farm track as it crosses a field. Where the entrance to Old Park Farm bears off to the right, keep straight on across a cattle grid. There is a sign here saying Private Road, No Unauthorised Vehicles, but this is a public footpath. This track goes across the middle of a field up a gentle slope. At (H) the path becomes a concrete track and rejoins the longer walk.

Walk 9
Ampleforth and Gilling East

This circular walk starts from Ampleforth and goes through a pleasant valley bordered by wooded hills to the village of Gilling East, overlooked by Gilling Castle. The route uses mainly field paths, skirting the edge of Gilling Forest Nature Reserve and the playing fields at the back of Ampleforth College. This is one of the major Roman Catholic public schools in the country and occupies a Benedictine abbey established by monks fleeing from the French Revolution. Allow 2 ¼ hours.

Ampleforth ★ (100) (58-78) is on **Tours 5 and 10**. It lies on an unclassified road 2 miles west of Oswaldkirk ★, which is on the B1363. Go south out of Ampleforth and park the car where the road turns sharp right **(A)**.

From **(A)**, take the sign-posted public footpath beside a house and walk down the edge of a field, making towards the wooded slope ahead. Where the hedge on the right bears away, go straight on. Head towards the two trees on the other side of the field and turn right by the right hand tree to follow the edge of the field towards a line of trees by a stream.

Cross a wooden footbridge at **(B)** and continue in the same direction, following a line of trees along the stream on your right. The route is waymarked by a red arrow on a post. Wild flowers grow in abundance on the banks of the stream.

Go over a stile by a gate. Do not be alarmed by the notice 'Private Grounds and Wildlife Sanctuary Not Open to Public without Permit': this warning only applies to the woods on the other side of the tarmac road, which runs at right angles across the stream. Turn left along this road at **(c)**. The lake which feeds the stream can be seen on your right through the trees. In spring the woods are carpeted with bluebells.

Soon the playing fields at the back of Ampleforth College become visible on the other side of the large field on your left. Go through Hunt House Farm and continue along the tarmac road, with rho-

Scale 1:50 000 or 1¼ INCHES to 1 MILE

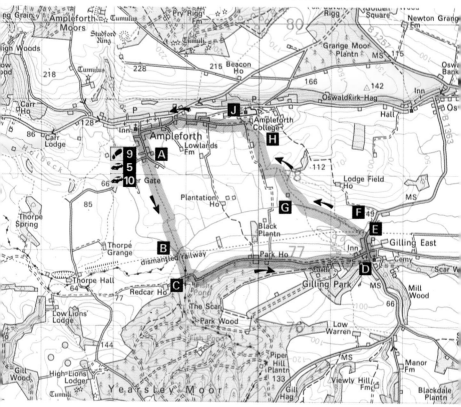

Bilberry (also called whortleberry) is a typical shrub of the uplands. It bears red flowers from April to June and purple fruits in late summer

dodendron bushes on the right. The path going off to your left to Ampleforth College is not a public right of way.

As you approach the village of Gilling East, the top of the castle can be seen above the trees on your right. Originally built by Roger de Mowbray, who provided the land for Byland Abbey ★ , it has had a succession of owners including the Fairfax family. It is now a preparatory school for Ampleforth but can be visited on weekday afternoons. The keep is Norman.

Walk down Pottergate and into the village. The road leading up to the castle is on your right. At the main road (**D**), turn left. The Fairfax Arms is on your right. Between the houses and the road runs a stream and each house has its own footbridge.

Just before the road bends right at (**E**), turn left through a gate, sign-posted by a yellow arrow. Go past a white house on your right. At this point there is a good view of the castle to your left. Follow an arrow through a second gate and continue across a field in the direction of the arrow until you reach a stream. Cross the stream and turn left to go down the left hand edge of a field. At the corner of the field (**F**) turn right to walk northwards, following a ditch which runs at the edge of the field.

At the next corner (**G**), follow the arrow to cross a wide stream by a footbridge and go over a stile. The land on either side of the bridge is rather overgrown.

Then turn left towards some playing fields and walk beside the stream on your left until you reach a fence. Follow the fence to meet another small stream, with a rugby pitch on the other side. Here turn right along the stream until you come to a cattle pen.

Turn left through a gate and walk round the side of the pen, with scrubland on your left, towards another gate and stile. Go through this gate and turn left almost at once to go past the school shooting range and tennis courts on the left. Where the track turns sharp right (**H**), turn left over a stile and cross a small concrete footbridge to walk along the edge of the cricket pitch.

Turn right onto the tarmac road at the end of the pitch and go up the slope towards the church of Ampleforth College. The architect, Sir Giles Gilbert Scott, also designed Liverpool Cathedral, new buildings for Clare College and the new library at Cambridge as well as additions to Magdalen College and the Bodleian Library at Oxford.

Follow the road as it bears left, keeping the college on your right. Looking back, there is a good view of the valley. At (**J**) don't go up the road to the right but carry straight on down the unmade road, leaving a bungalow on the right. This lane goes between some houses and eventually rejoins the road out of Ampleforth by the White Swan. Turn left to walk the short section back to the starting point at (**A**).

Walk 10
Kirkham Priory and the River Derwent

This is a circular walk starting at a ruined twelfth-century priory which lies on the banks of the River Derwent where it passes through a wooded gorge. The walk goes along the high ground to the west of the river, with fine views across the valley below, and returns along the river bank. Allow 2 ½ hours. (Note that the scale of this map is 1:50 000.)

Kirkham ★ (100) (SE 73-65) is on **Tours 4 and 6** and can also be reached by turning off the A64 at Whitwell-on-the-Hill, between York ★ and Malton ★ .

Park in the car park in front of the priory. This is now owned by English Heritage and is worth a visit, either at the beginning or the end of your walk. It was founded c.1122 and is the oldest of the three abbeys founded by Walter l'Espec, the others being Rievaulx ★ and Warden in Bedfordshire. Like Rievaulx, the site is outstanding. The best preserved section is the gatehouse which is late thirteenth century and has many fine features, including stone carvings of St George and the Dragon and David and Goliath. Parts of the priory church, rebuilt in 1180, are also preserved.

Leaving the priory, turn left down the hill and go over the River Derwent, passing the garden centre and tea rooms on the right. Cross the railway line by the level crossing, still manually controlled from a signalbox, and go on up the hill. As the road bends right at **(A)**, turn left down a track leading into the trees. After about 400 yards, bear right up an overgrown path running uphill and continue until you reach a stile marked with a yellow waymark arrow. Over the stile turn right and go down to the road. Turn left along the road and almost immediately turn left again at **(B)** just before a gate.

Follow the track up the hill, keeping close to the hedge on your right. At the top of the hill the priory and the river come into view on your left. The path bears to the right here to go through the hedge where it joins a track running along the side of a field. Almost immediately the track crosses a stile with a yellow waymark arrow and bears round to the right along the line of the valley.

You are now walking along the side of

the gorge with the river below. There are fine views across to Badger Hill on the other side of the valley. On the top of the hill Westow Hall ★ is visible. Keep the fence on your right and follow the waymark signs across two more stiles. The path goes through bracken but never becomes difficult.

At the second stile the path crosses over into a field, with the fence now on your left, and starts to descend again. A farm is visible ahead. Bear right across this field towards the telegraph post at the bend in the farm road below and then continue down the road away from the farm. This soon joins a quiet country road and continues in the same direction, crossing the railway line by a level crossing which still has its keeper's cottage. This section of the walk goes through some pleasant farmland typical of this part of Yorkshire.

Beyond the level crossing the river can be seen on the left over some fields. On the other side of the river the back of Howsham Hall ★ is visible. This is one of the many large houses built in the eighteenth century when the Yorkshire Wolds and surrounding country became fashionable and land was cheap. Opposite the Hall at **(C)** there is a gap in the hedge on the left, with a path leading through two fields down to the river bank. There may well be some cars parked by the roadside at this point, as the path is much used by anglers. Between the two fields is a ditch spanned by a concrete bridge – broken at the time this walk was done but with luck mended by now.

At **(D)** turn left to walk along the bank of the river Derwent. The river was opened up to navigation in Queen Anne's reign and Malton, 12 miles upstream from here, became a prosperous trading centre for the West Riding. Note that the river is not flowing east to the sea at this point, as one might expect, but inland. South of York it joins the river Ouse and finally exits into the North Sea at Hull. The river carries all the rainwater off the southern half of the Moors and flooding used to be a major problem. In the eighteenth century a short 'sea cut' was dug, just north of Scarborough ★ , which acts as a sluice gate to drain off the excess water.

Follow the path along the river bank, crossing between fields by stiles or planks. Where the low-lying ground becomes muddy, bear left onto slightly higher ground. The wooded slopes of Howsham Wood on the opposite bank come right down to the river bank and just after a sharp bend to the left the river

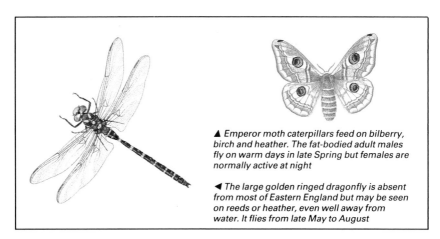

▲ Emperor moth caterpillars feed on bilberry, birch and heather. The fat-bodied adult males fly on warm days in late Spring but females are normally active at night

◄ The large golden ringed dragonfly is absent from most of Eastern England but may be seen on reeds or heather, even well away from water. It flies from late May to August

enters Kirkham Gorge. The path now goes into the wood which covers the hill on this side of the river and leaves it through a gate by the weir. A second gate leads onto the road near the level crossing. Turn right to return to the car park.

Scale 1:50 000 or 1¼ INCHES to 1 MILE

Walk 11
Hovingham, 'the prettiest village in Yorkshire'

Two circular walks, both taking about 1½ hours, explore the rich agricultural land which surrounds the charming village of Hovingham in West Ryedale. The village is England at its most appealing, with a green framed by large trees, old houses and a magnificent eighteenth century mansion, Hovingham Hall. The walks take in part of the long distance Ebor Way and go past the spot on which a Victorian entrepreneur tried to create a spa. (Note that the scale of this map is 1:50 000.)

Hovingham ★ (100) (SE 66-75) lies on the B1257 between Helmsley ★ and Malton ★ and is on **Tours 4, 6 and 7**. Apart from Hovingham Hall, the village contains the remains of a Roman villa.

There is no public car park but cars can be parked by the green near the Spa Garage. Cross the footbridge over the stream here and turn left. In front of Suitor's Cottage at **(A)** a right of way sign directs one to the right between two houses. Beyond the houses turn left through the gate at the sign for the Ebor Way. This is one of the many long distance footpaths and runs 70 miles from Helmsley to Ilkley via York ★. The grounds of Hovingham Park can be seen on the hill on the left. The track runs between fields in a
Hovingham

westerly direction. On a clear day the moors can be seen over to the north.

As the track goes through a small copse, it passes an isolated house on the right. This is Spa House which dates from the attempt to create a spa in Hovingham to rival Harrogate. Once out of the trees the village of Stonegrave ★ can be seen over on the right and shortly afterwards the houses of Cawton become visible ahead of you over a slight rise in the ground.

In Cawton turn right at **(B)** and go up the country lane which heads north between fields in the direction of Stonegrave. Just before the bridge at the edge of the village, turn right at **(C)** over a stile by a public footpath sign-post. After about 25 yards there is a ford for cattle across the stream on your left. Turn right here and go through the metal gate ahead of you. Walk down the right hand edge of the field and continue in a straight line through another field until you come to a drainage ditch. Turn left and walk along the edge of the ditch. Cross the footbridge at **(D)** and turn left. Where the ditch bears left, turn right towards two barns which are marked on the map below Hovingham Carrs, making for the gap in the hedge on the left hand side of the field. Beyond the gap follow the farm track towards the barns, going through two gates. Turn right past the barns and walk down the right hand edge of a field. Go through the gate and turn left along the disused railway line. Just past the bridge at **(E)** turn right through a wooden gate into a field. Cross the field, passing three large trees, and go through

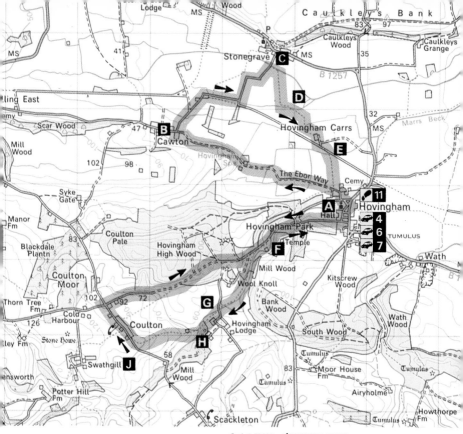

a second wooden gate onto a farm track. Follow this through two more gates and turn left along the Ebor Way to return to Hovingham.

The second walk goes south-west of the village. From the Spa Garage go south, passing the green on your left and the entrance to Hovingham Hall on your right. The Hall was built by Thomas Worsley around 1760 in local yellow sandstone and is Palladian in style. Its most unusual feature is the attached riding school which forms the entrance to the main house. This is what you see from the village. The acoustics of the riding school are so good that it has been used for music festivals. The Worsley family have owned the estate since the sixteenth century: the late Sir William Worsley captained Yorkshire at cricket and there is a fine cricket pitch in the grounds of the Hall. His daughter is the present Duchess of Kent.

Turn right along a country road, past the high wall of Hovingham Hall on your right. The road goes through Hovingham Park, passing a charming Italianate bridge in the park grounds on your right. As the road starts to go up hill turn left at (F) down the sign-posted footpath. Go through a gate and follow the path through the wood, keeping the stream on your left hand side. Come out of the wood and at (G) turn left down a dirt track leading to Hovingham Lodge.

Cross the stream and almost immediately turn right into a field over a stile with a yellow waymark arrow. Go through the field towards a second stile (also marked with an arrow). Go over this stile and past a pond on the right. Keep to the left of the next field, and three quarters of the way down, cross a stile into a group of trees. Go over the stream by the footbridge at (H) and follow the direction of the arrow on the footbridge away from the wood across a field and up the hill. Halfway up this field on the right hand side is another stile. Climb over this, turn sharp left and follow the farm track up to the farmhouse. A yellow arrow by the path indicates that this is the correct route.

At (J) climb over a stile and turn right down the country road. Walk through the village of Coulton to the cross-roads. Turn right here towards Hovingham and follow the road which runs over the hill and through Hovingham High Wood. Beyond (F) retrace your steps into Hovingham. As you come down into the village Hovingham Hall is ahead of you, with the cricket ground in front of it.

Walk 12
Bransdale and the edge of Bilsdale East Moor

Two circular walks are possible, both starting from the same point and taking about 1 ½ hours each. One goes up onto the high wild moorland which surrounds this sheltered dale and offers fine views of the Yorkshire Wolds to the south and Rudland Rigg to the east. The other dips down into the dale and up the other side, passing an old mill, and returns via the stream which runs through the bottom of the dale. The rich farmland of the sheltered south-facing dale provides a startling contrast to the lonely splendour of the moors. The north end of the valley is owned by the National Trust.

Cockayne ★ (94,100) (SE 62-98) lies on Tour 7 and is approached by a minor country road which runs almost due north from Helmsley ★ , passing through the village of Carlton. It consists of a tiny church and a few houses clustered at the northern end of Bransdale.

The walk starts halfway up the road running up the west side of Bransdale. Park at a parking place quarried out of the side of the hillside. Just to the north of this at **(A)** there is a sign marking the Bridleway to Bilsdale. Looking down from here one can see the entire dale, with the mill at the bottom. For the moorland walk, turn left up the bridleway. The track starts steeply, following the side of the quarry, and then becomes a path through the heather. Make for the ridge above you, following the route marked by cairns as this avoids the boggy patches. You will see a plantation on your right and on the left there are good views across to the

Scale 1:25 000 or 2½ INCHES to 1 MILE

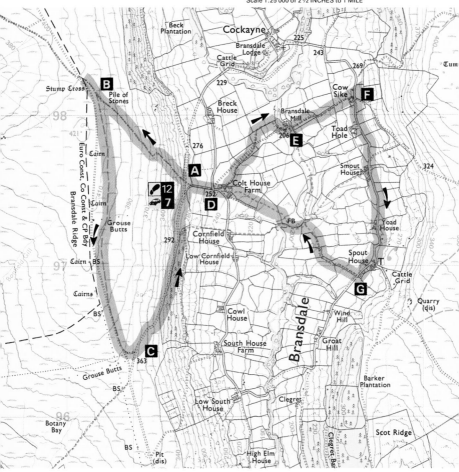

Yorkshire Wolds on the other side of the Vale of Pickering. The dale behind you quickly disappears as you climb and the heather stretches away in every direction.

The right of way which runs south across the moors starts at **(B)** and is marked by cairns which are shown on the map. You can turn left here but it is worth a short detour to look at Stump Cross, visible ahead of you up the bridleway. The cross marks one of the old tracks across the moors but the track that exists today is an access road for the grouse butts and is no longer a right of way at this point (although further south it merges with the right of way across the moors as they both descend to the road below).

Turn left at **(C)** and walk back along the road. There is very little traffic along this country road and the wide grassy bank on the dale side of the road makes for easy walking. In some places the side of the road has been planted with conifers but for most of the way Bransdale is visible below you and it seems remarkable that such fertile farmland should manage to exist in this small hollow in the moors.

To explore the dale, turn right down the hill at **(A)**. The bridleway is not sign-posted here but is easily identified by a gate opposite the parking place. Beyond the gate is a path which goes straight down the hill between two drystone walls and comes out onto the road below just to the north of Colt House Farm.

Opposite the bridleway at **(D)** you will see some wooden steps over a wall.

Climb over these and head down through the field towards the mill below you. A stone post with a hole in the middle indicates the pathway into a second field and there is another post marking the way into a third field.

When you reach the mill buildings at **(E)**, go through a gate into the mill yard. Although a mill has been here since the thirteenth century, most of the buildings you see are nineteenth century and date from the expansion of the mill by William Strickland. His son Emmanuel, who became vicar of Ingleby Greenhow ★, is responsible for the pious quotations in Latin, Greek and Hebrew which are inscribed on the buildings. The mill has been restored, mainly by the Acorn Volunteers, and is now owned by the National Trust. Walk through the yard and climb the steep bank ahead of you. At the top cross over the wall by some steps and walk across the field towards Cow Sike, crossing into a second field by another set of steps.

Turn right at **(F)** and walk along the road. To the left is rough ground sloping up towards Shaw Ridge and to the right the farmland drops down to the stream running through the dale. Just past Spout House at **(G)** there is a footpath sign on a gate on the right-hand side of the road. Turn right here by a stone wall and follow the track which runs down into the valley. When you reach the stream, turn left and follow its banks until you reach the footbridge shown on the map. Cross the stream and return to Colt House Farm.

Bog rosemary forms a low shrub 10 inches high and is found flowering in upland sphagnum bogs from April through to September

CONVENTIONAL SIGNS   1:250 000 or 1 INCH to 4 MILES

ROADS
Not necessarily rights of way

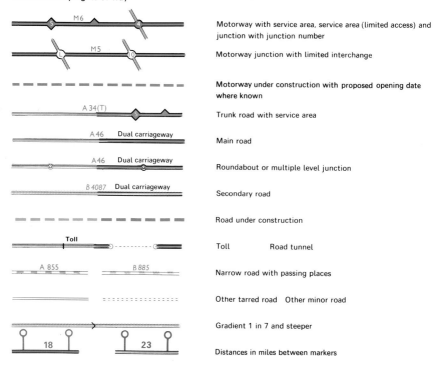

Motorway with service area, service area (limited access) and junction with junction number

Motorway junction with limited interchange

Motorway under construction with proposed opening date where known

Trunk road with service area

Main road

Roundabout or multiple level junction

Secondary road

Road under construction

Toll   Road tunnel

Narrow road with passing places

Other tarred road   Other minor road

Gradient 1 in 7 and steeper

Distances in miles between markers

The representation of a road is no evidence of the existence of a right of way

PRIMARY ROUTES

These form a national network of recommended through routes which complement the motorway system. Selected places of major traffic importance are known as Primary Route Destinations and are shown thus YORK Distances and directions to such destinations are repeated on traffic signs which, on primary routes, have a green background or, on motorways, have a blue background.
To continue on a primary route through or past a place which has appeared as a destination on previous signs, follow the directions to the next primary destination shown on the green-backed signs.

RAILWAYS

Standard gauge track   Road crossing under or over

Narrow gauge track   Level crossing

Tunnel   Station

WATER FEATURES

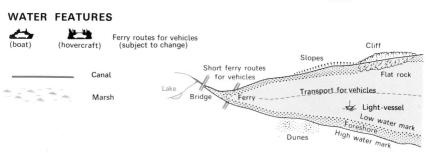

(boat)   (hovercraft)   Ferry routes for vehicles (subject to change)

Canal

Lake

Marsh

Bridge

Short ferry routes for vehicles

Ferry

Cliff

Slopes

Flat rock

Transport for vehicles

Light-vessel

Low water mark

Foreshore

High water mark

Dunes

ANTIQUITIES

※ Native fortress   ⚔ Site of battle (with date)   ------ Roman road (course of)   CANOVIUM • Roman antiquity

Castle • Other antiquities

𝔪 Ancient Monuments and Historic Buildings in the care of the Secretaries of State for the Environment, for Scotland and for Wales and that are open to the public.

BOUNDARIES

+ — + — + — + — National   — — — — — — — { County, Region or Islands Area

GENERAL FEATURES

Buildings

Wood

Lighthouse (in use)

Lighthouse (disused)

Windmill

Radio or TV mast

▲ Youth hostel

⊕ Civil aerodrome { with Customs facilities
+   { without Customs facilities

Ⓗ Heliport

✆ Public telephone

✆ Motoring organisation telephone

+ Intersection, latitude & longitude at 30' intervals (not shown where it confuses important detail)

TOURIST INFORMATION

✝	Abbey, Cathedral, Priory	✿	Garden	☆	Other tourist feature
🐟	Aquarium	▶	Golf course or links	✕	Picnic site
⋀	Camp site	🏛	Historic house		Preserved railway
	Caravan site	ℹ	Information centre	🏃	Racecourse
🏰	Castle	🏁	Motor racing	⛷	Skiing
	Cave	🖼	Museum	☀	Viewpoint
⛺	Country park	❗	Nature or forest trail		Wildlife park
	Craft centre	🦆	Nature reserve	🐘	Zoo

WALKS, CYCLE & MOTOR TOURS
Applicable to all scales

🔦1 Start point of walk

➡ Route of walk

Featured walk

🚗1 Start point of tour

➡ Route of tour

Featured tour

🚗 Start point of mini-walk

FOLLOW THE COUNTRY CODE
Enjoy the countryside and respect its life and work

Guard against all risk of fire

Fasten all gates

Keep your dogs under close control

Keep to public paths across farmland

Leave livestock, crops and machinery alone

Use gates and stiles to cross fences, hedges and walls

Take your litter home

Help to keep all water clean

Protect wildlife, plants and trees

Take special care on country roads

Make no unnecessary noise

Reproduced by permission of the Countryside Commission

CONVENTIONAL SIGNS — 1:25 000 or 2½ INCHES to 1 MILE

ROADS AND PATHS

Not necessarily rights of way

M I or A 6(M)	M I or A 6(M)	Motorway	
A 31 (T)	A 31 (T)	Trunk road	Narrow roads with passing places are annotated
A 35	A 35	Main road	
B 3074	B 3074	Secondary road	
A 35	A 35	Dual carriageway	

Road generally more than 4m wide

Road generally less than 4m wide

Other road, drive or track

Unfenced roads and tracks are shown by pecked lines

.... Path

RAILWAYS

	Multiple track	Standard gauge
	Single track	
	Narrow gauge	
	Siding	
	Cutting	
	Embankment	
	Tunnel	
	Road over & under	
	Level crossing; station	

PUBLIC RIGHTS OF WAY

Public rights of way may not be evident on the ground

Public paths { Footpath / Bridleway }

+ + + + + Byway open to all traffic

Road used as a public path

DANGER AREA
MOD ranges in the area
Danger!
Observe warning notices

The indication of a towpath in this book does not necessarily imply a public right of way
The representation of any other road, track or path is no evidence of the existence of a right of way

BOUNDARIES

— · — · — · — County (England and Wales)

— — — — — District

–o–o–o–o–o– London Borough

················· Civil Parish (England)* Community (Wales)

— — — — — — Constituency (County, Borough, Burgh or European Assembly)

Coincident boundaries are shown by the first appropriate symbol

*For Ordnance Survey purposes County Boundary is deemed to be the limit of the parish structure whether or not a parish area adjoins

SYMBOLS

Church or chapel { with tower / with spire / without tower or spire }

Glasshouse; youth hostel

Bus or coach station

Lighthouse; lightship; beacon

Triangulation station

Triangulation point on { church or chapel / lighthouse, beacon / building; chimney }

Electricity transmission line — pylon / pole

VILLA — Roman antiquity (AD 43 to AD 420)

Castle — Other antiquities

Site of antiquity

✕ 1066 Site of battle (with date)

Gravel pit

Sand pit

Chalk pit, clay pit or quarry

Refuse or slag heap

Sloping wall

Water		Mud
	Sand; sand & shingle	
	National Park or Forest Park Boundary	
NT	National Trust always open	
NT	National Trust opening restricted	
FC	Forestry Commission	

VEGETATION

Limits of vegetation are defined by positioning of the symbols but may be delineated also by pecks or dots

Coniferous trees

Non-coniferous trees

Coppice

Orchard

Scrub

Bracken, rough grassland

In some areas bracken (⌐) and rough grassland (······) are shown separately — Shown collectively as rough grassland on some sheets

Heath

Reeds

Marsh

Saltings

HEIGHTS AND ROCK FEATURES

50 · Determined by { ground survey }
285 · { air survey }

Surface heights are to the nearest metre above mean sea level. Heights shown close to a triangulation pillar refer to the station height at ground level and not necessarily to the summit

Vertical face

Loose rock / Boulders / Outcrop / Scree

Contours are at 5 metres vertical interval

ABBREVIATIONS

1:25 000 or 2½ INCHES to 1 MILE also 1:10 000/1:10 560 or 6 INCHES to 1 MILE

BP,BS	Boundary Post or Stone	P	Post Office	A,R	Telephone, AA or RAC
CH	Club House	Pol Sta	Police Station	TH	Town Hall
F V	Ferry Foot or Vehicle	PC	Public Convenience	Twr	Tower
FB	Foot Bridge	PH	Public House	W	Well
HO	House	Sch	School	Wd Pp	Wind Pump
MP,MS	Mile Post or Stone	Spr	Spring		
Mon	Monument	T	Telephone, public		

Abbreviations applicable only to 1:10 000/1:10 560 or 6 INCHES to 1 MILE

Ch	Church	GP	Guide Post	TCB	Telephone Call Box
F Sta	Fire Station	P	Pole or Post	TCP	Telephone Call Post
Fn	Fountain	S	Stone	Y	Youth Hostel

Maps and Mapping

Most early maps of the area covered by this guide were published on a county basis, and if you wish to follow their development in detail R. V. Tooley's Maps and Map Makers will be found most useful. The first significant county maps were produced by Christopher Saxton in the 1570s, the whole of England and Wales being covered in only six years. Although he did not cover the whole country, John Norden, working at the end of the sixteenth century, was the first map-maker to show roads. In 1611-12, John Speed, making use of Saxton and Norden's pioneer work, produced his 'Theatre of the Empire of Great Britaine', adding excellent town plans, battle scenes, and magnificent coats of arms. The next great English map-maker was John Ogilby, and in 1675 he published Britannia, Volume I, in which all the roads of England and Wales were engraved on a scale of one inch to the mile, in a massive series of strip maps. From this time onwards, no map was published without roads, and throughout the eighteenth century, steady progress was made in accuracy, if not always in the beauty of presentation.

The first Ordnance Survey maps came about as a result of Bonnie Prince Charlie's Jacobite rebellion of 1745. It was, however, in 1791, following the successful completion of the military survey of Scotland by General Roy that the Ordnance Survey was formally established. The threat of invasion by Napoleon in the early nineteenth century spurred on the demand for accurate and detailed mapping for military purposes, and to meet this need the first Ordnance Survey one-inch map, covering part of Essex, was published in 1805 in a single colour. This was the first numbered sheet in the First Series of one-inch maps.

Over the next seventy years the one-inch map was extended to cover the whole of Great Britain. Reprints of some of these First Series maps incorporating various later nineteenth century amendments, have been published by David & Charles. The reprinted sheets covering most of our area are Numbers 17, 18, 22 and 23.

The Ordnance Survey's one-inch maps evolved through a number of 'Series' and 'Editions', to the Seventh Series which was replaced in 1974 by the metric 1:50 000 scale Landranger Series. Between the First Series one-inch and the current Landranger maps many changes in style, format, content and purpose have taken place. Colour, for example, first appeared with the timid use of light brown for hill shading on the 1889 one-inch sheets. By 1892 as many as five colours were being used for this scale and at one stage the Seventh Series was being printed in no less than ten colours. Recent developments in 'process printing' – a technique in which four basic colours produce almost any required tint – are now used to produce Ordnance Survey Landranger and other map series. Through the years the one-inch Series has gradually turned away

from its military origins and has developed to meet a wider user demand. The modern detailed full colour Landranger maps at 1:50 000 scale incorporate Rights of Way and Tourist Information and are much used for both leisure and business purposes. To compare the old and new approach to changing demand, see the two map extracts of Scarborough on the following pages.

Modern Ordnance Survey Maps of the Area

York and the Moors are covered by Ordnance Survey 1: 50 000 scale (1¼ inches to 1 mile) Landranger map sheets 99, 100, 101, 105 and 106. These all purpose maps are packed full of information to help you explore the area. Viewpoints, picnic sites, places of interest, caravan and camping sites are shown as are public rights of way information such as footpaths and bridleways.

The North York Moors National Park area is also covered by a single map in the Ordnance Survey Tourist Map series at 1 inch to 1 mile scale.

To examine York and the Moors in more detail and especially if you are planning walks, Ordnance Survey 1:25 000 scale (2½ inches to 1 mile) Pathfinder maps which include public rights of way information are ideal. There are special Outdoor Leisure Maps also at 1:25 000 scale of the North York Moors National Park. Two such maps cover the area:

Sheet 26 – Western Area
Sheet 27 – Eastern Area

To look at the area surrounding York and the Moors Ordnance Survey 1 inch to 4 miles, Routemaster maps will prove most useful. Sheet 5 Northern England and Sheet 6 East Midlands and Yorkshire are relevant. An alternative will be found in the form of the OS Motoring Atlas of Great Britain at the larger scale of 1 inch to 3 miles.

To place the area in an historical context the following Ordnance Survey Archaeological and Historical Maps will also be useful: Ancient Britain, Roman Britain, Roman and Anglian York, and Viking and Medieval York.

Ordnance Survey maps are available from officially appointed agents, local agents (see below) and from most booksellers, stationers and newsagents.

Thomas C. Godfrey Ltd.,
32 Stonegate,
York,
YO1 2AP.
Telephone: 0904 24531

A. Sokell,
52-53 Middle Street South,
Great Driffield,
Humberside.
Telephone: 0377 42101

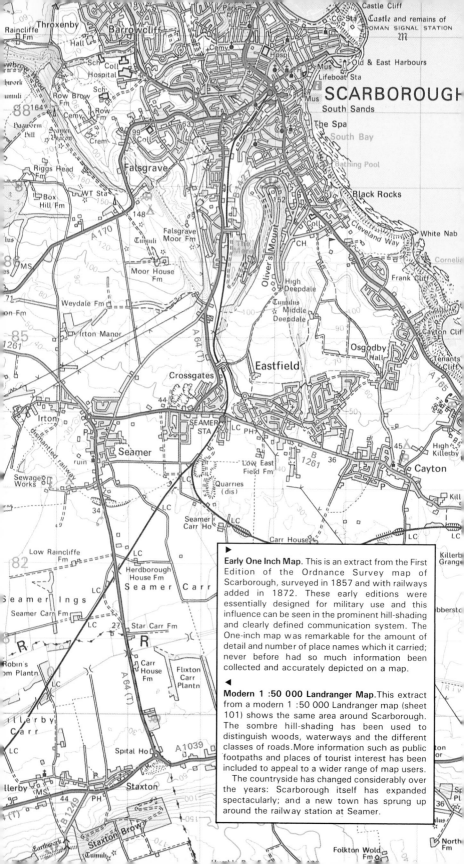

Early One Inch Map. This is an extract from the First Edition of the Ordnance Survey map of Scarborough, surveyed in 1857 and with railways added in 1872. These early editions were essentially designed for military use and this influence can be seen in the prominent hill-shading and clearly defined communication system. The One-inch map was remarkable for the amount of detail and number of place names which it carried; never before had so much information been collected and accurately depicted on a map.

Modern 1:50 000 Landranger Map. This extract from a modern 1:50 000 Landranger map (sheet 101) shows the same area around Scarborough. The sombre hill-shading has been used to distinguish woods, waterways and the different classes of roads. More information such as public footpaths and places of tourist interest has been included to appeal to a wider range of map users.

The countryside has changed considerably over the years: Scarborough itself has expanded spectacularly; and a new town has sprung up around the railway station at Seamer.

Index